Changing Your Mind

Changing Your Mind

The Bible, the Brain, and Spiritual Growth

VICTOR COPAN

CASCADE *Books* · Eugene, Oregon

CHANGING YOUR MIND
The Bible, the Brain, and Spiritual Growth

Cascade Books
An Imprint of Wipf and Stock Publishers
199 W. 8th Ave., Suite 3
Eugene, OR 97401

www.wipfandstock.com

ISBN 13: 978-1-55635-879-1

Cataloging-in-Publication data:

Copan, Victor A.

Changing your mind : the Bible, the brain, and spiritual growth / Victor Copan.

xx + 292 p.; 23 cm—Includes bibliographical references and index.

ISBN 13: 978-1-55635-879-1

1. Mind and body—Religious aspects. 2. Spiritual direction—Biblical teaching. 3. Spiritual life—Christianity. 4. Religion and science. I. Title.

BT702 C673 2016

Manufactured in the USA.

To Kathy:
The love of my life.
I owe you a debt of gratitude beyond words.

To Annaliesa, Andreas, and Benjamin:
My pride and joy.
I have learned so much from all of you.

Contents

List of Tables and Figures

Acknowledgements

THERE ARE A NUMBER of people that have contributed to this book in direct and indirect ways. Pride of place goes to my wife, Kathy, who read every word and gave such valuable critique, correction, and insight. Your willingness to question what I wrote and how I wrote it helped me express things more simply and clearly. Your *long-suffering* endurance throughout the months and years of writing qualifies you for sainthood! From the bottom of my heart, thank you.

Another person who read the entire manuscript and whose comments were invaluable is my former student, Drew Frazier. Your reading this manuscript from a student's perspective helped tremendously. Thank you for this labor of love, Drew!

My colleagues at Palm Beach Atlantic University, especially my brother Paul, were a constant source of encouragement and insight. Dean Randy Richards has been marvelous to work with and is ever supportive of those in his care. I am grateful to work with such a wonderful group of scholars—and friends. What a marvelous place to serve!

Perhaps the most formative influence on this book comes from a person I met only once in passing but whose writings have left an indelible impression on my life: Dallas Willard. Especially his *Renovation of the Heart* caused a paradigm shift in my thinking, literally changing my life. His influence runs like a silent, yet steadily flowing stream throughout these pages. Just as his last words, before he succumbed to cancer on May 8, 2013, were "thank you," so I want to say "thank you" to him for his impact on my life.

I am grateful to have been awarded a Quality Initiative Grant from PBA in 2013 that allowed me a summer of research at the libraries of Luther Theological Seminary and Bethel Seminary in St. Paul, Minnesota. Thanks also go to Paul and Dolly Smyth, who housed me while I was there. The conversations with you and your care for me meant a lot.

Lastly, I want to thank Robin Parry, my editor, for his encouragement and his expert advice throughout this project.

Abbreviations

AMP	Amplified Version
ASV	American Standard Version
BBE	Bible in Basic English
CEB	Common English Bible
CJB	Complete Jewish Bible
CSB	Christian Standard Bible
ESV	English Standard Version
GWN	God's Word to the Nations
KJV	King James Version
The Message	The Message Bible: The Bible in Contemporary Language
MIT	The Idiomatic Translation of the New Testament
NAB	New American Bible
NASB	The New American Standard Bible (1995)
NET	New English Translation
NIRV	New International Revised Version
NIV	New International Version (2011)
NJB	New Jerusalem Bible
NLT	New Living Translation
NRS	New Revised Standard Version
Phillips	J. B. Phillips New Testament
TNIV	Today's New International Version (2001)
WEB	World English Bible

Introduction

Setting the Stage

IT WAS AN ACCIDENT. I backed into spiritual formation. I didn't intend to. The main reason I got interested in it, I have to admit, was out of my own personal brokenness—and desperation.

When I was a young teenager, I once experienced an overwhelming sense of the presence of God. At that time, my heart said "yes" to him. I would follow him, heart, soul, mind, and strength. But over time, I discovered that the "yes" I said to God had slowly and imperceptibly morphed. I found myself believing in the presence of God much like I believed that the chemical formula of water was H_2O: it was good to know, but it wasn't a lived-out reality that shaped what I thought, how I felt, and how I lived. My actual day-to-day life was often miles away from what I said "yes" to in my head. Sometimes it even ran 180 degrees in the opposite direction!

Why does that happen? Why is it so difficult for me to live out my relationship to God in my everyday life? How is it possible to bring together what I have come to know in my head with how I live?

This incongruity of, on the one hand, wanting to live for God and, on the other hand, often doing exactly the things I knew were pulling me away from him, caused so much internal pain and anguish that I frankly don't know how I survived my teen years! The guilt I felt about living at odds with what I knew was true and good just about killed me.

I backed into spiritual formation because of this personal pain. It drove me to want to find out whether I could live with and for God every moment of every day. I wanted to bring together the thoughts and desires I had about how to live in God's presence with my actual experience. Is that even possible? If so, how is it possible? To me that is what spiritual formation is all about. This book is the result of my searching for answers to these questions.

My story with God, however, began much earlier. The first divine encounter I recall having was with my grandmother. Let me tell you her story.

Anna Helene Kirsch

Anna Helene was born in 1891 in Lithuania, into a family whose history could be traced back to Austria during the time of the Protestant Reformation under Martin Luther. When Catholic Counter-Reformation backlash arose, Protestants in Austria were given a choice: convert back, leave, or die. Anna Helene's forefathers chose to emigrate north and eventually found their way to Lithuania and Latvia. Anna Helene's life was filled with the difficulty and hardship that comes to those forced to live as a foreigner in another land.

Anna Helene came to faith early in life. She wrote in her diary, "On the 11th of October 1904 I came to faith and in April 1905 I was baptized. The happiest day of my life was when I came to faith. The most festive day of my life was my baptism."

Anna Helene married a man who loved her but was not always easy to live with. He didn't, let's say, always exude warmth. When she was about fifty, her husband died unexpectedly of a heart attack. She found herself alone, without a job, without income, and with three children to feed.

Then came World War II. Her only son was drafted into the army and sent to fight in the frontline. He was never heard from again. When the Russian army advanced on the Baltic States, Anna Helene had to flee, leaving her home and all her possessions behind. She spent most of the war as a refugee in Germany—constantly fleeing from one place to the next, in order to find food and shelter. She saw and experienced the horrors of war.

At the end of the war, Anna Helene was helpless and alone. Her daughter took her in and together they emigrated to America.

In the years that followed, she contracted Parkinson's disease, and because of it, she could not feed herself. On top of that, she fell and broke her hip, and from that time on, she could not walk alone. She could do nothing for herself, and had to be dependent upon others even to go to the bathroom.

That was Anna Helene, my "Oma." She lived with our family all through my childhood until the day she died.

Even though Oma was in constant pain, I never recall her complaining or falling into self-pity. Never!

Once, when I was about seven or eight years old, I slept in her room. In the middle of the night, I heard someone groaning, and I realized it was Oma. Physical pain had woken her up, as it often did, and she couldn't sleep.

In the dark I could make out her figure in bed, and I stared intently at her and noticed that she was praying passionately and fervently for each of us seven kids and for my parents. I remember a feeling of awe came over me when I heard her pray for me.

After the prayer, in a half-whisper, she sang her favorite song:

> *Solang mein Jesus lebt*
> *und Seine Kraft mich hebt,*
> *muß Furcht und Sorge von mir fliehn,*
> *mein Herz in Lieb erglühn.*

> As long as Jesus lives
> And His strength lifts me up
> Then fear and worry need to flee
> My heart will glow in love.

In many ways, life had treated Anna Helene badly: the horrors of war, a refugee without a home, meager possessions, bad health, and the humiliation of being totally dependent on others for all of her needs. Yet, despite all this, she had the spiritual resources to sing in the pain and experience joy in Jesus' presence.

This night is etched deep in my mind. As a seven-year old kid, it planted a seed idea of what it looked like when God's presence within a person was a reality. I remember thinking to myself back then, "I want to be the kind of person who has that kind of experience with God."

In a real sense, this story captures for me what spiritual formation is all about. Spiritual formation is about asking and answering the following questions:

- How can my life be formed and transformed so that—no matter what happens to me, or what circumstances I find myself in—I grow to become a person with the inner life and disposition of an Anna Helene?

- How can I develop ways of thinking and being that will steer me steadily toward this goal?

- What are practices and habits of mind, soul, body, and social relationships that can shape me toward that end?

Behind this Book

This book grew out of a course on spiritual formation that I have been teaching at a Christian university every semester for the past decade. In many ways, this book follows the same path as the course itself. The goal of this book (as in my class) is to take you on a journey to explore what spiritual formation is and how it unfolds, with the ultimate aim of setting you on your own path toward genuine, personal spiritual transformation.

Quite a number of great books on spiritual formation have been written (I will be pointing some of them out as we go along), so why write another one? There are primarily three reasons.

First, some books are very detailed about spiritual formation, and so it's easy to miss the forest for all the trees. Other books talk about spiritual formation in more general ways. This book tries to steer a course between those two.

Second, the aim of this book is to give you all the tools that you need—biblical, scientific, and practical—in order to develop your own pathway for spiritual growth. I hope to make clear what are the essentials to put yourself on a trajectory of spiritual development that fits who you are.

The third reason for writing this book is to bring recent findings of brain research[1] as well as social science research into conversation with spiritual formation. These fields have uncovered some significant insights about human transformation, which could be useful in our own

---

1. Brain research actually goes by a bewildering number of names: neuroscience, neuropsychology, neurobiology, etc. I will generally use the term "neuroscience" as a blanket term relating to the study of the brain and how it functions. My apologies in advance to specialists in this field who would want more nuancing of terms.

spiritual transformation. These two fields of research deal with the following questions:

- What are the natural, normal change processes that take place in our mind and body?

- How do our thoughts affect the structure of our brain?

- How do our actions and interactions with others affect us physically—our brain structure and our body composition?

- What are the effects of our thoughts and our emotions on our brain and body chemistry?

- Have brain research and social science research discovered mechanisms of how we function that could help lead to genuine and lasting change in us—mentally, emotionally, socially, and spiritually?

The answers to these and other questions that these fields of science have uncovered also hold significant insights for how we change spiritually. If God has made us a unity of body, soul, and spirit—then the insights about how we change in one dimension may very well apply in the other dimensions. An openness to learn from them helps us cooperate with how God made us, rather than working against how God made us.

Roadmap

We will begin our journey into spiritual formation by first clarifying what spirituality and spiritual formation are—and what they are not. We will explore contemporary understandings of spirituality and compare it with a biblical understanding.

Part 1 of the book will lay out the biblical foundations of spiritual formation. We will look at key texts from the Bible that speak to the goal, purpose, dynamics, and process of spiritual formation.

Part 2 will then explore the scientific foundations of spiritual formation. Here is where we will look at how current neurobiological research can inform and support us in the spiritual transformation process.

Part 3 looks at the various dimensions of the human person—our heart, our mind, our body, our soul, and our relationships—and explores the transformation process in each of these dimensions. Understanding the dynamics of transformation in each of these areas will go a long way toward helping us experience transformation.

Part 4, the final section of the book, will seek to be very practical, drawing from all that we discussed earlier. Here we will connect what we discovered about the social-scientific foundations of spiritual formation to our understanding of how habits develop. We will also sketch out how to develop a pathway for your own spiritual growth that is tailored to who you are and where you find yourself on your spiritual journey right now.

Just a couple notes before we start: First, I will be using the New International Version 2011 translation throughout the book. If I cite another version, I will let you know.

Second, throughout the book, footnotes will include additional information and additional resources that you can use to follow up on what I have mentioned in the main text. If you don't like footnotes, you can happily skip over them without missing anything substantial.

With that out of the way, let's begin.

1

Spirituality: What It Is and What It Isn't

Understanding Spirituality and Spiritual Formation

FOR MORE THAN TWO decades now, there has been an increasing fascination about all things spiritual in the Western world—and it is everywhere. The term *spirituality* is a buzz-word in popular culture, and the phrase *spiritual formation* is increasingly a "buzz-phrase" in the church. But what do we mean when we use the word "spirituality"? What does the phrase "spiritual formation" actually mean? And more importantly for us: What is a biblical understanding of spirituality and spiritual formation? We will explore these questions in this chapter.

It is one of the astonishing developments of the last decades that spirituality has made a strong comeback after years of being out of vogue. Do a Google search on the term *spirituality,* and you'll get you over 141,000,000 hits. And when you look closer, you'll find all different shades and types of spirituality for virtually every interest group and personality type imaginable. Even if you are an out-and-out atheist, like Janna Saliger, it is no shame anymore to talk about your spirituality. In a blog post, she wrote this:

> I was diagnosed with major clinical depression and generalized anxiety disorder two years ago. . . . After scouring dozens of self-help books, I've found one piece of advice from them all to be rather consistent: be spiritual. At first, I scoffed at this idea. I don't believe in a god. I'm an atheist. Spiritualism and atheism just didn't seem to fit together. I kept on reading, though, and I

discovered that perhaps even an atheist like myself could benefit from getting in touch with my spiritual side.

Now, let's get things straight—being spiritual does not mean being religious. Religion can be a component, yes, but that's not all there is to it. Spirituality does have connotations of belief in a higher power, but just because you don't believe in any gods doesn't mean you can't have faith in something larger than yourself.... I'm a spiritual atheist![1]

Spirituality is *in* . . . but that has both a positive and a negative side.[2] On the positive side, renewed interest in spirituality shows people are hungry to connect with and experience God. A few decades ago, you could feel the disdain for religion and spirituality on college campuses and among the culture leaders across the country. You just couldn't talk about those things without being looked at like you had a third eye! That has thankfully changed.

But the negative side to this spirituality boom is that spirituality can mean virtually anything you want it to. Donald Carson writes that today

"spirituality" has become such an ill-defined, amorphous entity that it covers all kinds of phenomena that an earlier generation of Christians . . . would have dismissed as error, or even as "paganism" or "heathenism." It is becoming exceedingly difficult to exclude absolutely anything from the purview [domain] of spirituality, provided that there is some sort of experiential component in the mix.[3]

Notice the last part of the quotation: for the average person *experience* is the key to what makes something spiritual. Virtually anything that gives you a good feeling can be chalked up as a spiritual experience, no matter what it is: a rock concert, a patriotic moment, a chat with a friend—even an fabulous meal!

Notice how Rebecca Wells' book, *Divine Secrets of the YaYa Sisterhood*, views spirituality and religious experiences in these two entries on her YaYa blog.

Dear Sweetnesses,

I've just come back from a walk outside on this evening in early summer in the Pacific Northwest. . . . So, anyway. It was on

1. Seliger, "Spiritual Atheist."
2. Carson, *Gagging of God*, 555.
3. Ibid., 558.

Sunday that I saw the rainbow. Out on the waters on which I live. I could see the beginning and the end of the rainbow all at once! I think it was a double rainbow, had so many levels I jumped up and down, and though I was on the phone with two dear pals, I said, "Scuse me, but I'm having a quasi-religious experience with this rainbow and I'm going to have to talk to yall later."[4]

In another post, her understanding of spirituality comes out even clearer,

Dahlins!

How are yall?! Here in the Pacific Northwest, La Luna [the moon] was shooting down so much clarity and power last night that I made a big decision that I'd been praying about. I think she helped me, as she always does. Tonight, clouds are in front of her, but I know she is there, just like I know she is shining down on each of you, loving you with infinite tenderness and compassion. More and more, when I pray (or meditate or chant or whatever it is), I try to remember that the Divine KNOWS what I cannot put into words. And that the Divine loves me just as much when I am a screaming, crying mess as when I do something brave and heroic. We are all perfectly imperfect creatures, doing the best we can. Can you sometimes stand in the moonlight and let the love in? Sometimes I block it—with fear or anger or any number of things. Other times an opening occurs and then I know it: I am beloved. Just as you all are.[5]

What is Rebecca Wells' understanding of spirituality? It's a bit squishy and hard to nail down! Certainly, nature is on center stage. It has a divine quality that overwhelms her.

And it's also true for me: there is something in an experience of a rainbow or a full moon on a cloudless night that evokes something deep within us. I've had the same types of overpowering "senses of the divine" in nature as well, and I resonate a lot with what she says, even though I don't describe it the way she does. My take on her spirituality, though, is that she confuses the *creation* with the *creator*—or perhaps fuses them together.

Now, as Christians we are not called to a jelly-like spirituality as many in our culture define it. The question we need to ask ourselves is

---

4. Wells, "Dear Sweetnesses."
5. Wells, "Dahlins."

this: How can we think biblically about the concepts of spirituality and spiritual formation?

Spiritual Formation Happens . . .

Of all the writers I have read over the last decades, Dallas Willard has done some of the most careful, biblically rooted thinking on spirituality and spiritual formation.

In one of his discussions on this topic, Dallas makes the point that there is nothing special about the term *spiritual formation*. He writes:

> We could forget the phrase "spiritual formation," but the fact and need would still be there to be dealt with. The spiritual side of the human being, Christian and non-Christian alike, develops into the reality which it becomes, for good or ill. Everyone receives spiritual formation, just as everyone gets an education. The only question is whether it is a good one or a bad one.[6]

What is Willard driving at here? Simply stated, *spiritual formation happens!* (I was thinking of creating a bumper sticker with this on it, but I don't think it would catch on!) Spiritual formation is something that happens to every human being, and it happens through every thought we think and every step we take. Whether we want to be or not, every one of us is being formed each and every minute of our lives. Yes, Hitler was spiritually formed, and Mother Teresa was spiritually formed. But their spiritual formation was profoundly different!

Spiritual formation, then, is not tied to any one religious tradition, but is what inevitably happens to each one of us, whether we are atheists or devout Christians. That is why Dallas Willard writes: "We all become a certain kind of person, gain a specific character, and that is the outcome of a process of 'spiritual formation'"[7] *Spiritual formation happens*—and we can't do anything to stop it.

Spiritual Formation Happens . . . But We Can Influence the Direction and Outcome

Even though it is inescapable that we will be spiritually formed, we *can* do things that directly influence *how* we are being spiritually formed. We can

6. Willard, "Spiritual Formation in Christ," 254.

7. Willard, *The Great Omission*, 105.

engage in practices that reshape our interior and exterior lives that will then aim our lives in certain directions. In other words, there are things we can do that lead us in the direction of becoming like a Mother Teresa, and that will keep us from ending up like a Hitler.

So, let's summarize what we have been saying up to now and take it a step further: We have said that spiritual formation happens to all of us, but we are not simply passive in the process. We can actively participate in our own spiritual formation in order to aim ourselves in the direction we want to go.

But what specifically is that direction? That is what we want to explore next.

From Generic Spiritual Formation— to Christian Spiritual Formation

As followers of Jesus, we want to ask the question: What is *Christian* spiritual formation? What, in other words, does spiritual formation look like that is fully, truly, and unmistakably *Christian*? After scouring the way authors who write about spiritual formation understand Christian spiritual formation, I have found the working definition that Dallas Willard offers to be the most helpful. He views Christian spiritual formation as *the redemptive process of forming the inner human world so that we take on the character of the inner being of Christ himself.* [8]

I think this is right on, but I would like to add a bit more nuance to Dallas Willard's description. I see Christian spiritual formation as *the redemptive process of intentionally forming our interior and exterior life so that so that we increasingly take on (acquire, develop) the character of the inner being of Christ himself.*

Every part of this definition is significant, so let's explore what each word or phrase means.

Spiritual Formation is Redemptive.

The word "redemptive" implies something about us humans: it implies that we humans are estranged from God in our spirits, thoughts, actions,

8. He modified his definition of Christian spiritual formation slightly in *Renovation of the Heart* to the following: "*spiritual formation for the Christian basically refers to the Spirit-driven process of forming the inner world of the human self in such a way that it becomes like the inner being of Christ himself*" (22).

and attitudes. Jeremiah talks about the heart being "deceitful above all things and beyond all cure" (Jer 17:9), and Paul tells us that we were at one time dead in our trespasses and sins (Eph 2:1). In other words, something has gone fundamentally gone wrong in us. To fix it, we don't merely need to try a little harder. We don't just need therapy. We need to be given a new life. We need to be redeemed.

Spiritual Formation is a Process

The word *process* implies a number of things: It implies development and progression; it implies struggle and learning; and it implies that we have not yet reached a goal that we are aiming at.

Redemption begins with conversion—being reconciled to God. But redemption does not end there. It is a *process* that takes place over time. Sometimes a very long time. Spiritual formation isn't granted to us once-and-for-all when we first said "yes" to God. It is a daily, step-by-small-step sort of thing.

Spiritual Formation is Intentional

Spiritual formation is conscious and deliberate. This implies that we are not merely passive agents waiting for it to happen to us. We need to actively engage in the process. We become fully involved participants with God in this process. God has a part to play in our spiritual formation, and so do we. Paul explains it this way: "continue to work out your salvation with fear and trembling, for it is God who works in you" (Phil 2:12–13). But our part in this process of spiritual formation is not simply related to our thoughts. It is not just agreeing with God about certain spiritual truths—as I had originally believed in my teen years. It is an intentional process that encompasses the transformation of every dimension of our being—both our inner and outer human world.

Spiritual Formation is about Forming

The term "forming" is also significant, and it too implies something about us. This word indicates that we all are, in some sense, "*de*-formed" and are in the need of becoming *re*-shaped. There are areas in our lives that are not the way God intended for us to be. The apostle Paul talks about our need to be con*form*ed to the image of Jesus (Rom 8:28), and of our minds needing to be trans*form*ed (Rom 12:2). Jeremiah uses the imagery of humans as clay that has been badly marred (Jer 18:4). This clay needs to be re*form*ed and re*shape*d into the image of God that was marred in the Garden of Eden.

Spiritual Formation is about Forming the Interior and Exterior Life

This part of the definition identifies the specific dimensions that need to be re-formed: our inner and outer human world. Why both interior and exterior? Because our relationship with God goes far beyond what happens between our ears or even, as we often say, in our hearts. It extends to every nook and cranny of our lives: what is going on within us and how we are living our lives through our bodies as we interact with the "outside world" around us. That is why Jesus speaks of loving God with all our heart, soul, mind, and strength, and loving our neighbors (Mark 12:30). He indicates with this comment that the sum total of all of who we are needs to be transformed.

Spiritual Formation has a Purpose

The words *so that* signal the purpose of Christian spiritual formation. It tells us why we should even be interested in spiritual formation in the first place: *so that* our inner lives become like the inner life of Jesus himself.

Spiritual Formation is about Becoming Something We Are Not

The phrase "take on" implies there is something we do not have that we need to acquire. Dallas Willard describes this as "the character of the inner being of Christ himself." What we *take on* is Christ himself.

It is challenging to convey the right understanding of the phrase, *take on*. It does not refer to "putting something on"—as in the phrase, "he's just putting on a show." Rather, it refers to acquiring something that is absent: the life of Christ in us. It is the reality of Christ within us that we can nurture and grow—like a seed that we plant, water, and care for.

We are not, contrary to much of modern psychology, complete in ourselves. We lack something. We don't have all the resources within ourselves to solve all of our problems, to heal ourselves, and be whole persons. There is something that must come from outside ourselves that we need to *take on*: the life of Christ within us.

It is at this point that Christian spiritual formation runs into conflict with our culture's understanding of spirituality that we mentioned earlier. Our culture approaches spirituality with a "what's in it for me" mentality, whose ultimate aim is for *me* to feel good about *myself* through warm spiritual experiences.[9]

True, Jesus' early followers were often full of joy and had warm spiritual experiences, but that was not their primary *aim*. If we make it our primary aim, it will lead to frustration, guilt, and disappointment. The New Testament is packed with joyful people, who had "warm spiritual experiences"—but these were often encountered *in the midst of* suffering, challenge, pain, and sometimes death. Christian spirituality is marked both by joy and suffering.

The promise of New Testament spirituality is that through taking on the inner being of Christ himself, though it may lead us down a path marked by suffering, it will ultimately lead us to joy. Peter expresses this well: "Dear friends, do not be surprised at the fiery ordeal that has come on you to test you, as though something strange were happening to you. But rejoice inasmuch as you participate in the sufferings of Christ, so that you may be overjoyed when his glory is revealed" (1 Pet 4:12–13).

Spiritual Formation is about Acquiring the Character of Jesus

What is character? The topic is actually quite a complex one,[10] but I understand character as the settled way of being and responding that a person has developed over time that becomes *character*istic of them. It refers to the unique set of virtues and qualities of an individual that consistently manifests itself in the way they order their lives, the choices they make, and the way they interact with others. All of this refers to a person's character.

Spiritual formation is about examining our own character and bringing it into alignment with the character of Jesus. It speaks of our

9. This is a bit of a caricature—but not by much!

10. See the helpful discussion of this topic by Cox and Kallenberg, "Character," 127.

need to develop specific ways of thinking, feeling, and acting that conform us to the way Jesus himself lived.

These character qualities are often referred to as *virtues*. In the ancient world, Greeks and Romans (speaking very generally now) held to the four ideals of wisdom, courage, moderation, and justice.[11] Judaism also had its own set of forty-eight virtues.

Although these are noble virtues to strive for, these are not the virtues Christian spiritual formation aims at. Christian spiritual formation is aimed at *taking on the virtues and character qualities of Christ himself.* That means it is Jesus

- who **establishes** the content and shape of the character we are striving for;
- who **determines** which virtues we are to strive for;
- who **defines** what those virtues are;
- and who **exemplifies** how we are to live these virtues out in the real world.

So, it is not, for example, "goodness" as society around us defines goodness that we are to strive for. We want to have *Christ's kind of goodness* formed in us. And so, we need to ask ourselves: How was Jesus good? How did *he* show goodness to others?

In the process of reflecting on Christ's kind of goodness, we may need to shake off our culture's understandings of what goodness is. In fact, Christ's kind of goodness and our culture's understanding of goodness may conflict with each other. We need to have Jesus define our understanding of those virtues.

Spiritual Formation Aims at Transforming the Heart

The final aspect of our understanding of spiritual formation zeroes in on developing our character that is in line with *the inner being of Christ himself.*

The reason it is important to emphasize the *inner being* of Christ is that it will keep us from falling into three traps—traps that are actually close cousins to each other.

11. See Plato's *Republic* 427e for his description of these; see also Seneca, *De Inventione* II and LIII.

The first trap we might call *externalism*.[12] Externalism is when people think that how they act on the outside is all that counts. The focus is on doing things that others can observe—whether or not it's in line with who we are on the inside. Who we are on the outside is disconnected from who we are on the inside. They don't mirror each other.

Have you ever seen a mother or father make their child smile or behave nicely when in the company of others—even though it is obvious that on the inside the kid wants to kick somebody or say something nasty? It is possible to say and do the right things on the outside, while being the complete opposite on the inside.

Jesus calls people who pretend to be religious on the outside, but who are not genuine about it on the inside, "white-washed tombs." Their external actions mask the brokenness below the surface.

The second cousin of this first trap is *legalism*. The mindset of a legalist is: "I have to do the right thing in order to be a good Christian." It is the grit-your-teeth, white-knuckled approach to spiritual formation. It emphasizes human responsibility and self-discipline, but cuts God out of the equation. It focuses on self-reliance, disregarding God's empowering presence within us.

When we focus on taking on the inner being of Christ, it also helps us avoid a third trap: *judgmentalism*. Judgmentalism is an orientation of the heart that is based on *comparison* with others. It is performance-based, competitive, and driven by the question, "Am I doing all the things that *a good Christian* should be doing—and am I doing it *better* than other people?"

When we focus on the external performance, it often leads to two polar-opposite reactions. *On the one hand*, we become proud. We pat ourselves on the back for all the things that we have done—and we look down on others who, well, just aren't as holy as we are. We look at others, and in our hearts we pray the prayer of the Pharisee in Luke 18:11: "God, I thank you that I am not like other people—robbers, evildoers, adulterers—or even like this tax collector."

On the other hand, when we meet someone who is even more externally holy than we are, we become jealous, angry, or depressed.

In order to avoid these three traps, we need to focus exclusively on ever increasingly taking on and developing the character of the inner life of Christ within us.

12. This is a helpful term that I believe Dallas Willard has coined. Willard, *Renovation*, 23.

Although I have mentioned three traps to avoid as we seek to take on the inner character of Christ, I still have not told you what the phrase, "taking on the inner being of Christ," actually means. The best way to do this is with an illustration.

When Jesus was hanging on the cross, after he has been brutally beaten, mocked, jeered at, and verbally abused; after he had endured a trial that was a mockery of justice—after all of this, what did Jesus say as he looked at the people who did that to him? He said "Father, forgive them. They don't know what they are doing."

From the way the Gospel writers tell the story, these words just flowed out of him—as if this was nothing unusual for him to say. His first and natural response when people abused him was to bless and not to curse.

Taking on the character of the inner being of Christ has to do with developing the same "heart condition" that Jesus had, which made his spontaneous reaction possible as he hung on the cross. It is a condition of the heart, where forgiveness, love, and mercy flow out of us—instead of us gritting our teeth, trying to say words that sound forgiving and loving, but inside wishing we could destroy someone.

The ultimate goal of spiritual formation is developing the same heart attitudes that Jesus has so that we begin to live out the kinds of external responses that Jesus would have were he in our situation today.

So, in this first chapter, we've introduced the topic of spiritual formation by noting the following:

- We've seen the increasing interest and openness to spirituality, but this has an upside and a downside.

- Spirituality is understood by our culture as an *experience* we have, regardless of the content.

- Everyone is spiritually formed, whether they actively seek it or not: Hitler, Mother Teresa, and you.

- Christian spiritual formation is about "the redemptive process of intentionally forming our interior and exterior life so that we increasingly take on (acquire, develop) the character of the inner being of Christ himself."

- In our quest for this, we need to avoid the traps of externalism, legalism, and judgmentalism.

In the next section, we'll examine the biblical foundations of spiritual formation.

PART 1

Biblical Foundations of Spiritual Formation

2

The Biblical Backdrop of Spiritual Formation

Understanding Spiritual Formation on the Canvas
of What God Is Doing in the World

To SET THE STAGE for this chapter, let me start with three analogies. The *first* one is as old as Jesus. Imagine you are building a house. If you want it to last a long time, you have to invest time and effort in laying a strong foundation that will handle all kinds of situations. If the foundation is deficient, your house will fall apart.

Second, imagine someone gave you a thousand-piece puzzle—but they didn't give you the box top with the picture of it. You're an avid puzzler, and so you have a go at it. You notice some pieces that have the same colors, and you are able to put that section together. That leaves you with, say, nine-hundred other pieces that you can't figure out how they go together. You won't be able to fully appreciate and understand the section you did put together without placing it within the larger picture.

Third, imagine you go to a play that you've never heard of before, but you happen to arrive during the fifth and final act. You can tell by the faces of everyone in the audience that the play is moving and meaningful. You, however, are clueless. You understand the words they are saying, but the overall flow of the story doesn't make sense to you. Why? Because you have no understanding or experience of the first part of the play.

A house, a puzzle, a play. How do these analogies connect to spiritual formation? It's probably obvious, but let me spell it out: spiritual formation won't make real sense to us unless we see it on the grand canvas of the story that the Bible is telling us. If spiritual formation does not have this backdrop, then our understanding, practice, and experience of spiritual formation may be hindered, incomplete, or even harmful.

My own working title for this story is "The Story of God and His World." It's not a snappy title, but it conveys what is happening from Genesis through Revelation.[1] This overarching story tells us

- who God is
- who we are
- what God planned for the world
- where history is heading
- how he designed us to live[2]

It is this last point that ties in directly with spiritual formation! So, we'll need to have a good grasp of the key parts of this story in order to give us the right perspective on what spiritual formation is, what its goals are, and then what we can do to form ourselves spiritually so we can take up our role in this unfinished drama.

In this chapter we will look at the big picture and we'll place spiritual formation within that grand story.

To do that, it would be helpful if we could find one text that captures the big picture and connects it with spiritual formation. Is there such a text? I think there is, but there are two challenges with it: first, the connection to the story of God and his world is not immediately apparent; and second, it's quite a challenging text to understand because it contains some concepts that are easily misunderstood. If we deal with these two things, we can see how strongly this text relates to spiritual formation.

I would suggest the text that does this is Rom 8:29: "For those God foreknew he also predestined to be conformed to the image of his Son, that he might be the firstborn among many brothers and sisters."

I believe this verse takes us to the heart and center of the grand story the Bible is telling us. I think of this verse as the pinnacle of a tall mountain. When you climb to the top of a mountain, you can see everything

---

1. Some theologians argue that it's better to think in terms of the Bible being a play, in which we are invited to be actors in this not-yet-finished drama. Vanhoozer makes this point in *The Drama of Doctrine*. A similar point is made by Wells in *Improvisation*. I think they're on to something!

2. There is a lot more to it, but we'll keep it basic. If you want to read more about this, see Vang and Carter, *Telling God's Story*; Bartholomew and Goheen, *The Drama of Scripture*; Wright, *New Testament and the People of God*, 215–43.

around you for miles! It becomes possible to notice how all the hills, valleys, rivers, lakes, and streams are connected to each other. You can make sense of the whole region because of your wide perspective. In many ways, Rom 8:29 is like that. It describes the grand vision that God intended for his world. Once we understand what Paul is communicating in this verse, I believe we will be able to see how all the main bits of the Bible fit together into this grand vision and how spiritual formation fits into that grand vision.

However, the trek up to this pinnacle will not be easy. In Rom 8:29 we will encounter some rather steep sections that might confuse and frustrate us, so that we might be tempted to give up the climb! But, I promise you, if you make it to the top, you will see that it was worth the hike! So, put on your hiking boots and get ready for some serious climbing!

The Letter to the Romans—Why Paul Wrote This Letter

Before we can make sense of Rom 8:29, we need to put it into the overall context of why Paul wrote the book of Romans in the first place. Paul's main purpose in writing this letter is to deal with a number of core issues that were causing deep rifts within the church in Rome. Two clear factions—one Jewish and one Gentile—had developed around these issues. Each group had radically different ideas of what it meant to be a follower of Jesus.[3] Each group had their own set of questions and viewpoints that were at odds with the other faction.

They could not figure out what it meant for Jesus to be both a Jewish Savior and, at the same time, a Gentile Savior—that is, the Savior of the entire world. The key question they were wrestling with was: *how do Gentiles, who have come to believe in Jesus, fit into the promises God made to Abraham and the nation of Israel in Gen 12:1–2?* The answers these two factions came up with were:

- The Jewish believers in Rome held that Gentile believers needed to become Jewish and follow the Jewish laws and customs.

---

3. I am simplifying a lot here. This view of the reason for Romans is controversial, but you can read a defense of it in N. T. Wright, *Romans: Part One*, which is quite readable. If you want something a bit more challenging, see Wright's "Romans, Theology of Paul."

- The Gentile believers in Rome held that they could be faithful followers of Jesus without having to become Jewish or having to follow Jewish laws and customs.

The view these Gentiles held raised serious questions for the Jews:

- If Gentiles don't have to follow Jewish laws and customs, what does that mean for the Jewish people, who are God's "chosen people"?
- Is God now setting the Jewish nation aside?
- If so, then is God being unfaithful to his promises to Abraham and to Israel, that they would be his chosen people forever?

You can see from this set of questions that the character and the justice of God were at stake: Is God going back on his promise to Abraham? How can God be just if he does that?

These issues and questions were swirling around in the church at Rome. Paul had his work cut out for him in this letter to answer these burning issues.

But in an inspired move, Paul tells both Jews and Gentiles that each group had the wrong starting point! They shouldn't start with Abraham, as the Jews had been doing. They needed to travel back to a time *before* Abraham—back to the very beginning. Paul takes them back to creation itself and reexamines the purpose why God created the heavens, the earth, and humanity in the first place.

I think Paul's answers to both factions can be summed up in this way:

If you understand God's original intent for human beings at creation, then it will make sense:

- *why God chose Abraham and the Jewish nation*
- *what role the laws and customs of Israel played*
- *why Jesus came*
- *how Jews and Gentiles relate to God and each other in the body of Christ*

The details of Paul's answer are spelled out in chapters 1–8.[4] These eight chapters form one long, intricate but unified argument that answers

---

4. He has to deal with one final big problem in chapters 9–11, but the major arc of his answer is completed in 1–8.

the questions each faction had. Paul's explanation reaches its main point and climax at the end of Rom 8.

The metaphor of a music score might help us think about what Paul is doing in these chapters. Imagine that Paul is composing a symphony in Romans 1–8 with various themes strung together that recur in various forms throughout the first eight-and-a-half chapters. Then, in Rom 8:18–29, Paul weaves all of these musical themes together bringing them to a dramatic crescendo. This image of a musical score helps me understand our verse, Rom 8:29. I believe it is the highpoint of Paul's symphonic crescendo. Let's look at the verse.

Reading Romans 8:29 in one Breath: Grasping God's Vision for Us

In order to grasp what Paul is trying to communicate, it is really important to read this verse in one breath. Don't stop, pause, or even slow down until you arrive at the period of the sentence. If you stop anywhere along the way, you may miss Paul's point. So, go ahead, read it out loud now: *"For those whom God foreknew he also predestined to be conformed to the image of his Son in order that he might be the firstborn within a large family."*[5]

Now, while keeping in mind that this is one complete thought, let's break this verse down into four parts to help us understand it better:

(1) For those whom God foreknew he also predestined
(2) to be conformed to the image of his Son,
(3) in order that
(4) he might be the firstborn within a large family.

Now, let me comment on each of these parts:

- First, at some time in the past, God intended to do something: *for those whom he foreknew he also predestined.* (What does he mean by that!? Hold on, we'll come back to that in a moment.)

- Second, Paul tells us specifically what he intended to do: to have people who would *be conformed to the image of his Son.*

---

5. This is the NRS version. The NIV has "firstborn among many brothers and sisters."

- Third, this intention for people to be conformed to the image of Jesus is connected to an even larger purpose: it is *in order that* something else might happen—which leads us to the fourth point.

- And fourth, that larger purpose is in order that Jesus *might be the firstborn within a large family.*

If you take some time to reflect on this verse, you will notice that it reveals a grand vision that God has for humanity that he wants to accomplish—a vision that relates to the story of God and his world and to spiritual formation. But first we have to deal with two pesky little words that crop up in this verse, because they tend to mess with our minds and blind us to the actual point Paul is making. This is why I said we will need to put on our hiking boots and get ready for some serious mountain climbing!

Those Puzzling Words in Romans
8:29—"Foreknew" and "Predestined"

As soon as people read words like "foreknew" and "predestined," all sorts of questions arise, and problems invade our minds because of what *we think* they mean. And, although this seems like a topic to cover in systematic theology, it also has a deep impact on our understanding of spiritual formation.

Why is it important to think carefully about this—especially with regard to spiritual formation? I see at least two reasons.

First, I know people who have lost their faith because they believed that God had not predestined them. They did not feel like they were part of "the chosen." They concluded that they must not have been predestined because they didn't feel the presence of God or didn't sense that they were a child of God. Yes, they prayed. Yes, they committed their life to Christ. And yes, they went to church faithfully. But when that didn't result in feeling or experiencing anything with God, they concluded that they must not be "predestined" or "chosen."

The second reason it is important to wrestle with this as it relates to spiritual formation is this: If God predestines everything, then it seems that nothing that I do really matters. If God foreknew everything, then whatever God intended to happen will happen. If my actions are all pre-determined by God, then I can't change anything. This can lead to a fatalistic outlook on life and to spiritual passivity.

My description of these theological ideas may seem somewhat like an overstated caricature. However, many of the students I have taught and people I've known have come to these conclusions when they read such "predestination" passages in the Bible.

If we don't take a closer look at these words and clarify their meaning, it could have serious consequences for how we experience faith and understand spiritual formation.

So what do these terms mean? Does this verse teach that God pre-selects in advance which individuals he wants to save and which persons will not be saved?

If you read the book of Romans beginning in chapter 1, verse 1 all the way up to our verse, Rom 8:29, it becomes apparent that Paul is not focusing on individual salvation at all.

Two important principles along with two observations about grammar sandwiched between them help us understand what is going on here.

The *first principle:* Understand the passage you are reading in light of the overall reason the author wrote the book or letter. If we don't, we are in real danger of misinterpreting the passage.

As I indicated above, the main reason Paul wrote this letter was to address a fundamental issue that runs throughout the book: how does the church—that is composed of both believing Jews and Gentiles together—fit into the plan and promises that God had for the children of Abraham in the Old Testament?

In Romans, Paul is not talking about Schlemiel, the individual Jew, or Aristobulus, the individual Greek. He is talking about "Jews" and "Gentiles" collectively *as a group.* How do we know that? We know it by paying attention to the Greek grammar of the text.

First, in Greek, every verb, noun or pronoun is clearly either singular or plural. A Greek reader knows immediately knows if a word refers to an individual or a group. Greek can distinguish between "you" the individual and "y'all" (if you're from the South), or "yous guys" (if you're from the Northeast). English can't do that. What is significant is that in Rom 8, as in the seven previous chapters, Paul consistently uses the plural "you all" when he refers to the Romans. Paul is clearly not talking about individual salvation here.

Why does Paul use "you all"? This leads us to a *second* grammar-related observation. Recall throughout the book, Paul addresses two divided factions—Jews and Gentiles—and explains how they are now one new group—"one body" he calls them.[6] Particularly in the first eight chapters, Paul repeatedly refers to Jews and Gentiles as distinct groups that God wants to bring together into one. Notice how often he repeats this:

- "... first to the Jew, then to the Gentile." (1:16; 2:9, 10)
- "Jews and Gentiles alike are all under the power of sin." (3:9)
- "There is no difference between Jew and Gentile." (3:22; 10:12)[7]

Again, I believe it is clear that Paul's focus is not on individuals. He's not thinking in terms of, "I choose Jim and Sue, but I don't choose John and Sarah." Rather, he's thinking in terms of how God has decided that the Jews *as a group* and the Gentiles *as a group* should become the one new people of God together. Do you see how important it is to get this straight in our heads at the outset?

The second principle is that when you come to a puzzling word in the Bible, it is important to slow down and examine how the concept is understood throughout the Old and New Testaments. So before I tell you what I think "foreknew" and "predestined" mean, we need to try and connect Rom 8:29 with the big story of God and his world.

How Does Romans 8:29 Fit into the Story of God and His World?

I believe that Rom 8:29 gives us a glimpse into God's fundamental vision for humanity. What was God's vision? To find that out, we need to go back to the beginning—the very beginning, when God created humanity. Let's look at some verses that relate to this and see what we discover.

6. As he describes them in Rom 12:4–8.

7. In addition, he also addresses these groups directly and individually as well. *Gentiles*: Rom 1:14; *Jews*: Rom 2:17, 28, 29; 3:1, 29; 9:24.

The first one is perhaps the most significant: Gen 1:26–27. As you read it, ask yourself, what do these verses tell us about God's original vision for why he created humanity?

> Then God said, "Let us make mankind in our image, in our likeness, so that they may rule over the fish in the sea and the birds in the sky, over the livestock and all the wild animals, and over all the creatures that move along the ground." So God created mankind in his own image, in the image of God he created them; male and female he created them. (Gen 1:26–27)

These verses tell us that God wanted to create a people that *bear his image*.

Although we'll be nuancing later what the Hebrew word for image (*ṣelem*) means, for now let's just focus on the central idea of this word. Both the Hebrew word *ṣelem* and the English word "image" convey the idea of reflecting or reproducing something of the form or essence of a person or thing.

The writer of Genesis tells us that it was God's desire when he created humanity that *all* humans represent God. What that specifically means has been discussed and debated for centuries.[8] Although I'll present my case for this in the next chapter, I would suggest that a major part of what it means to be made in the image of God has to do with human beings reflecting God's character and values in how we live and in the way we relate to others.

But notice also that the writer underscores that God made them *male* and *female* in his image. Why does he do that? I think one primary reason was to indicate that God intended to have a large family to relate to. Why else do you have male and female? Male and female together create families. That is why he tells them in the next verse to "be fruitful and increase in number"!

Another significant passage that gives us a further insight into God's original vision for why he created humanity is Gen 3:8. Although this comes right after Adam and Eve disobeyed God, notice what this verse implies about God's relationship with Adam and Eve: "Then the man and his wife heard the sound of the LORD God as he was walking in the

---

8. For what may be seen as a definitive discussion of the concept of "the image of God," see Middleton, *The Liberating Image*. For a more dated, but useful discussion see McDonald, *Christian View of Man*, 32–41.

garden in the cool of the day, and they hid from the LORD God among the trees of the garden."

This verse describes a scene in which God is portrayed as "visiting" with the people he created. From the Hebrew grammar of the phrase "walking in the garden," it is clear that God did this on a regular basis: He was constantly "visiting" with them. Why? He wanted to be in deep relationship with them. He wanted to go through life together with them.

The Old Testament scholar John Walton has a number of publications arguing that the author of Genesis views the Garden of Eden as a temple.[9] The purpose of a temple is to be a place where God and humans meet to relate to one another. You can see this desire of God cropping up throughout the entire Bible. Here are some passages that express this:

- "I will put my dwelling place among you. . . . I will walk among you and be your God, and you will be my people." (Lev 26:11–12)

- "Many nations will be joined with the LORD in that day and will become my people. I will live among you and you will know that the LORD Almighty has sent me to you." (Zech 2:11)

- "For we are the temple of the living God. As God has said: 'I will live with them and walk among them, and I will be their God, and they will be my people.'" (2 Cor 6:16)

And when we come to a description of our future experience when God returns to make things as he originally intended them to be, notice what it says:

> And I heard a loud voice from the throne saying, "Look! God's dwelling place is now among the people, and he will dwell with them. They will be his people, and God himself will be with them and be their God." (Rev 21:3)

All these verses make *explicit* what is *implicit* in Gen 3:8: from the very beginning to the very end of the Bible, God's desire is to dwell with his people. So, when we summarize God's original vision for creation as we see it reflected in Gen 1:26–27 and Gen 3:8, we can express it this way:

God's original vision was to create a family of brothers and sisters, who share his character qualities, his values, and his way of life

---

9. Walton, *Ancient Near Eastern Thought*; Walton, "Creation in Genesis 1:1–2:3," 48–63; Walton, *Lost World of Genesis One*; Walton, *Genesis 1 as Ancient Cosmology*.

and who walk with him and with each other in unhindered and
open relationship.

That is what God envisioned before the world began. However . . .
the introduction of sin into humanity messed up God's vision. Adam and
Eve broke their relationship with God by turning away from God to seek
their own way. This caused fundamental damage in the relationship between God and people that has been with us ever since. Something happened to humanity that makes it impossible for them to remain alive in
the presence of a God who is characterized by utter purity and goodness.

So, what was God to do? (I am summarizing most of the Old and
much of the New Testament into one sentence here.) He sends his Son
on a cosmic mission to restore the relationships that were damaged: our
relationship with God and our relationships with each other.

That, in a nutshell, is the backdrop to Rom 8:29.

And now we're ready to think about what the words *foreknew* and *predes-*
tined mean. Let's look at them one at a time.

Foreknew

In light of what we have said, what does it mean that God *foreknew?* The
word suggests God *knew* something *in advance.* But, what—or, more precisely—*whom* did God know in advance? With this background in mind,
let's read the passage again to try to answer this question:

> For those whom God foreknew he also predestined to be con-
> formed to the image of his Son, in order that he might be the
> firstborn within a large family. (Rom 8:29)

I would suggest that the identity of the people referred to in this
verse—the people that God knew in advance—is directly related to God's
original vision in the first chapters of Genesis that I sketched out in the
preceding section: God's original vision was to have a large family of
brothers and sisters, who all reflected his image and that responded to
him in faith. Though Adam and Eve did not respond in faith to God
and marred that image, that doesn't deter God! He sends Jesus—the true
image of God—to accomplish his original vision of having a large family

who did, in fact, reflect his image and respond to him in faith! It is these people that God envisioned at creation. It is these he *knew in advance*.

It might be helpful to think about this "knowing something in advance" the way an engaged couple "knows in advance" that they want to have children. Imagine this scenario: an engaged couple go out on a date on a starry night on a hill overlooking a beautiful landscape—and both of them start dreaming about the future. They dream about the family they want to start. How many kids do they want? They're not sure, but they know they want a lot! And they begin to dream about the character qualities they want their children to have and how they hope that their kids will reflect the values and character of their parents.

This is, I would suggest, how Paul is using the word "foreknow" here. Paul understands God as *knowing in advance* that he wanted to have a large family in which all the brothers and sisters reflect his character and values. Although that original vision was damaged, God never gave up on it. Jesus came to earth to turn that original vision into a reality. In and through Jesus, humanity can now be restored to the image of God as reflected in the image of his Son! That is what God envisioned from the very beginning.

Predestined

And what he *envisioned—knew in advance* is what he also "predestined." Now, what does this word mean? I think what Paul means by the word "predestined" is that God *determined in advance* to accomplish something. Or to say it another way, the word *predestined* simply refers to something that God had *resolved to do*.

At the end of Rom 8:29 Paul lays out two things God resolved to accomplish:

1. "*to be conformed to the image of his Son,*

2. "in order that he might be the firstborn *within a large family.*"

God *envisioned* ("foreknew") from before creation, and he also *determined in advance/resolved to accomplish* ("predestined") that he would have a large family (point 2) and that the children in this large family would share in, reflect, and be conformed to the image of his Son (point 1).

Paul's intent in Rom 8:29 is not to indicate that certain people are predestined to be saved and others are not. That would not fit the flow of Paul's letter, nor does it fit the big story of God and his world, nor would it fit with the grammar Paul uses in Romans. Rather, God has determined in advance that he would have a great big family of these Jesus-image-bearing kind of people as his people.

Since God "predestined"—determined in advance—a family full of children who share the same character traits as Jesus had, anyone who says "yes" to God becomes part of that family that God envisioned and determined in advance to have.

This way of understanding these words not only resolves the problems often associated with these terms; it also helps us grasp the vision God has for us—a vision that liberates and inspires, and that our hearts long to embrace! In contrast, if we understand these words as they are popularly understood, and if we don't understand this passage in light of Paul's overarching concern throughout Romans, we may create a theology that causes fear and judgmentalism instead of a theology that brings rejoicing and hope.

Whew! That was a long climb up to the top of this mountain. I hope we have left the rough terrain behind, gotten out of the fog, and now have a better panoramic view of what God envisioned for his creation—and for us.

Now we are ready to circle back and see how Rom 8:29 relates to spiritual formation. But since it relates specifically to the *goal* of spiritual formation, we'll save that for the next chapter, where we will examine passages that speak directly to the goal of spiritual formation.

3

The Goal of Spiritual Formation

How does the New Testament describe the goal of spiritual formation? What language does it use to describe what we are to aim at when we think about spiritual growth? Let's look at some key texts that capture and describe this goal, starting with the apostle Paul's writing and then looking at one exemplary text in the Gospels.

I do want to let you know up front that all of these texts point to the same goal, with each text adding depth and richness to what the goal of spiritual formation is.

We will first look briefly, once again, at Rom 8:29 to see what it tells us about the *goal* of spiritual formation.

Romans 8:29

The part of this verse that directly relates to the goal of spiritual formation comes in the middle of the sentence: "For those God foreknew he also predestined *to be conformed to the image of his Son*, that he might be the firstborn among many brothers and sisters." From the very beginning, God envisioned and intended us to be conformed to the image of his Son. Let's reflect on what that means.

As we noted in the last chapter, when God first created the world, he created Adam and Eve "in his own image and after his own likeness"

(Gen 1:26). We touched on some of what the word "image" means, but we need to develop this more fully here.

Looking at how the words "image" and "likeness" are used in the Old Testament helps us grasp the point Gen 1:26–27 is driving at. There are two aspects to the way this word "image" was used in the Old Testament.

First: in the Old Testament, the word "image" can refer to idols that represented a pagan god.[1] It is also used to refer to humans, which makes the meaning clearer. It's helpful for us that the exact same words in Gen 1:26–27—"image" and "likeness"—appear together a few chapters later, but this time these words are referring to Adam and his son, Seth: "When Adam had lived 130 years, he had a son in his own *likeness*, in his own *image*" (Gen 5:3). Adam's son is described as reflecting who Adam was. In other words, when they see Seth, they will see the *character* and *essence* of Adam, with his flaws and wayward tendencies—yet also with the glory that God shared with him. So, being made in the image and likeness of God, means that humans are to reflect in some way God's character, essence, and values. But that is not all.

Second: There is another dimension to the word "image" that is somewhat foreign to our way of thinking today: in the ancient Near East, it was understood that kings were made in the image of the gods and that kings were the representative of a god on this earth in order to rule the world on that god's behalf. They were to re-*present* their god to the people: the king was the visible presentation of god; and so, when the king said or did something, it was as if that god himself were saying or doing it.

We see this, interestingly, in the name of the ancient Egyptian pharaoh we have nicknamed King Tut. His full name is *Tutankhamon*, which literally means "living image of Amon," who is the Egyptian god of the sun.[2] In fact, one ancient Egyptian document has the god Amon addressing another pharaoh by the name of Amenhotep III with these words: "You are my beloved son, who came forth from my members, my image, whom I have put on earth. I have given to you to rule the earth in peace."[3] Both of these pharaohs were considered the visible and official representations of Amon, the sun god, ruling on his behalf.

1. Num 33:52 "Destroy all their carved images and their cast idols, and demolish all their high places." Other examples are 1 Sam 6:5, 11 and 2 Kgs 11:18.

2. See the helpful Wikipedia page on King Tut at http://en.wikipedia.org/wiki/Tutankhamun.

3. Middleton, *The Liberating Image*, 109.

In Gen 1:27, the writer tells us that it's not just kings who are to rule and be God's representatives. In fact, *everyone*—male and female—is made in the image of God. This would have been a shocking claim at that time. God did not create a human pyramid with certain people having more value being placed above others of less value. Rather, *all* people bear the image of God, not just kings and nobles, and not just males.[4] *Every* human being is a representative of God and rules the earth on God's behalf.

Note also the next verse: "God blessed them and said to them, 'Be fruitful and increase in number; fill the earth and *subdue* it. *Rule over* the fish in the sea and the birds in the sky and over every living creature that moves on the ground'" (Gen 1:28). When God tells Adam and Eve to "subdue the earth," and "rule over it," he is not telling them to do whatever they wanted with the earth. Some have interpreted this command as a license to "trash the place," with no concern about destroying nature. That, however, is not at all what the passage conveys.

Back then, large stretches of the earth were wild, untamed, and un-inhabitable. In order for humans to live in those areas, the wild animals needed to be "subdued" and the land needed be tamed and cultivated. In other words, the command to "subdue" and "rule" was the command to make the earth habitable so that human life could flourish. Just as God who created this world "ruled" it with care and wisdom, so humans were to reflect God's way of rulership over the earth, treating it with the same care and wisdom God displayed. They were, after all, made in his image.[5]

So, to sum up: the word "image" indicates, on the one hand, that we are to reflect the essence, character, and values of God in the way we live our lives, and, on the other hand, that it is not a select few that have the dignity of being God's representative on this earth. All human beings do.

But that image became distorted. Adam and Eve turned their back on God, and in doing so, they no longer fully reflected the image of God

---

4. I think Paul gets at this point when he tells us in Gal 3:27 that "in Christ there is neither Jew nor Gentile, slave or free, nor is there male and female, for you are all one in Christ Jesus."

5. Gordon Wenham explains it this way, "humanity is made in God's image to be his representative on earth, that is, to act in a godlike way in caring for the earth and the other creatures in it. Kings in ancient times were expected to rule their people in a way that benefited their subjects and in particular kings had a duty to look after the poor and weak members of their realm. It is this language that Genesis is echoing here. Or to put it another way, humanity is expected to manage the earth for God in a way that pleases him." Wenham, *Exploring the Old Testament, Vol. 1*, 20.

THE GOAL OF SPIRITUAL FORMATION: PART 1   31

to the world around them. The Greek word for image is *eikōn*, and so Scot McKnight speaks of human beings as "cracked eikons" of God,[6] whose image has now been distorted, cracked, and marred.

What did God do about this problem? He sent his Son, Jesus, who is described as "the image of the invisible God."[7] God did this for three connected reasons. *First*, he did it so that we might see what the image of God looks like when it is lived out in real time on this earth. *Second*, he did it so that we would have an example to pattern our own lives after as we live on this earth. *Third*, he did it so that humanity would have a power source, helping us to be recreated in his image through his Spirit living inside of us.

Athanasius, an early church father, makes a brilliant comment about this. In a treatise on the incarnation of Jesus, he wrestles with the problem that human sinfulness marred the image of God in man and writes:

> What, then, was God to do? What else could He possibly do, being God, but renew His Image in mankind, so that through it [humanity] might once more come to know Him? And how could this be done save by the coming of the very Image Himself, our Savior Jesus Christ? [Humanity] could not have done it, for they are only made after the Image; nor could angels have done it, for they are not the images of God. The Word of God came in His own Person, because it was He alone, the Image of the Father Who could recreate [humanity] made after the Image.[8]

Athanasius agrees with Paul's statement in Rom 8:29 that God's original goal for us to share his image is now made possible through Jesus' life, death, and resurrection. By being "conformed to the image of his Son," we can now become what Adam and Eve were intended to be. This doesn't happen all at once, but is a process that happens over time. Paul points to this being a process in 2 Cor 3:18, where he describes us as contemplating Jesus' glory, and as we do we "are *being transformed* into his image with *ever-increasing* glory, which comes from the Lord, who is the Spirit."

So, to summarize, the goal of spiritual formation given in this passage is that our lives increasingly should look like, act like, and be like Jesus. Our inner world (our outlook, priorities, values, motivations) and

6. McKnight, *Embracing Grace*, 52–63.

7. Col 1:15.

8. Athanasius, *On the Incarnation*, 3.14. Available at http://www.ccel.org/ccel/athanasius/incarnation.html.

outer world (our lifestyle, actions, speech, and relationships) should reflect the pattern of life that Jesus embodied in his life on earth.

Let's look at another significant verse. It's a short one, but there's a lot in it!

Galatians 4:19

Let me give you the context of this verse before we read it. The theme running through Paul's entire letter to the Galatians is that the Galatian Christians had been pressured by certain Jewish believers to follow the Old Testament Jewish law as a means of salvation. Paul explains that if they try to blend human effort with the free gift of God, human effort nullifies God's gift.

In this context, you can sense Paul's exasperation, as he utters these words expressing his deepest longing for these believers: "My dear children, for whom I am again in the pains of childbirth until Christ is formed in you."

The phrase "again in the pains of childbirth" expresses Paul's deep agony. (I was in the room each time my wife gave birth to our kids. Let's just say, I'm glad she was giving birth, not me! I think it would have killed me.) When a woman is in the pains of childbirth, she suffers deep personal pain for the sake of another. Paul is so concerned about the believers in Galatia, that he feels a similar sense of agony with regard to his deep wish that *Christ will be formed in them.*

What does Paul mean by this? The early church fathers wrestled with what it meant for Christ to be formed in us and came up with some pretty startling formulations, which might sound heretical at first.[9]

- "The Word (became) man ... and the Son of God (became) son of man so that man ... might become a son of God." (Irenaeus)

- "God became man in order that we may become gods." (Athanasius)

- "You were God from the beginning, and You became man later in order to make me god." (Gregory of Nazianzus)

9. The Russian Orthodox Metropolit Hilarion Alfeyev has gathered citations from early church fathers relating to this in a helpful article entitled "Deification in Christ" at http://hilarion.ru/en/2010/02/25/1081. I am using his wording here. The quotations are from Irenaeus, *Against Heresies*, 5. Preface; Athanasius, *On the Incarnation*, 54.3; Gregory of Nazianzus, "Poemata historica," in *Patrologia Graeca* 37, 971.

Archbishop Alfeyev summarizes what these early church fathers were saying with this helpful formulation: "through the Incarnation of the Word, the human person becomes by adoption what the Son of God is by nature."[10] The concept that these quotations capture is what the Orthodox Church calls *deification*, the process of becoming more and more like God. Not that we are becoming God, but we are progressively becoming more and more *like* him.

So, Gal 4:19 and these sayings of early Christians point out that our major aim is to become like Christ.

At this point, however, we need to wrestle with a difficult question: *how can we become like Jesus, if he was God?* This would seem to be an exercise in frustration, like telling someone to leap a tall building in a single bound, when everyone knows only Superman can do that, only it's worse because even Superman isn't God. How can we, fallen human beings, become like Christ, who was God in the flesh? Is it even possible? Since this will take us on a bit of a tangent that is not directly related to the topic of this chapter, I will pick up this topic in the next chapter. In the meantime, let's look at a few more passages that speak to the goal of spiritual formation.

Ephesians 3:16–19

In Paul's letter to the Ephesians, he talks about his ultimate goal in life using language similar to Phil 3, which we will look at shortly. In Ephesians, however, Paul goes into more descriptive detail about the nature of his experience of Jesus. Paul is overwhelmed by Jesus' love for him, and he prays that the Ephesians will experience this love the same way he has. Notice Paul's description in Eph 3:16–19.

> I pray that out of his glorious riches he may strengthen you with power through his Spirit in your inner being, so that Christ may dwell in your hearts through faith. And I pray that you, being rooted and established in love, may have power, together with all the Lord's holy people, to grasp how wide and long and high and deep is the love of Christ, and to know this love that surpasses knowledge—that you may be filled to the measure of all the fullness of God.

10. Alfeyev, "Deification in Christ."

Christ's love is so powerful and wonderful that Paul struggles for ways to convey what he has experienced. Like the limitless sky, Paul says we will never fathom the full expanse of Christ's love, and he prays that we would experience what words cannot describe. But Paul's wish for the Ephesian believers doesn't end there. In the last half of verse 19, the ultimate goal of experiencing the love of Christ is that we will be "be filled to the measure of all the fullness of God."

Well, that *sounds* grand . . . but what does it actually *mean*? If we were to translate these Greek words directly and literally, it would read "in order that you would be filled to/into/with all the fullness of God." It is challenging to convey what Paul is getting at, so let's compare how different translations render this:

- "May you experience the love of Christ, though it is too great to understand fully. *Then you will be made complete with all the fullness of life and power that comes from God.*" (NLT)

- ". . . and thus to know the love of Christ that surpasses knowledge, *so that you may be filled up to all the fullness of God.*" (NET)

- "You will know Christ's love, which goes far beyond any knowledge. I am praying this *so that you may be completely filled with God.*" (GWN)

These translations seek to convey Paul's prayer that we would experience God fully and directly in our lives, so that we would be, so to speak, "in-godded"—that God would fill our entire being.[11] Now *that* is astonishing! But that is what Paul says that he experienced, and he indicates that it can be our experience as well.

Philippians 3:7–12

Paul's letter to the Philippians is the most individual and personal of all of Paul's letters.[12] In it we get the clearest insight into what mattered most to him. In Phil 3:7–12 he bears his soul more than in any other passage. Notice how Paul describes his personal life aim.

---

11. This notion of being *in-godded* has been developed in the Eastern Orthodox tradition of *theosis*. We'll pick this up later.

12. "Philippians, though the opening greetings are by Paul and Timothy, must be considered the most individual of Paul's letters." Llewelyn, ed., *Ammonius*, 171–72.

But whatever were gains to me I now consider loss for the sake of Christ. What is more, I consider everything a loss because of the surpassing worth of knowing Christ Jesus my Lord, for whose sake I have lost all things. I consider them garbage, that I may gain Christ and be found in him, not having a righteousness of my own that comes from the law, but that which is through faith in Christ—the righteousness that comes from God on the basis of faith. I want to know Christ—yes, to know the power of his resurrection and participation in his sufferings, becoming like him in his death, and so, somehow, attaining to the resurrection from the dead. Not that I have already obtained all this, or have already arrived at my goal, but I press on to take hold of that for which Christ Jesus took hold of me.

It comes through loud and clear in this passage that, for Paul, nothing in life matters more than knowing Christ as fully and deeply as possible. What makes this even more compelling is that just a few verses earlier Paul lists all of his credentials and accomplishments. From the standpoint of Jewish society at that time, it is an impressive list! It reads like Paul was certainly someone on the "Who's Who in the Jewish World" list of his day.

And yet Paul's opinion of these credentials and accomplishments is that they are "garbage" compared to knowing Christ. Behind the English word "garbage" in this passage is the Greek word *skuballon*, a term that indicates "useless or undesirable material" that someone intends to throw out. Ancient writers used it to refer to "excrement, manure, garbage, or kitchen scraps."[13] That is how Paul viewed his trophy case of Jewish credentials when set alongside the value of knowing Christ: *skuballon!* What he once held to be of highest value, he now sees as stuff to be thrown into the garbage can! Paul found something so much more valuable that it makes all of his other accomplishment seem worthless in contrast.

Paul reveals for us in this passage his ultimate goal in life: He wants to "gain Christ" and he wants to "know Christ." But what does he mean by that? Paul was Jewish, so his understanding of what it means to "know" something was steeped in the language and ways of thinking of the Hebrew Scriptures. In some contexts, the Hebrew word *yada'*, which we translate as "know," carries the meaning of deep, personal, and intimate knowledge. For example, notice how the TNIV translates the word *yada'* in these passages:

13. Bauer et al., eds., *Greek-English Lexicon of the New Testament*, 932.

- "Then the eyes of both of them were opened, and they *realized* they were naked." (Gen 3:7)

- "Adam *made love to* his wife Eve, and she became pregnant and gave birth to Cain." (Gen 4:1)

- "And the LORD said to Moses, 'I will do the very thing you have asked, because I am pleased with you and I *know* you by name.'" (Exod 33:17)

- "Since then, no prophet has risen in Israel like Moses, whom the LORD *knew* face to face." (Deut 34:10)

- "You *know* when I sit and when I rise; you perceive my thoughts from afar." (Ps 139:2)

All of the words in bold italics above are translations of the word *yada'*. In each passage the word indicates a deep, personal, and intimate acquaintance with someone. And that is how Paul used this term "know" in Phil 3. Paul's desire is to know Christ as deeply and as personally as possible. He doesn't simply want to know *about* Christ. He doesn't want to become a Bible quiz champion knowing all the facts about the life of Jesus. He wants to *experience* Christ directly and personally. That is Paul's ultimate goal in life. And he wants it to be our life goal too.

John 17

When we circle back to the Gospels in search of texts that communicate the "spiritual formation" goals that Jesus had for his followers, perhaps the most significant text is found in John 17.

At the end of the Gospel of John, Jesus, knowing that his final hour has come, gathers his disciples together for a meal. While they share a final meal together, he gives what scholars often refer to as his "farewell discourse." Besides the Sermon on the Mount in Matthew 5–7, this is the longest teaching of Jesus in the Gospels, stretching from chapters 14–16, and it ends with the longest recorded prayer of Jesus, which spans all twenty-six verses of chapter 17. In this prayer we catch a glimpse of Jesus' ultimate desire for his followers—and for the entire world. Notice two things in this passage: first, what Jesus emphasizes; second, how that compares with the passages we just looked at from Paul.

Father, the hour has come. Glorify your Son, that your Son may glorify you. For you granted him authority over all people that he might give eternal life to all those you have given him. Now this is eternal life: that they know you, the only true God, and Jesus Christ, whom you have sent. . . .

Holy Father, protect them by the power of your name, the name you gave me, so that they may be one as we are one . . . that all of them may be one, Father, just as you are in me and I am in you. May they also be in us so that the world may believe that you have sent me. I have given them the glory that you gave me, that they may be one as we are one—I in them and you in me—so that they may be brought to complete unity. Then the world will know that you sent me and have loved them even as you have loved me. Father, I want those you have given me to be with me where I am, and to see my glory, the glory you have given me because you loved me before the creation of the world. . . .

I have made you known to them, and will continue to make you known in order that the love you have for me may be in them and that I myself may be in them. (John 17:1–26)

We see that Paul and Jesus shared the same vision and goal for humanity that God had at creation.[14] The emphasis and even the language they use is the same. Notice especially the phrases "that they know you," "I in them and you in me," "in order that the love you have for me may also be in them and that I myself may be in them." Jesus wants his disciples to know God and his love personally and experientially and to be *in-godded* much like Paul described.

Summary

Let me summarize the main thrust of each of these passages regarding the goal of spiritual formation:

- To conform our lives to the image of Jesus so that who we are on the inside and the outside reflects Jesus, inside and out. (Rom 8:29)

- For Christ to be formed in us. (Gal 4:19)

14. See verses 5 and 24.

- To have Christ dwell in us so that we experience his immeasurable love and are fully "in-godded"—or filled up with God. (Eph 3:16–19)

- To strive to know Christ (as intimate experience) and his power and become like him (Phil 3:7–12).

- To know God, be in him, and experience the love of God in ourselves. (John 17)

These passages, which are just the tip of the New Testament iceberg, speak with one voice: the goal of every follower of Jesus is to experience him and his love in ever deepening ways, so that every thought, act, and every relationship is infused with the love of Christ who lives within us.

If this is the goal of spiritual formation, then it is important to think through the implications of this. One implication stands out loud and clear. Everything that stands in the way of deep intimacy with Jesus has got to go. One of the key tasks in our own spiritual formation is to identify those areas in our lives that hinder us from experiencing the love of Jesus and develop a plan to deal radically with them.

So, whatever else we can say about spiritual formation in the New Testament, one of the top goals has to be knowing and loving God in Jesus as deeply and intimately as possible and bringing all of our life into alignment with his life. We want our inner world (our outlook, priorities, values, motivations) and our outer world (lifestyle, actions, speech, social relationships) to reflect the pattern that Jesus embodied in his life on earth. In other words, spiritual formation is about being made into the image of God as embodied in Jesus. Our goal is to become like Jesus himself.

How we do that, we will cover in the rest of the book, but now I want to pick up the question I raised earlier in this chapter: *how can we become like Christ, if he was God?* After that, we'll try to get a better handle on what it means to become like Christ in a more practical and tangible way.

4

An Aside: But Can We Really Become Like Christ?

"He [became] one of us as man in order that we also might be like Him, that is, gods and sons."

CYRIL OF ALEXANDRIA[1]

SO, CAN I BECOME like Jesus, even though he was God and I am not? The first step in solving this problem, I would argue, is to look carefully at the first part of what Cyril of Alexandria wrote: *he [became] one of us as man.*[2]

So, let's think about this: *What does it mean that Jesus became like us?*

When we look at the New Testament, we see over and over again that Jesus is our example. Note the following passages. In 1 Cor 11:1, Paul tells the Corinthians, "follow my example, as I follow the example of Christ." John tells believers in 1 John 2:6 that "whoever claims to live in him must live as Jesus did."

The Greek phrase "live as Jesus did" is more literally rendered by the ESV as "ought to *walk* in the same way in which [Jesus] *walked.*" It is important to stop and think about this little word *walk*, because in New Testament times, it had a particular meaning. It was used by Jewish

1. Cyril of Alexandria, *Commentary on John*, 663.

2. Ron Habermas, has a helpful blog post, "The Greatest Story Never Told," and some of his thoughts flow into and through this chapter. You can read the blog post at http://www.koinoniablog.net/2009/05/habermas-1.html. He explores this in more depth in his book *Complete Disciple*, 119–39.

39

rabbis and their disciples to describe the *entire way of life* that the rabbi had. Everything the rabbi did and said was to be the pattern for the lives of the rabbi's followers.

John tells his audience that Jesus is to function as an example for us in every dimension of our lives. Paul says the same thing when he tells the Corinthians to follow his example as he is following Christ's example in every aspect of life.

But again, if Jesus is God, how can he function as an example for us humans? For this we need to think—again—about what it meant for Jesus to become man.

Take a look at the following list and ask yourself, which of these is true of Jesus?

• He wept	• He prayed
• He became angry	• His prayer wasn't answered
• He experienced hunger	• He was tempted
• He learned new things	• He suffered
• He grew in wisdom	• He was disappointed when
• He became tired and slept	he felt the absence of God's
• He was surprised	presence
• He depended on God's guidance	• He was dependent on others
to know what to do and say	• He was influenced by others

Answer: All of these were true of Jesus—just as they are true of us. And yet he was divine—fully God. How do we put these two truths together?

Perhaps the most significant passage to help us understand how Jesus can be our example is Phil 2:5–11. Notice what it says about Jesus' humanity and his divinity:

> Have the same mindset as Christ Jesus: Who, being in very nature God, did not consider equality with God something to be used to his own advantage; rather, he *made himself nothing* [NRS: *emptied himself*] by taking the very nature of a servant, *being made in human likeness*. And being found in appearance as a man, he humbled himself by becoming obedient to death— even death on a cross!
>
> Therefore God exalted him to the highest place and gave him the name that is above every name, that at the name of Jesus every knee should bow, in heaven and on earth and under the earth, and every tongue acknowledge that Jesus Christ is Lord, to the glory of God the Father.

This passage is very clear that Jesus was God in every way. He was "in very nature God." But verse 7 contains two critical phrases:

- *made himself nothing (emptied himself)*
- *being made in human likeness*

This leads us to ask two important questions.

- Emptied himself of what?
- What did it mean for Jesus to be *made in human likeness*?

It is important to figure out what the Greek term for emptied, *kenoō*, means. The term in Paul's day was used in the following ways:[3]

1. literally *remove the content of* something;

2. figuratively,

   a. as taking away the effectiveness of something: *deprive of power*;

   b. as taking away the significance of something: *destroy, make invalid, empty*;

   c. as taking away the prerogatives of status or position: *empty, divest*.

Scholars debate which meaning, or combination of meanings, Paul was referring to in Phil 2. Unfortunately, Phil 2 doesn't give us enough context to nail down the precise meaning with confidence. We can, however, look at how the rest of the New Testament describes Jesus to gain insight into what this "emptying" actually entailed. Then we can come back to Phil 2 and figure out which usage make most sense.

Let's begin by looking at Luke 2. Notice these two passages:

- "And the child grew and became strong; he was filled with wisdom, and the grace of God was on him." (Luke 2:40)
- "And Jesus grew in wisdom and stature, and in favor with God and man." (Luke 2:52)

What does it imply that Jesus "grew" in wisdom? It indicates that at that time, he did not have all wisdom. I have encountered many Christians who assume that Jesus, when he was on earth, knew everything possible to know. If that is the case, Jesus couldn't have grown in wisdom,

---

3. Friberg, Friberg, and Miller, *Analytical Lexicon to the Greek New Testament*, Vol. 4, 228.

since his wisdom and knowledge would have been complete. Yet, this passage indicates Jesus gradually acquired something that he did not previously have.

Now, look at another passage: "But about that day or hour no one knows, not even the angels in heaven, nor the Son, but only the Father" (Matt 24:36). Why doesn't the Son know? We might assume that Jesus knew everything because he was God. So, why doesn't he know? I think the answer is that Jesus didn't know because he gave up any use of his divine powers, deliberately declining to draw on any of the attributes of God that would have given him an advantage over people. He took on humanity and its limitations fully and completely.

Although this is hotly debated, I would suggest that it means that *when Jesus was on earth, he only knew what other human beings could have known—unless God revealed it to him.* This may seem like a wild claim to make, because many have gotten so used to assuming Jesus drew on all his divine powers when he lived on earth, and yet, I think that is what this verse indicates. It boggles my mind every time I think about it.

Now, let's look at Heb 2:14–18. Key in particularly on the words in italics and think about the implications:

> Since the children have flesh and blood, he too *shared in their humanity* so that by his death he might break the power of him who holds the power of death—that is, the devil—and free those who all their lives were held in slavery by their fear of death. . . . For this reason he had to be *made like them, fully human in every way*, in order that he might become a merciful and faithful high priest in service to God, and that he might make atonement for the sins of the people. Because *he himself suffered when he was tempted*, he is able to help those who are being tempted.

The writer of Hebrews says that Jesus identified with humanity *in every way*. In his earthly life, Jesus was fully human like you and I are—with no "supernatural" advantages over us in this life. He was tempted just like you and I are tempted, and he had to resist temptation just like you and I need to resist.

This is emphasized again in another passage in Hebrews: "For we do not have a high priest who is unable to empathize with our weaknesses, but we have one who *has been tempted in every way, just as we are*—yet he did not sin" (Heb 4:15). The writer of Hebrews is emphasizing the 100 percent identification between Jesus and us: Jesus was like us *in every way*. He was tempted like us in every way—but he did not sin.

Let's look at one more passage describing Jesus' temptation. Reflecting on it is somewhat unsettling: "Then Jesus was led by the Spirit into the wilderness to be tempted by the devil. After fasting forty days and forty nights, he was hungry. The tempter came to him and said . . ." (Matt 4:1–3a). These verses set the stage for Jesus to be tempted three times by Satan. Were these real temptations for Jesus or not? Could Jesus *really* have been tempted—and *fallen*? Before you immediately think "No way!" think through the options:

> *Option 1*: If Jesus were functioning *in his capacity as God*, this would not have been a temptation for him at all.[4] But if that is the case, then he could not have been an example for us to resist temptation. It would be like Superman telling a normal human being to leap over a tall building in a single bound. It would be setting up a standard that would be impossible for us to keep.

> *Option 2*: If Jesus were functioning in his capacity *as a human being*, then these were real temptations, and he could have fallen. If that is the case, then Jesus becomes a real example for us to follow in how to resist temptation.

Isn't Option 2 exactly what Heb 2:14–18 and 4:14 tell us? All the temptations Jesus experienced really were temptations just like you and I experience.[5]

But then, some would argue: Those are the temptations, but how do you explain all the miracles Jesus did? How do you explain the things that Jesus knew about people that he couldn't have known as a mere human being? Aren't these proofs that Jesus really was God? Let's look at John 14:12: "Very truly I tell you, whoever believes in me will do *the works* I have been doing, and they will do even greater things than these, because I am going to the Father." The *works* that Jesus refers to are the miracles that he performed. This verse indicates two things. *First*, Jesus viewed the miracles he performed as a pattern that his followers should imitate. *Second*, Jesus performed these miracles as a human being who trusted in God. The faith Jesus displayed in God when he performed these miracles is the same type of faith that Jesus' followers can have to perform miracles.

---

4. That is actually the argument that James makes when he tells us that "God cannot be tempted" (Jas 1:13).

5. Here is a challenge for you: can you think the following thought? *Jesus really could have, as a fully human being, given in to Satan. If that is the case (and it seems like it is), do you realize the risk that God took in order to save us?*

In fact, this is exactly what happens in Luke 10. Jesus sends out seventy-two of his followers to do what he had been doing, saying, "Heal the sick" (Luke 10:9). And the disciples returned amazed that they could do the same sorts of miracles that Jesus had been doing, even driving out demons (Luke 10:17). And later, in the book of Acts, the disciples and other Christ-followers continued to do the same type of "works" that Jesus had done:

- Peter heals a lame man (Acts 3:1–11) (Jesus: John 5:5–9).

- Peter has supernatural knowledge (Acts 5:1–10) (Jesus: John 4:17–19).

- The apostles "performed many signs and wonders" (Acts 5:12) (Jesus: Matt 15:30–31).

- Peter and John pray and people receive the Holy Spirit (Acts 8:15) (Jesus: John 20:22).

- Peter heals someone who was paralyzed (Act 9:33) (Jesus: Luke 5:18–25).

- Peter and Paul raise people from the dead (Acts 9:36–41; 20:9–12) (Jesus: Mark 5:41).

- Peter and Paul cast out demons (Acts 5:16; 19:12) (Jesus: Matt 8:16).

- Ananias heals Paul of blindness (Acts 9:17–18) (Jesus: John 9).

- Paul heals many people of various diseases (Act 19:11–12) (Jesus: Mark 6:56).

All of these miracles recorded in Acts are identical to Jesus' miracles!

So, let's ask the question again: Did Jesus perform his miracles (and for that matter, everything else he did) through his own powers *as God*? Or did Jesus perform these miracles by faith in God—just as Jesus' followers in Acts did? What makes best sense of this evidence? As hard as it is to fathom or accept this, I think it is the second option.

The New Testament scholar, N. T. Wright, in his careful study of Jesus, comes to this conclusion:

> I do not think Jesus "knew he was God" in the same sense that one knows one is tired or happy, male or female. He did not sit back and say to himself, "Well, I never! I'm the second person of the Trinity!" Rather, "as part of his human vocation, grasped in faith, sustained in prayer, implemented in action, he believed he

had to do and be, for Israel and the world, that which according
to Scripture only [God] himself could do and be.[6]

Since Jesus gave up the exercise of every divine power that would
separate him from humanity, it meant that he had to discover who he
was—God incarnate—and act on that in faith.

If you are like me, the first time I thought this thought, it was so out-
of-sync with how I had grown up that it just felt wrong. Then it dawned
on me that I had grown up with a fuzzy notion of Jesus being God that I
had never seriously thought about. The more I read the New Testament,
the more I saw that this new perspective made more sense—as challenging as it was for me to come to terms with. But don't take my word for it.
Re-read the New Testament and see what you think.

⚖

After reflecting on the passages we just looked at, what would you say
now about how Paul uses the word *kenoō* (emptied himself) in Phil 2?

1. literally *remove the content of* something;

2. figuratively,

    a. as taking away the effectiveness of something *deprive of power*;

    b. as taking away the significance of something *destroy, make in-
    valid, empty*;

    c. as taking away the prerogatives of status or position *empty, divest*.

My conclusion is that the emptying Paul refers to is "2a" and "2c"
combined—of giving up the power and knowledge that Jesus had as God
and giving up the prerogatives of his status and position as God and not
making use of them. These two together seem to make sense of all that
the New Testament says of Jesus:

- Jesus was fully God and fully man during his time on earth.

- Yet, he set aside/didn't avail himself of any of the dimensions of his
  divinity in his time on earth.

- He lived his life on earth fully as a human being.

6. Borg and Wright, *The Meaning of Jesus*, 166. See also Wright, *Jesus and the
Victory of God*, 654.

- Everything that Jesus did while on earth—including all the supernatural things—he did as a human being, who put his full trust in his heavenly Father.

What does this teaching about Jesus becoming human and emptying himself have to do with our understanding and practice of spiritual formation? Only if Jesus was human in every way that we are, could he become the pattern for every dimension of our lives.

- His way of life should be our way of life.

- His values should be our values.

- His concerns should be our concern.

- His character should become our character.

- His teachings should be what we follow.

- His actions should be the actions that we also engage in.

- His relationship with God is a template for our relationship with God.

- His relationship with others is a model for our own relationships.

How do we discover these things? Have you ever asked yourself, *why* Matthew, Mark, Luke, and John were written? Why do we need four books about the same thing? And have you ever wondered *what kind of writing* they actually are?

The New Testament scholar, Richard Burridge wrote his doctoral dissertation researching the question, *what are the Gospels*? He concludes that each of these four writings fit into the genre of ancient Greco-Roman biographies, called *bioi*.[7] He also notes that these ancient biographies were written for two primary reasons:

First, by selecting historical facts, stories, incidents, sayings, sermons, and weaving these incidents together in a certain way, the author intended to paint a portrait of an extraordinary individual and help others understand what that individual stood for. Most people get this.

The *second* reason, however, we might have missed: the writers of these ancient biographies deliberately present a person's life and teachings, as well as how they encountered challenges, *as an example for others to imitate.* It was, in fact, the discovery of this that led Richard Burridge

---

7. Burridge, *What Are the Gospels?*, 145–48, 180–83.

eventually to write his book *Imitating Jesus*, where he examines the life of Jesus in all its dimensions as a model for how to live.[8] Burridge claims that the authors of the four Gospels wrote so that we would *see* how Jesus lived every facet of his life and *hear* what he said and how he said it, in order that we would have a *pattern* for how we should live. Having four Gospels adds depth-perception: four different vantage points that help us grasp who Jesus is and how we can live like him.

So, let's briefly summarize what we've said up to now. We've discovered that the primary goal of spiritual formation is for each of us to become like Christ. The Bible indicates that, yes, it is possible to increasingly become like Christ because he was truly human, just as we are. We will not attain Christ-likeness fully in this life, but it is possible to become more and more like him.

Now let's turn to look at what becoming like Christ means in a more practical and tangible way.

8. See especially pages 28–30 and 73–79 in Burridge, *Imitating Jesus*, on this topic.

5

The Goal of Spiritual Formation

PART 2: GETTING SPECIFIC

What Does It Mean to Become Like Christ?

SINCE IT IS POSSIBLE to become more and more like Jesus, let's drill further down into what that means. We can get at this by reflecting on the values that Jesus held and lived out. I find it helpful to ask the question, *What were Jesus' central concerns?* Thankfully, Jesus gave a clear and straightforward answer to this.

A legal expert in Jewish law once asked Jesus, "Of all the commandments, which is the most important?" (Mark 12:28). The rabbis of Jesus' day frequently debated about what were the "weightiest" (more important) commands in the law of Moses, and what where the "lighter" (less important) commands. This teacher wanted to know what Jesus saw as "the spiritual center of Judaism."[1] Jesus uses this opportunity to explain what most mattered to him.[2]

As was often the case, Jesus answered in a way that caught his listeners off-guard. His answer contains both something expected and unexpected:

> "The most important one," answered Jesus, "is this: 'Hear, O Israel: The Lord our God, the Lord is one. Love the Lord your God with all your heart and with all your soul and with all your mind and with all your strength.' The second is this: 'Love your

1. McKnight, *Jesus Creed*, 8.
2. Morris, *Matthew*, 563.

neighbor as yourself." There is no commandment greater than these." (Mark 12:29–31)

Quite possibly, this legal expert expected Jesus to cite one of the Ten Commandments. Jesus, instead, chose something more foundational—something that precedes and encompasses those commandments. Jesus began his answer by citing something every Jewish person of his day would have been intimately familiar with—the *Shema*, the most ancient Jewish creed.

From Moses' day, through the time of Jesus, and up to the present day, every morning and evening devout Jews recite the *Shema*. The word *shema*, which means "hear," is taken from the first word of this creed recorded in Deut 4:4–9:

> Hear (*Shema*), O Israel: The LORD our God, the LORD is one. Love the LORD your God with all your heart and with all your soul and with all your strength. These commandments that I give you today are to be on your hearts. Impress them on your children. Talk about them when you sit at home and when you walk along the road, when you lie down and when you get up. Tie them as symbols on your hands and bind them on your foreheads. Write them on the doorframes of your houses and on your gates.

These verses are the closest thing Jews have to a common creed.[3] Through daily repetition, these words became ingrained in the minds and hearts of Jesus' hearers. They became, in fact, the Jewish pathway for spiritual formation, and quite a comprehensive one, at that.[4] Notice how these instructions aim at shaping and transforming the internal and external dimensions of a person's life. These instructions:

- target our desires ("love the Lord")

- incorporate our entire being ("heart . . . soul . . . strength")

- focus on our inner being ("on your hearts")

- are instilled into the warp and woof of daily life ("Impress them on your children. Talk about them when you sit . . . walk . . . lie down . . . get up")

---

3. McKnight, *Jesus Creed*, 7.
4. Ibid.

- assist in integrating these concepts into their lives by incorporating multiple and multidimensional reinforcements:

  - verbal ("impress on" "talk about")

  - social ("children" = family)

  - physical/bodily ("*tie* them as symbols on your hands" "*bind* them on your foreheads" "*write* them on the doorframes . . .")

  - visual ("*symbols* on . . . *hands* . . . *forehead*" "on the *doorframes* of your *houses* and on your *gates*.")

This is quite an effective, comprehensive program of Jewish spiritual formation. Then Jesus did the unexpected: he meddled with this ancient creed, by adding to it. That would have taken this legal expert and other listeners aback. Everyone knows, creeds are sacred. They come with a "do not tamper with the contents" label on them.[5] That didn't stop Jesus.

What did Jesus do? He added "love your neighbor as yourself."[6] That's not in the creed. So, why did Jesus add that? Scot McKnight explains it this way and, at the same time, ties it in to Jesus' understanding of spiritual formation:

> What Jesus adds is not unknown to Judaism, and he is not criticizing Judaism. Jesus is setting up his very own shop within Judaism. Loving others is central to Judaism, but . . . the emphasis on loving others is not found in Judaism's creed the way it is found in the Jesus Creed. Making the love of others part of his own version of the Shema shows that he sees *love of others as central to spiritual formation.*[7]

Jesus directly connected love of others with love of God. To him, they are inseparable. Love for others is so essential for Jesus, he placed it right next to and on the same level as this ancient Jewish Creed.

5. Scot McKnight suggests it would be like tampering with the Apostles' Creed, by after the closing word, "and life everlasting" adding "and in supporting your local church by giving a tithe of income, before taxes!" Ibid., 9.

6. This is actually a direct quotation from Lev 19:18.

7. Ibid. (My italics in the last section)

When Jesus did this, something unusual took place: Jesus formed a new creed.[8] Scot McKnight calls it *The Jesus Creed* and sees what Jesus did here as so momentous, he devotes an entire book to exploring this.[9]

In this creed, Jesus staked his claim that love is the most important thing in life. Why? Because God himself is love (1 John 4:8), and he intended the structure of everything in the universe to be a reflection and a conduit of that love.[10]

But What is Love, Actually?

Love, however, is a challenging term to define because we use it in so many ways. We "love chocolate" and "love kittens," but mean different things, since we eat chocolate but (hopefully) not our kittens!

The definition that best captures what Jesus meant by "loving God" and "loving people" is one that Thomas Aquinas suggests. Love, Aquinas writes, is "to will the good of another."[11] Love begins with the choice to act for the well-being of another. This is how God loves in John 3:16, "For God so loved the world that he gave . . . ." God chooses to act for the good of the world.

This God-like kind of love accepts others unconditionally and is the kind of love Jesus embodied in all his interactions with God and people. It is the kind of love that marks us off as followers of Jesus.

As human beings, tainted by sin, this is unnatural for us. Unlike God, we may have to begin this kind of love with a sheer act of the will, with no positive emotions behind it. Yet the wonder of this kind of love is that, over time, our emotions often become transformed as we choose to *think* thoughts of goodwill toward others we initially felt no affection

---

8. Some people argue that Jesus isn't proposing a change to how the Shema is recited, since he doesn't explicitly state that he is doing that. That may well be the case. At the very least, however, we can say that Jesus links these two statements together and insists they are the most important commandments.

9. Great book, by the way! I would encourage you to read it.

10. That means John Lennon and Paul McCartney of the Beetles weren't far off when they sang, "Love is all you need." The big difference, however, is that it is a Jesus-directed and a Jesus-filled kind of love.

11. Aquinas, *Summa Theologica*, 26.4. He is following Aristotle who wrote, "Let loving, then, be defined as wishing for anyone the things which we believe to be good, for his sake but not for our own, and procuring them for him as far as lies in our power" (*Rhetoric* 2.4.2).

for, and as we choose to *act* for their good. (We will cover this more fully a bit later.)

When Jesus combined loving God with loving people, he boiled down the Ten Commandments to their very essence.[12] The first four commandments target our relationship with God; the rest target our relationship with other people:

Love God (verses 3–11)	Love neighbor (verses 12–17)
You shall have no other gods before me	Honor your father and your mother
You shall not make for yourself an image	You shall not murder
You shall not misuse the name of the LORD your God	You shall not commit adultery
	You shall not steal
Remember the Sabbath day by keeping it holy	You shall not give false testimony against your neighbor
	You shall not covet

Jesus said in his creed: "Focus all your effort on loving God with all your heart, soul, mind, and strength, and loving your neighbor as yourself. If you aim at these two things, you will automatically keep the ten." By this he was indicating that you don't need law if you just focus on loving God and people. That is why Paul could say, "For the entire law is fulfilled in keeping this one command: 'Love your neighbor as yourself'" (Gal 5:14).

A story I once heard underscores this. Once upon a time—long before the days of the women's equal rights movement—there was a woman who was married to a tyrant. Her husband would write lists of tasks for her to accomplish while he was gone. She would study the lists and do her best to complete them. When he returned, he would beat her if he found things not to his liking.

One day, this ogre of a husband died. Some years later, this woman married again. This man was everything her first husband was not: kind, caring, and loving. When this husband went out to the fields to work, he trusted her judgment of what to do in the house—without any lists.

As this woman was cleaning one day, she moved a dresser to dust behind it. She noticed a scrap of paper and picked it up. It was one of the lists that her first husband had written for her. As she read through the list, she discovered that she was actually doing all of these things without

---

12. Davies and Allison, *Matthew*, 3:238.

even thinking in terms of lists. But now, rather than doing these tasks under pressure or fear of punishment, she did them with joy and freedom out of love for her second husband and out of gratitude for his kindness toward her.

Even though this is an antiquated picture of marital relationships, I hope the point of this little parable is clear: when we focus on doing what is loving toward God and toward others, we won't need a list of rules. Love is the fulfillment of the law.

What Does It Mean to Love God and Neighbor: Beliefs, Practices, Character

If Christlikeness means we have the same concerns as Jesus, and if Jesus' concerns are summed up in loving God and loving people, then what does that mean in practice? We can break the answer down into three interconnected dimensions.[13] These dimensions have to do with our beliefs, practices, and virtues.

- *Our Beliefs* refer to our fundamental view of life: how we *understand* God, ourselves, others, and how to live in this world.
- *Our Practices* refer to those things that we *repeatedly do* so that they become ingrained in our heart, mind, and body that reflect our beliefs.
- *Our Virtues* refer to the *character qualities* that have become part of who we are that have been shaped by our practices as they have been informed by our beliefs.

All three of these dimensions are related to each other: what we *believe* influences how we *behave*, and how we behave then shapes the person we *become*. And all three need to be reshaped and aimed at becoming like Christ in the way he sought to love God and love people.

We can map it out in the following way:[14]

13. Randy Frazee and Scott Duvall both use these three categories, but use different terms for them. Randy talks about beliefs, practices, and virtues in *The Christian Life Profile Assessment Tool Workbook*. Scott uses the terms believing, behaving, and becoming in *Experiencing God's Story*.

14. For convenience, I will use the terms "believe, behave, and become" from Scott Duvall, *Experiencing God's Story*, though they are not original with him.

Believing what Jesus believed (about God, ourselves, and others)	Behaving the way Jesus behaved (about God, ourselves, and others)	Becoming like Jesus (through our relationship to God, ourselves, and others)
• The Story of God • Core ideas • Beliefs • Convictions	• Habits • Practices	• Character Qualities • Virtues

Living this out is a lifelong process of absorbing the teachings of the Bible and then allowing them to reshape us. How does this work?

How the Bible Reshapes Us

Let me illustrate how this way of approaching the Bible can work by giving an example. Once you get the hang of it, you can easily use this approach on your own.[15]

In Exod 19–20, God gave Moses instructions to the people to prepare them for receiving the Ten Commandments. God instructed them to purify themselves and not to come too near the mountain where God will meet with Moses. As Moses prepared to meet with God, lightning flashed, thunder crashed, a thick cloud settled over the mountain, and the people began to tremble.

Let's approach this passage in terms of believe, behave, and become, by concentrating on how God is revealed in this passage. We can ask ourselves,

- What do we learn about God from this passage that we should believe about him?

- What are the implications of what we learn about God for how we should behave?

- And what is the ultimate goal of how we behave for the type of people we should become?

Let's try to answer each question briefly. What do we learn about God from this passage that we should believe about him? By looking carefully at the passage, we discover God deeply cares for his people (Exod

15. The idea from this comes from Scott Duvall's book, ibid., 16–17.

19:3) and he showed it by rescuing them from slavery in Egypt. We are moved by reading that God "carried them on eagle's wings" (Exod 19:4). We also discover the whole world belongs to God (Exod 19:5), that he is powerful, has authority, and is holy (Exod 19:16, 22–24; 20:18–19).

How might this description of God influence our *behavior* (our actions)? One of the implications from this passage is that God is worthy of *worship*. His character and what he has done for us calls for a response of thankfulness and worship, giving him the honor due to him. Worship, however, shouldn't be confined to certain hours of the week. It calls for us to live all the moments of our day in ways that honor him.

What effect should discovering these things about God and developing a lifestyle of worship have on what kind of people we are to *become*? We can see throughout these two chapters, that the people were called to consecrate themselves (19:14) and to be holy (19:6). In fact, all of the Ten Commandments, when we summarize them, indicate that followers of God are called to live lives of purity.

So, let's summarize the flow from what we believe, to how we behave, to what we become, based on these observations:

Believe	Behave	Become
God as loving creator and ruler of the world	Leads us to worship	Shapes us to become pure and holy

Review

So far, we have looked at biblical texts relating to the *goal* of spiritual formation. In this section, we looked at a number of passages that spoke about being conformed to the image of Christ. Then we asked ourselves, what does it mean to become like Christ? We said that Jesus answered this for us when he focused on the two major commandments: *love God with all your heart, soul, mind, and strength* and *love your neighbor as yourself*. We also said that another way to look at becoming like Christ was to understand it in term of *believing* what Jesus believed, *behaving* like Jesus behaved, and *becoming* like the character of Jesus. Now, we want to turn and explore the *dynamics* of spiritual formation.

6

The *Dynamics* of Spiritual Formation

Does God Do It All? Do I Do It All? Do Both of Us Do It?
Understanding Our Role and the Role of the Holy Spirit in the
Transformation Process

WHEN IT COMES TO understanding what the Bible says about spiritual growth, a tension seems to run through the New Testament. Two texts in Philippians get at this tension with respect to the dynamics of spiritual formation.

Philippians 1:6

First, observe how Phil 1:6 describes the dynamic of transformation—that is, who is the active agent in the transformation process: *"being confident of this, that he [God] who began a good work in you will carry it on to completion until the day of Christ Jesus."*

This passage emphasizes *God's role* in transforming us. Black on white, God is responsible for transformation. But wait. Does it mean that I don't do anything? This verse seems to indicate God does it all, which seems to imply that we don't need to do anything. Is that true?

An important truth about Scripture is this: never build a "belief" based on one verse of Scripture without bringing the rest of Scripture into the conversation. The Bible has a lot more to say about the dynamics of transformation than this one verse. For instance, note what Paul says in the next chapter of Philippians.

Philippians 2:12-13

Notice how Phil 2:12-13 describes the dynamic of the transformation process here: *"Therefore, my dear friends, as you have always obeyed—not only in my presence, but now much more in my absence—continue to work out your salvation with fear and trembling, for it is God who works in you to will and to act in order to fulfill his good purpose."*

Paul tells the Philippians—and us today—that *we* are to work out our salvation *and* that God is working in us. It is "both—and," not "either—or."

Is Paul telling us we are to earn our salvation? Not at all! Salvation is a free gift: "It is by grace you have been saved," Paul says. We are saved "through faith—and this is not from yourselves [i.e., you can't produce it], it is a gift of God—not by works, so that no one can boast" (Eph 2:8-9).

When Paul uses the phrase *"work out* your salvation," he is talking about how saved people *live out and express the salvation they have received as a free gift* in their lives.

The salvation God gives us implies a certain way of living and behaving that is inherent in the nature of that salvation. Paul wants us to examine our life to see if it reflects the way of life that that salvation calls for. If not, we need to bring our lives into alignment with that salvation— we are to work that salvation out in our lives.

In this text, notice who is responsible for "working out" our salvation? Paul's grammar is unmistakable: *We* are the ones responsible for working it out! Not God. But this text also talks about God's role: "God is at work in us." God, in other words, is the actual power source within us for the actual transformation.

The New Testament speaks of "God" working in us, but when it is more specific, it indicates that it is God's Spirit, who dwells in and empowers us.

Romans 8:11-13

Notice the claims that Paul is making in Rom 8:11-13 about the Holy Spirit's role and our role:

> And if the Spirit of him who raised Jesus from the dead is living in you, he who raised Christ from the dead will also give life to your mortal bodies because of his Spirit who lives in you. Therefore, brothers and sisters, we have an obligation—but it is

not to the flesh, to live according to it. For if you live according to the flesh, you will die; but if by the Spirit you put to death the misdeeds of the body, you will live.

There are many facets of this passage worth exploring, but I want to focus on two of them. The *first* important fact is that the Spirit dwells in us (8:11), and since he dwells in us, we have the power to live the way God intended for us to live.

The *second* fact is that we have a choice to make—a choice that is at the same time a responsibility: the decision is *up to us* whether we live according to the flesh or live according to the Spirit. It is *our* responsibility, not God's.

How do we understand the interaction between our part and God's part? This is often a puzzling question.

Two Chairs and a Table

To illustrate how this works, Mindy Caliguire, founder of Soul Care, uses an analogy of a table with two chairs.[1] In a business context, people talk about what employees of a company bring to the table—the strengths and skills they have ensure the project will succeed. Adapting this analogy for spiritual formation, Mindy asks:

1. What is on the table?

2. What does God bring to the table?

3. What do we bring to the table?

In this project of personal spiritual formation, *what is on the table* is our soul being restored to what God originally intended it to be.

God brings to the table his desire for our transformation, his forgiveness, grace, and above all his power to change us.

We bring to the table our brokenness and our willingness to be transformed. We bring all of ourselves—our heart, mind, and body—and *present* it to him.

It is our *brokenness* that opens us up to God working in us. *Presenting ourselves* to God allows God to reshape us.

---

1. Caliguire, "Two Chairs: The Process of Spiritual Formation."

This language of "presenting ourselves"—or as the NIV renders it, "to *offer* our bodies"—is important to Paul. He uses this phrase a few times in the book of Romans:

- "Therefore, I urge you, brothers and sisters, in view of God's mercy, to *offer* your bodies as a living sacrifice, holy and pleasing to God." (Rom 12:1)

- "Therefore do not let sin reign in your mortal body so that you obey its evil desires. Do not *offer* any part of yourself to sin as an instrument of wickedness, but rather *offer* yourselves to God as those who have been brought from death to life; and *offer* every part of yourself to him as an instrument of righteousness." (Rom 6:12–13)

This imagery of *offering our bodies* is taken directly from what priests did in the temple: they offered up grain or sheep on the altar as a sacrifice to God. Paul reworks this imagery for followers of Jesus and says that *we* are now priests. Instead of a priest offering God a sheep, *we* now present our bodies to God to be used only for purposes that align with his.

This isn't just a cute metaphor. It is something we physically do. Paul wants us to change the way we use our bodies in our day-to-day life. Whereas we once used our bodies to engage in (for example) lying, taking advantage of others, harboring angry or hateful grudges, looking at questionable sites online, having sex outside of marriage, we no longer do those kinds of things anymore. When we use our body in these ways, we are making our body, in Paul's language, an "instrument of wickedness." Eugene Peterson expresses it this way: "You must not give sin a vote in the way you conduct your lives. Don't give it the time of day. Don't even run little errands that are connected with that old way of life."[2]

Instead, Paul wants us to replace those damaging ways of using our body by using our body to bring healing and restoration—as an "instrument of righteousness." In other words, "throw yourselves wholeheartedly and full-time . . . into God's way of doing things."[3] That means:

- instead of lying—we tell the truth;

- instead of taking advantage of others—we look for ways that we can do something helpful for them;

---

2. Rom 6:13 (The Message).
3. Ibid.

- instead of harboring angry or hateful grudges—we commit to praying for God to bless them;

- instead of looking at questionable sites online—we invest in deep relationships with fellow believers;

- instead of having sex outside of marriage—we choose to enjoy sex only within the boundaries of a marriage commitment.

Summary

The main idea in this chapter was to wrestle with the question, *"Who is the active agent in the transformation process? Is God or am I the active agent?"* The answer to this question is Yes! *Both* God *and* we are active in the transformation process. Our roles are different, but both of us are participants in this project. Transformation can't happen unless we are both fully invested. Although God is the actual power source for transformation, we block his power to transform us if we do not actively *present* ourselves—every part of us—to him.

7

The Process of Spiritual Formation

SO FAR WE LOOKED at texts relating to the goal of spiritual formation, all of which focus on becoming like Christ. We saw Jesus' main concerns were loving God and loving your neighbor, and talked about practicing this in terms of believing, behaving, and becoming. Then we examined texts that addressed the dynamics of spiritual formation, which indicated that both God and we are active in this project of our spiritual formation. Now, let's look at the *process* of spiritual formation.

Several texts in the New Testament describe the process of transformation in different but complementary ways. Together they provide a full picture of the journey of spiritual transformation. My hope is that, by the end of this chapter, you'll see all the elements of the journey of spiritual formation laid out in way that you can say, "That makes sense! I can do that!"

Hebrews 12:1–3

> *Therefore, since we are surrounded by such a great cloud of witnesses, let us throw off everything that hinders and the sin that so easily entangles. And let us run with perseverance the race marked out for us fixing our eyes on Jesus, the pioneer and perfecter of faith. For the joy set before him he endured the cross, scorning its shame, and sat down at the right hand of the throne of God. Consider him . . .*

The author of Hebrews is writing to a group of Christians probably living in Rome, who had been believers for some time.[1] But instead of entering

---

1. That they were most likely living in Italy comes out in Heb 13:24, where the

deeper into their understanding and practice of their faith, they had gone in reverse, and were in danger of losing it all.[2] The author focused on three crucial questions as he wrote to these Christians:

1. How can I help them mature in their faith?

2. How can I encourage them in the midst of the difficulties they are facing?

3. How can I persuade them to remain faithful even though they are tempted to go back to their former life?[3]

Hebrews 12:1–3 is the heart of the letter and gives his answer to the first question. Here I see a five-step roadmap for spiritual maturity.[4]

Our Role Models: Identifying and Reflecting on Role Models for How to Live a Faithful Life

"Since we are surrounded by so great a cloud of witnesses" (Heb 12:1)

The author paints a picture of a stadium of spectators watching a race. The "cloud of witnesses" are the Old Testament saints whom he described in the previous chapter, who exhibited faith in the midst of difficulty and uncertainty.

By the time the author finished his moving description of the difficulties they encountered and their persistence despite those difficulties,[5] the readers must have been thinking, "I thought *I* had it rough. My difficulties are minor in comparison to theirs. If they could do it, then maybe I can too."

---

author writes that "those from Italy send you their greetings." The most natural understanding of this is "as a greeting from certain Italian Christians who are currently absent from their homeland that is being communicated by the author to the members of the house church in or near Rome." Lane, "Hebrews," 446.

2. Heb 5:11–14; 6:1–8; 10:29.

3. This comes out quite clearly in Heb 2:1–2; 3:12–14; 4:11; 5:12–6:8; 10:19–39.

4. There's a lot more detail we could go into in this passage, but these are the five major points the writer highlights.

5. It gets pretty graphic: "Some faced jeers and flogging, and even chains and imprisonment. They were put to death by stoning; they were sawed in two; they were killed by the sword. They went about in sheepskins and goatskins, destitute, persecuted and mistreated—the world was not worthy of them. They wandered in deserts and mountains, living in caves and in holes in the ground" (Heb 11:36–38).

The first step in the process of spiritual growth is to look back at those who went before us and reflect on their lives of faithfulness.

This author reflects a deep insight into human nature: *humans are born imitators!*[6] We learn by observing other people in how they live their lives—whether it is by seeing them physically, or by reading about them, or by watching them on film. The writer of Hebrews picks this up and says, "choose your models carefully. Meditate deeply on their lives. Visualize what they went through. Make real to yourself what they endured and reflect on how they dealt with the challenges of life. Learn by example."

Our Blockages: Getting Rid of the Hindrances to Your Spiritual Walk

"let us also lay aside every weight and the sin that clings so closely"
(Heb 12:1)

The second step in the process of spiritual formation in this passage is to deal with hindrances to our spiritual walk: throw off "everything that hinders" and "sin" that easily entangles. I call this the "Drano" step: dealing with the garbage that stops up our relationship with God.

I don't think many people take this as seriously as Isaiah does when he writes, "But your iniquities have separated you from your God; your sins have hidden his face from you, so that he will not hear" (Isa 59:2). The prophet Isaiah is clear and direct: the wrong we do directly affects our relationship with God. The things we do—how we think, the activities we engage in—directly impact our relationship with God, and we need to deal with things that block that relationship.

The author identifies two blockages: "everything that hinders" and the "sin" that easily entangles. It's brilliant that he begins by telling them to *throw off everything that hinders.* Why doesn't he list specific things that hinder? Because my list is different than yours.

This list could include any number of things—whether wrong, neutral, or even good. If it is hindering *your* relationship to God, it's got to go. By leaving this wide open, the author calls each of us to examine

---

6. There is solid scientific evidence that learning by imitation is our primary mode of real learning—learning that transforms, as opposed to learning for a test. We'll talk about this research in a few chapters.

everything in our lives and inspect it to see whether anything might be blocking our relationship to God.

Our Frame of Mind: Living like You Are in a Long Distance Run

"run with perseverance the race set before us" (Heb 12:2)

The third step in the process of spiritual formation is to "run with perseverance the race set before us." He is talking about the race of life—specifically, how much time we have before we die.

The word "race" is an interesting one. The Greek word is *agōn*, from which we get the English words *"agony"* and *"agonizing."* In certain contexts, as in Hebrews 12, *agōn* can mean "race." But in 2 Tim 4:7 Paul uses it to refer to the battle of life he was engaging in. In 1 Thess 2:2 Paul is talking about a major conflict he encountered when he was speaking about Jesus. In Col 2:1 Paul uses the word *agōn* to describe the intense investment of time and labor he poured into serving others for Jesus' sake.

What all these meanings have in common is that, no matter how you slice it, what lies ahead of Paul's readers will be a *challenge* and a *struggle*. Life is not a casual stroll. It is a marathon. But right at this point, we need to flag some dangers of viewing life as an agonizing struggle.

Dangers in Viewing Life as a Race

I see three dangers in viewing life as a race. The *first* danger is that *this mindset makes the Christian life seem exhausting!* It could have the psychological effect of making the spiritual life feel like an endless treadmill of work, work, work. There is no stopping, no letting up. It just goes on, and on and on . . . and then you die.

The *second* danger with thinking in terms of this race metaphor is that *it makes the Christian life to be about self-punishment and renouncing all that brings joy to life*. This emphasis on self-discipline and asceticism often leads to one of two reactions. On the one hand, it can lead to *pride*: "Look at how sold out I am to God! Look at all the things I have given up for God. I must be really spiritual." It can lead to *judgmentalism and comparison*: "That person there isn't as dedicated to God as I am." These people look down their righteous noses at those poor people, who just aren't as disciplined, and sold out to God as they are.[7] On the other hand, if people can't live up to the standard they think they ought to reach, it can lead to *despair and hopelessness*: "I will never measure up. I am not good enough. There must be something deeply wrong with me." Both reactions are a sign that we haven't truly comprehended what God's grace is, and as a result, we haven't truly experienced it.

The *third* and final danger of viewing life as a marathon is that *it could lead to an unhealthy perspective on the good gifts God wants to give us*. Some Christians conclude we have to reject things that bring pleasure to our lives. Implicit in this psychologically damaging perspective is that anything in life that evokes a sense of pleasure is evil. Is that what the author of Hebrews is saying? Nowhere in the entire book does he indicate this.

As with every teaching in the Bible, we need to bring it into conversation with all the other passages in order to more fully understand what the Bible says. In 1 Tim 6:17 Paul underscores that God "richly provides us with *everything* to enjoy." In other words, it was God's intention that we experience joy and pleasure in the creation that he made! We need to reframe our thinking about the Christian life to encompass this teaching of Paul in 1 Tim 6.[8]

⚱

When the writer of Hebrews describes life as a race, he reminds us that the Christian life is challenging! No, it doesn't exclude pleasure, rest, and relaxation, or enjoyment of God's good gifts. The author simply acknowledges that endurance and persistence will be required, if we are going to finish life well. Addressing this fact is meant to cause us to prepare for the challenge so we are ready for it and don't get side-tracked by lesser things.

7. Paul has some strong words to say about this whole mindset that leads people to pride, judgmentalism, and despair. Paul tells the Roman Christians, who were caught up in this way of thinking, that no one is to play this game. All of us are servants of God, and only God is the judge of our actions. Paul says: "Who are you to judge someone else's servant? They stand or fall before their own Lord." (Rom 14:4, CEB)

8. We could also add Pss 34:10; 84:11–12; 85: Jas 1:17.

Our Focus and Goal: Concentrating on Jesus as Our Target and Example

"fixing our eyes on Jesus, the pioneer and perfecter of faith. For the joy set before him he endured the cross, scorning its shame, and sat down at the right hand of the throne of God." (Heb 12:2)

In this verse the author intentionally describes how Jesus lived as an example for the readers to follow. He underscores the following points about Jesus:

- Just as Jesus believed that God would come through in the end, so should we.

- Just as Jesus' trust in the future promises of God gave him the strength and commitment to endure the pain and shame of life in the present, we should do the same.

- Just as Jesus was honored for his faithfulness to God (he "sat down at the right hand of the throne of God"), so we can expect to be honored if we remain faithful.

In this *fourth* step, the writer of Hebrews wants us to study, reflect, and meditate on the life of Jesus, *so that* we can absorb the way Jesus lived his life and keep a picture of how he lived constantly before us.[9] When we do this, the result will be that, whatever we encounter, we will more naturally respond like Jesus would.[10]

Our Companions: Experiencing Accountability in Community

One final element in the process of spiritual formation in this passage is the need for community and accountability. Although it is not explicit in our text, this need for community and accountability operates as an assumption throughout the book. Recall that this letter was written as a "word of exhortation" (Heb 13:22) addressed to an actual community. When letters were sent to a group or community in the ancient world,

---

9. In an upcoming chapter, we will talk more about scientific research into the role of images and *imagination* in the transformation process.

10. This, by the way, is one of the reasons why I try every day to read a passage about the life of Jesus from the Gospels—so that I am constantly filling my thoughts and imagination with the example of Jesus so that it begins to reshape how I think and feel and act.

the members would gather together to hear the letter carrier (most likely) read the letter to them. Since the "exhortation" was read aloud, the brothers and sisters in the congregation would remind each other of its contents in the future and keep each other accountable to follow them.

Another indication of this need for community and accountability comes by noticing that there is a straight line of thought we can trace from Heb 12:1–3 directly back to the final verses in chapter 10: "Let us consider how we may spur one another on toward love and good deeds, not giving up meeting together, as some are in the habit of doing, but encouraging one another—and all the more as you see the Day approaching" (Heb 10:4–25). This passage in chapter 10, which encourages us to live faithful lives, sets up the "cloud of witnesses" in chapter 11, who exemplified living faithfully, which is directly linked to our passage in chapter 12.

Hebrews 10:24–25 contains all the hallmarks of the concept of accountability: "spurring one another on toward love and good deeds," "meeting together," "encouraging one another." Spiritual growth happens best in the context of a supportive community marked by these characteristics, where each individual sees it as their responsibility to help each other to grow in their faith.[11]

2 Peter 1:3–9

At the beginning of Peter's second epistle, he outlines the process of spiritual formation.

> His [Jesus'] divine power has given us everything we need for [life and godliness] through our knowledge of him who called us by his own glory and goodness. Through these he has given us his very great and precious promises, so that through them you may participate in the divine nature, [and escape] the corruption in the world caused by evil desires.
>
> For this very reason, make every effort to add to your faith goodness; and to goodness, knowledge; and to knowledge, self-control; and to self-control, perseverance; and to perseverance, godliness; and to godliness, mutual affection; and to mutual affection, love.

---

11. This dimension of community accountability that we see in the book of Hebrews is also operating implicitly in the next two passages that we will look at, though we won't take time to discuss them.

For if you possess these qualities in increasing measure, they will keep you from being ineffective and unproductive in your knowledge of our Lord Jesus Christ. But if any of you do not have them, you are nearsighted and blind, and you have forgotten that you have been cleansed from your past sins. (2 Pet 1:3–9 NIV)

Peter understands the process of spiritual growth as having three parts. *First*, he describes what God has done for our spiritual growth. *Second*, he describes our part in the process. *Third*, he describes the results of the process.

God's Part in Our Spiritual Growth

"His divine power has given us everything needed [for life and godliness] through our knowledge of him who called us by his own glory and goodness." (2 Pet 1:3)

As Peter lays the foundation for his understanding of the process of spiritual formation, he highlights five things God does.

The Source of Power: Jesus Himself

"His divine power" (2 Pet 1:3)

The phrase *his divine power* refers to the power Jesus displayed in his life, his defeat of Satan on the cross, and the resurrection power that was working in him.[12] It is that same power that is available to us, not only for our spiritual transformation, but for our entire life.

The Power is for a Particular Purpose

"for life and godliness" (2 Pet 1:3)

The purpose for which God gives us power is not visions, out-of-body experiences, or other miraculous displays of power. Rather, it is power

---

12. Although this is debated, the last words of verse 2 refer to Jesus, which introduces vv. 3–9. Then at the end of the passage, it indicates that by doing what Peter recommends in 3–8, this will keep us "from being ineffective and unproductive in [our] knowledge of *our Lord Jesus Christ.*" This seems to indicate Jesus is the source of this divine power. This is the conclusion of Witherington, *Letters and Homilies: 1–2 Peter*, 303; Davids, *2 Peter and Jude*, 169.

aimed at accomplishing *two things*. Peter says simply, it's for "life and godliness."[13]

Power for life: The term "life" (*zōē*) refers to all things related to how we live our day-to-day lives—every aspect of it. When we remain connected to Jesus, he gives us the resources to live the way God designed us.

Power for godliness: Godliness (*eusebeia*) refers to expressing devotion and commitment to God through concrete acts. It is a "Mother Teresa-like power" that shows itself through actions that bless people and display our reverence for God. Remaining connected to Jesus, gives us power to *live a life of true devotion to God*.

God is the source of power for both of these things. *How* do we access the power to live in this way?

Accessing the Power: A Deep Relational Knowledge of Jesus.

"through our knowledge of him" (2 Pet 1:3)

We access this divine power *through our knowledge of him*. The word "knowledge" here is not the usual word for knowledge found in the New Testament. Peter takes the most common word for "knowledge" in the New Testament (*gnōsis*) and changes it slightly by sticking a preposition onto the front of it of the word: *epignōsis*.[14] The Greek language often does this to intensify the word. When Peter uses this word, he is referring to knowledge that is true, full, and complete.

As we saw earlier, the biblical understanding of knowledge is relational and experiential knowledge, not simply intellectual knowledge. In other words, we have access to this divine power *through a personal and living experience of Christ within us*.[15]

Peter indicates that when we experience Jesus' glory (the divine nature he shares with his Father) and his goodness (virtuous life that Jesus

13. Although the wording "life and godliness" reflects the actual wording of the Greek, the NIV merges these words into one concept, translating them as "a godly life." While that is a possible translation, it seems Peter is emphasizing two distinct spheres in which God gives us power.

14. The Greek language often creates new words by adding a preposition on the front end of another word.

15. Peter Davids suggests that this knowledge of Jesus is "coming to understand and acknowledge his significance." Davids, *2 Peter and Jude*, 170. Although this is correct as far as it goes, it is not simply cognitive knowledge that gives us access to God's divine power. It is through opening ourselves to Jesus and experiencing him that this divine power enters us.

lived), they function like a magnet that creates a desire to know Jesus personally.

Mediating the Power: Jesus' Spirit in Us

> "*through these things* [Jesus] *has given us his very great and precious promises*" (2 Pet 1:4a)

That true, relational knowledge of Jesus comes through *his very great and precious promises*. Peter's flow of thought here is complex and needs unpacking.

Peter tells us that it is *through these things*—referring to the supernatural quality of Jesus' life (his glory) and his compelling character (his goodness)—that Jesus gives us *his very great and precious promises*.

What these promises are, Peter doesn't tell us directly. He assumes his readers know. When we scan the Gospels, two intertwined promises stand out:

- Jesus' promise to send his Spirit to be with us, live in us, and empower us, as well as to be our comforter and advocate—someone who acts on our behalf.[16]

- Jesus' promise that he personally will be with us forever.[17]

It makes sense to think that Peter had these two things in mind (and possibly more besides).

Since these things are true—Jesus' glory and goodness—then we can take Jesus' promises to the bank that he will give us his Spirit and all the gifts the Spirit brings with him. In other words, Jesus' glory and goodness function like a guarantee for what Jesus promises—promises that are to Peter "precious and most magnificent" (NET).

The Aim of the Power

> "*so that . . . you may escape from the corruption that is in the world because of lust, and may become participants of the divine nature.*" (2 Pet 1:4b NRS)[18]

---

16. John 14:16–18; 16:7; Acts 1:8.

17. Matt 28:20.

18. The Greek grammar of this verse is a bit tricky. It can also be translated like the TNIV does: "so that through them you may participate in the divine nature, having

The words *so that* indicate the aim or outcome of the Spirit indwelling and empowering us. There is one outcome aimed at something positive, and one aimed at dealing with the negative things in our lives.

Positive: Sharing in the Life of God

"so that . . . you may become participants of the divine nature."
(2 Pet 1:4b NRS)

The positive outcome is that we will share in the nature and life of God. It's an astonishing claim: Jesus' desire is that we become in-godded. God gives himself to us, and we share in the essence of who he is. This is Peter's way of saying what Paul says in Eph 3:19, that we "may be filled to the measure of all the fullness of God."

Peter Davids explains that "participating in the divine nature" means that we share "some characteristic of God . . . that makes the readers more like the world of the divine (including the beings other than God inhabiting that world) than like the world of human beings."[19] Now, if that doesn't boggle the mind!

Negative: Breaking Free from Corrosive Influences

"so that . . . you may . . . escape from the corruption that is in the world because of lust." (2 Pet 1:4c NRS)

The second outcome is aimed at dealing with the negative things in our lives. Through the empowering presence of Jesus through his indwelling Spirit, we have both the perspective and the power to free us from the destructiveness and pull of sensual pleasures.

How do we come to share in the life of God and break free from the corrupting influences of the world? Peter goes on to explain how that happens.

---

escaped the corruption in the world caused by evil desires." This reading sees that "having escaped" as happening in the past. The NRS sees the escaping as continuing in the present. Even with the way the TNIV translates it, the reality of escaping the world still continues to be ongoing.

19. Davids, *2 Peter and Jude*, 174.

Our Part in our Spiritual Growth

"For this very reason, make every effort to add to your faith . . ."
(2 Pet 1:5)

Up to now everything Peter said focused on the resources we have in Christ. Now he turns and addresses our part in the process of spiritual formation. Peter highlights three things we are to do: (1) We need to do all we can for our growth, and (2) we need to go beyond "bare" faith (3) by living out virtues that undergird and strengthen our faith.

Doing All We Can for Our Growth

"make every effort" (2 Pet 1:5)

Peter begins by telling *us* that *we* are to "make every effort." In other words, what Peter is about to describe is clearly not in God's job description. It's in *ours*! *We* are the ones who are called to *make every effort*.[20]

In order to get a better picture of what this phrase *make every effort* means, it's helpful to compare how different versions translate it:[21]

- "do your utmost" (NJB)
- "you must do your utmost from your side" (Phillips)
- "take every care" (BBE)
- "try your hardest" (CJB)
- "giving all diligence" (KJV)

All these versions point to the same thing: we are responsible to do all we can for our spiritual growth.

Going Beyond a "Bare" Faith

"add to your faith" (2 Pet 1:5)

Our every effort is aimed at *adding to* our faith. Some versions translate this as:

---

20. Remember our discussion on "working out our salvation" in Phil 2:14? In the same way, Peter isn't talking about earning our way to heaven; he's talking about living more and more into the salvation we were given.

21. Noted in Arichea and Hatton, *Handbook on Jude and Second Peter,* 68.

- "support your faith" (NRS)
- "supply" (ASV)
- "supplement your faith" (CSB)

That's puzzling: How can we add anything to faith? The Greek word behind our English translation carries the idea of *supporting something that is already present.*[22] In other words, when you "add to" your faith, you are building on top of the faith that is already there.

Peter then goes on to tell us how.

Living Out Virtues That Strengthen Our Faith

> "add to your faith *goodness . . . knowledge . . . self-control . . . perseverance . . . godliness . . . mutual affection and . . . love.*"
> (2 Pet 1:5-7)

We undergird our faith by "engaging in virtues that undergird, maintain, and strengthen our faith—virtues that flow out of that faith and are implied in that faith."[23] When we put our faith in Jesus, that "Jesus-style-faith" carries with it also a particular "Jesus-way-of-life."

Faith is like an acorn. An acorn contains within it the DNA of the full-grown oak tree. Peter unpacks what is contained in our faith "acorn." It is a set of virtues he wants his readers to engage in:

Goodness

Knowledge

Self-control

Perseverance

Godliness

Mutual Affection

Love

The arrangement of these virtues does not seem to point to an intentional order or progression to them.[24] What Peter does emphasize is

22. The Greek word is *epichorēgeō. Analytical Lexicon to the Greek New Testament,* 169.

23. Arichea and Hatton, *Handbook on Jude and Second Peter,* 78.

24. Davids, *2 Peter and Jude,* 178. Why does Peter list eight qualities? There is debate whether we are to see this list as having eight (with *faith* included in the list) or seven. However, that seems to be inconsequential, for in the ancient Greco-Roman

that the Christian life begins with faith and ends in love as the "crowning virtue" that embraces all of the preceding virtues.[25] All these qualities are necessary to fully live out the Christian life.[26] They are part and parcel of what it means to be a follower of Jesus because they are the virtues Jesus embodies. As his followers, we reflect these qualities in our own lives.

2 Peter 1:3–9 begins by highlighting *God's part* in our spiritual growth, then shifts to emphasize *our part*—doing all we can to live into core virtues that are contained in our faith, and then concludes by underscoring what happens in our life as a *result* of this process.

The Results of this Process of Spiritual Growth

"For if you possess these qualities in increasing measure, they will keep you from being ineffective and unproductive in your knowledge of our Lord Jesus Christ." (1 Pet 1:8)

Peter describes the results of this process of spiritual growth as having a condition attached to it. If the condition is fulfilled, then the results will naturally follow. What is the condition?

The Condition: If These Qualities Are Increasing. . .

The condition is that these qualities that Peter has laid out here are *increasing in measure*. What he implies is subtle but significant. *First,* he implies these virtues are *not* something that we have once-for-all. That means, *second,* they are not permanent. *Third,* they are subject to change over the course of our lives: they can increase—but they can also decrease. *Fourth,* our challenge is to make sure that "these qualities are active and growing in our lives."[27]

It's brilliant psychology on Peter's part to have us focus on striving to become better and better at living these virtues out. When we adopt this mind-set, spiritual progress inevitably follows.

world the number 8 symbolized perfection, and in the Jewish world, the number 7 symbolized perfection. In other words, the message is this: in order for you to be a complete (i.e., "perfect") follower of Christ, *all* of these virtues need to be present in our lives. The message is clear: if you want to experience completeness, then concentrate on absorbing these virtues.

25. Bauckham, *Jude, 2 Peter,* 187.
26. Arichea and Hatton, *Handbook on Jude and Second Peter,* 79.
27. I am using the wording of The Message here.

*The Results: Then Your Knowledge of Jesus Will Be
Effective in Your Life*

Peter says as much in the second half of the verse: increasing in these qualities will *keep you from being ineffective and unproductive in your knowledge of our Lord Jesus Christ.*

Peter uses a figure of speech (litotes), common back then, that we rarely use today, so it rings a little off in our ears. Peter states something in the negative that is meant to be positive. Luke uses it in Acts 20:12 to refer to what happened when Eutychus, who was listening to Paul, sunk into a deep sleep, fell out the window, and died. When the boy was brought back to life the text says, "they were not a little comforted" (ASV). Many modern translations, however, render this as "greatly comforted" or "immeasurably comforted."[28]

When we flip it around, Peter is saying something like this: "if these qualities are ever increasing, *then your experience of Jesus will be marked by ever-growing fruitfulness in your life.*" That is the result of the process of spiritual formation that Peter is describing here.

☫

Let's summarize: since God commits himself to do his part in providing the power for spiritual growth, our job is to do all we can for our growth by going beyond "bare" faith and increasing in the virtues that we see embodied in Jesus. When we set ourselves to this task, our lives will be marked by continual fruitfulness. It is a powerful vision—and plan—for spiritual growth.

Colossian 3:1-12

The final passage we will look at is the most comprehensive description of the process of spiritual formation in the Bible. It is as simple and practical as it is psychologically sound.[29]

> So if you have been raised with Christ, seek the things that are above, where Christ is, seated at the right hand of God. Set your minds on things that are above, not on things that are on

28. BBE, CEB, CJB, GWN, NAB, NASB, TNIV.

29. I will be using the NRS translation instead of the TNIV because I find the NRS to be clearer.

earth. . . . Put to death, therefore, whatever in you is earthly: fornication, impurity, passion, evil desire, and greed (which is idolatry). . . . Do not lie to one another since you have put off the old man with its practices and have been clothed with the new man that is being renewed in knowledge according to the image of the one who created it. . . . As God's chosen ones, holy and beloved, clothe yourselves with compassion, kindness, humility, meekness, and patience. (Col 3:1–2, 5, 9–10, 12 NRS)

Here, Paul indicates there are four closely related steps we engage in in the process of spiritual formation.[30]

Recalibrating our Orientation and Motivation

"Seek the things that are above." (Col 3:1)

The first step is to "seek the things that are above." Packed into the word "seek" are the following ideas:

- the *orientation* of our hearts;
- the *desires* that drive us;
- the *direction* we are aiming at;
- the *motivations* of our heart that pull us in a particular direction.

I don't think it's an accident that Paul uses the same Greek word Jesus used in the Sermon on the Mount: "But *seek* first his kingdom and his righteousness" (Matt 6:33). Paul's words and Jesus' words are parallel expressions meaning essentially the same thing. Paul wants us to develop "a cast of mind, a settled way of looking at things, [and] a sustained devotion" that is oriented to God and life in his kingdom.[31]

This phrase, however, implies there is another motivation and orientation that competes with this one: *seeking* to please ourselves.

Paul's call to seek the things that are above challenges us to look within and ask: is my life defined by the desire to gratify my fallen ego, or is my heart aimed at, drawn toward, and in sync with God's desires?

This first step calls us to check and recalibrate the orientation and motivation of our hearts.

30. Although the passage actually extends to verse 14, the four movements are captured in the first twelve verses.

31. Dunn, *Colossians*, 205.

Redirecting our Mind and Thoughts

"Set your minds on things that are above." (Col 3:2)

In verse 2, Paul shifts his focus away from what motivates us and directs it to our thought-life: "Set your *minds* on things that are above." The second step Paul wants us to engage calls for recalibrating our *thought life.*

A more literal rendering of this verse would be *"keep thinking about things from above."* It is a call to intentionally and willfully direct your thoughts in a God-pleasing direction. *All spiritual transformation begins in the mind and what we choose to allow our thoughts to dwell on.*

This second step challenges us to ask: What have I been filling my mind with? Is it with thoughts, images, and ideas oriented toward what is good and godly? Or are my thoughts aimed at my own ego-motivated desires? This self-examination can lead to "changing our mind."

Re-Forming our Body: Battling our Vices (Negative Action)

"Put to death . . . whatever in you is earthly"
"Put off the old man with its practices." (Col 3:5, 9)

Verse 5 signals the third step in the process of spiritual formation: "Put to death, therefore, whatever in you is earthly." Paul expresses the same idea in verse 9, but with different imagery: "put off the old man with its practices."

Paul's thought-progression in Colossians 3 begins with our motivation/orientation (3:1), moves to how we use our minds (3:2), and then shifts to how we use our bodies (3:5–12).

This step aims at dealing with the negative use of our bodies: things we do that cause damage to ourselves and others. That's what sin is: a self-inflicted wound that also wounds others.[32]

When Paul says we should get rid of things that are *earthly*,[33] he refers to a way of living that is rooted on this *earth* and has its sight set on what happens here-and-now before we die. The range of vision for *earthly* people stops at the grave. *The things that are above* aren't on their

---

32. We'll look more carefully at sin later.

33. He is echoing what he said in verse 2, where our minds should not be oriented to and dwell on earthly things.

radar because they are fixated on feeding their physical appetites. As a result, they end up using and abusing others in the process.[34]

Two startling images capture Paul's strategy for dealing with our self-gratifying fallen desires: *put them to death* and *take them off*. He's talking about *murder* and *stripping*! Paul uses graphic word pictures for shock effect: he wants to get our attention! Let's unpack what Paul is conveying with this imagery.

Paul knows there are things we do with our body that hinder us in our movement toward God, inflict damage on ourselves, and ruin our relationship with God and others. The only way to deal with them is to stop these things *dead* in their tracks so that no further harm is done.

Notice what Paul tells us to put to death and take off:

List 1: Put to death whatever is earthly:

fornication

impurity

passion

evil desire

greed (which is idolatry)

List 2: Get rid of all such things:

anger

wrath

malice

slander

abusive language from your mouth

Do not lie to one another

List 1 focuses on selfish desires. List 2 focuses on what happens in my social relationships when my selfish desires are blocked: we become angry, rage wells up in us, etc.

The common denominator running through both lists is that everything is oriented toward the *self*: toward *self*-gratification, *self*-advancement, and satisfying *self*-centered desires. It's all about *me, me, me*! It's about using people for what *I* want—and lashing out if they block *my* way!

---

34. Dunn, *Colossians*, 205.

The things that we are told to put to death are technically known as *vices*—actions we engage in that are harmful and destructive.[35] These word pictures of "putting to death" and "stripping off" indicate that *we need to take strong and decisive action*. No half-measures will do. *These things have to die!*

How do we put something to death? One way—and this seems to be what Paul has in mind—is to simply *stop doing something*.

Let me use my own imagery to explain. If we don't feed our pets, they will starve. If we refuse to water our plants, they will wither up and die. If we stop using our muscles, they will atrophy.[36] And if we stop lying for long enough, we will eventually starve that practice out of existence in our lives.

Notice again, that this "putting to death" is something *we* do. God does not do it for us. It is *our* action. It is *our* responsibility.

But Paul does not stop with simply battling the negative. He knows that spiritual growth can't result if we simply dwell on the negative. That is why this movement must go hand-in-hand with the next step.

Reshaping Our Relationships: Cultivating Virtues (Positive Action)

"Clothe yourselves with compassion, kindness, humility, meekness, and patience." (Col 3:14)

The fourth and final step comes in verse 12: "As God's chosen ones, holy and beloved, *clothe yourselves* with compassion, kindness, humility, meekness, and patience."

This step shifts the focus from the negative to the positive. It is un-helpful to focus exclusively on avoidance. Let me illustrate.

Suppose I told you right now, "Stop thinking about pink elephants," and then kept on repeating: "Stop thinking about pink elephants!" "I told you to stop thinking about pink elephants!" "Aren't you listening to me? Stop thinking about pink elephants already!"

35. This term has a long history in the study of the spiritual life. We'll explore it more later.

36. James Dunn describes how this phrase *put to death* "seems to be derived from medical usage in reference to the atrophy of part of a body through sickness: in old age the body dies little by little." Dunn, *Colossians*, 212.

What happens? The constant effort to avoid something only results in intensifying its hold on us. Anytime you fixate on *not* doing something, it increases your longing to engage in it.

Instead, Paul advocates a "replacement strategy," filling the space of the negative with something positive. Paul knows that genuine spiritual transformation occurs by actively participating in things that fill our lives with goodness and bless others.

Paul uses this imagery of putting certain articles of clothing on. These are often referred to as "virtues"—things that enhance our relationship with God and others.

Notice Paul's two lists of virtues we should put on:[37]

List 1: clothe yourselves with
compassion
kindness
humility
meekness
patience

List 2: Bear with one another
forgive each other
Above all, clothe yourselves with love
let the peace of Christ rule in your hearts
be thankful
Let the word of Christ dwell in you richly
teach and admonish one another
with gratitude in your hearts sing . . .
do everything in the name of the Lord Jesus
give thanks to God (Col 3:12–17 NRS)

The vice lists and virtue lists stand in direct contrast to one another. We put the vices to death by actively engaging in acts of compassion, kindness, etc.

In contrast with the vice lists, which are oriented to gratifying selfish desires, the virtues lists are oriented towards *others*. But that makes sense, since when our horizon is expanded to include heaven rather than

37. The second list extends beyond the passage we are looking at but is still connected to it.

stopping with the grave, we gain a renewed perspective that allows us to extend grace and understanding to others.

Although we have been talking about this imagery of "clothing ourselves," we haven't yet explored what it means.

When we put clothes on, we take something that is not part of us—or hasn't been part of our lives—and we actively engage in doing it. We find ways to show compassion, and kindness to others. We don't need to wait for some spiritual feeling to overcome us in prayer, before we can be kind to others. We simply start doing it. The beauty of this is that, as we engage in these things, after a while our feelings begin to change—and we begin to feel kindly toward others. Feelings change as a result of our actions, not the reverse.

Notice—again—that this is something *we* do. God does not do this for us.

And notice also that as we practice these virtues, we cannot at the same time be engaged in the vices. By engaging in these virtues, we cancel the vices out—and slowly starve them out of existence. And by engaging in these virtues, we are being drawn into an ever-closer and deeper experience of God and others.

☩

We could go on looking at other significant texts,[38] but these three passages most clearly lay out the process of spiritual formation.

Putting the Ideas Together

When we integrate all the components of the spiritual formation process found in these three texts, the following emerges:

Process of Spiritual Formation in Hebrews 12, 2 Peter 1 and Colossians 3
  1. Laying the foundation for the process of spiritual formation:
     a. The source of power for transformation is Jesus himself (2 Pet 1:3)

---

38. For example: Matt 5–7; Rom 5–8, 12; Gal 5:6–26, Eph 4:17—5:21 and 6:10–18. These, however, do not describe the *process* of spiritual formation. They describe various aspects of life lived in a God-honoring way.

       b. This power is given for a specific purpose: to live in a God-honoring way in all aspects of daily life and to live out our devotion to God in concrete ways (2 Pet 1:3)

       c. The means of accessing the power comes through living in a relational experience with Jesus through his Spirit (2 Pet 1:3)

  2. Grasping the vision for our ultimate future

       a. The promise of participating in Jesus' kingdom both in the present and in the future reframes our focus (2 Pet 1:4)

       b. Participating in Jesus' kingdom in the present has two outcomes (2 Pet 1:4):

          i. Positive: we can share in the life of God himself

          ii. Negative: we can break free from the corrupting influences of the world that come through lust

  3. Doing our part for our spiritual formation

       a. How we do our part:

          i. Do all we can for our growth (2 Pet 1:5)

          ii. Identify and reflect on the lives of godly role models of faithful living (Heb 12:1)

          iii. Develop the perspective of a marathon runner (Heb 12:1)

          iv. Have as our focus the example of Jesus (Heb 12:2)

       b. What we actively do:

          i. Recalibrate our orientation and motivation: "Seek the things that are above" (Col 3:1)

          ii. Redirect our thoughts: "Set your minds on things that are above" (Col 3:2)

          iii. Deal with the negative (vices):

             a) Deal with the blockages that hinder our walk (or "run") (Heb 12:1)

             b) Re-form our body: battling our vices (negative action) (Col 3:5, 7; 2 Pet 1:4)

          iv. Shape our lives in a positive direction (virtues):

             a) Develop core Christian virtues (2 Pet 1:5)

             b) Reshaping our relationships: cultivating virtues (positive action) (Col 3:12–17)

          v. Doing all of this in the context of community accountability (Heb 12)

 4. Result of our engagement in the process of spiritual formation: experiencing continual growth (2 Pet 1:8)

This is a comprehensive and powerful vision of the process of spiritual transformation. From this, we can develop our own personal roadmap for spiritual growth.

What makes this vision of the New Testament even more compelling is to see how the discoveries of brain research are supporting the New Testament's understanding of the process of spiritual development. Let's turn and look at that now in the next part of this book.

PART 2

Brain Research, the Bible, and Spiritual Formation

Reviewing Recent Scientific Research on the Human Body, Particularly the Brain, as it Relates to Spiritual Formation

Part 2 will explore recent findings of scientists regarding how the brain works (neurobiology) as it relates to how we think, feel, and act. We will also reflect on how this research can inform and help us in the spiritual transformation process.

As we look at these topics, we will need to wrestle with a question that presents itself to us: What is the difference between *human* transformation, which comes about as a result of our natural human effort, and *spiritual* transformation, which is only possible as a result of God's Spirit living inside of us?

8

Insights for Spiritual Formation
from Brain Research

GENESIS 2:7 FASCINATES ME every time I read it: "Then the LORD God formed a man from the dust of the ground and breathed into his nostrils the breath of life, and the man became a living being."

The word "formed"—or "fashioned" as some translations render it—is the interesting Hebrew word *yatṣar*. Jeremiah uses this word when he describes a potter fashioning a pot out of a lump of clay.[1] It describes what sculptors, artists, and craftsmen do: after thoughtful planning, they take some material and fashion it with their hands. This is what God the master craftsman does in Gen 2:7 when he takes the dust of the ground and fashions a human being out of it.

This passage indicates that God skillfully creates us. He sculpts us—both inside and out—as an intricate masterpiece. We are his master creation! That means, when scientists discover new insights about how we are *created* and what leads to brain and body health, they are, in fact, discovering how God, the master craftsman, designed us to live. On the flip-side, when scientists discover patterns of thinking and living that cause damage to us in mind and body, they are helping us avoid the negative consequences of not living the way God designed us. Learning about what scientists have discovered can help us live in sync with God's intentions for how he planned life to be lived. And when we discover how God "wired" us to live, it makes it possible for us to make significant progress in our goal of becoming like Jesus.

---

1. Jer 18:2–4.

In this chapter, we will start, *first,* by telling some stories that show how the brain affects the body—and vice-versa—and reflecting on what we learn from those stories.

Second, we will explore why human beings are the way they are by highlighting recent research on the human brain that gives us an insight into how the brain and the body work together to explain human behavior—insights that can aid us in our desire for spiritual growth.

Since there are many relevant discoveries that I would love to dig into, this section could easily turn into a book itself, but I will seek to keep it tightly focused on what is relevant to spiritual growth.

Stories of Brains and Bodies and how they Work

I have chosen a few stories that highlight various dimensions of how the brain works as it interacts with the body as well as reveal aspects of how human beings develop—what we might call "personal growth."

Pedro Bach-y-Rita

Dr. Paul Bach-y-Rita, medical doctor and pioneer of modern brain research, launched his research into the brain's amazing ability to change itself because of his father.[2] In 1950, Pedro Bach-y-Rita, a Catalan poet and scholar, suffered a massive stroke at age sixty-five, which took away his ability to speak and left not only his face but also half his body paralyzed.

Since four weeks of rehab showed no effect on Pedro, Paul's brother, George (also a medical doctor) took him in. Fortunately, George knew nothing about standard rehabilitation practices, and he broke all the rules. He thought to himself, "How do children learn to walk?" So he told his father, "You started off crawling, you are going to crawl again for a while." George got his father knee-pads and helped him learn how to crawl again. After quite some time, Pedro was able to make his way to a wall and crawl along it. George describes what they did then:

2. This is a story told by Norman Doidge in *The Brain That Changes Itself,* 20–26. It's a fascinating book that tells a number of stories of human transformation in a number of areas, physically, mentally, morally, socially, etc.

> That crawling beside the wall went on for months. After that I even had him practicing in the garden, which led to problems with the neighbors, who were saying it wasn't nice, it was unseemly, to be making the professor crawl like a dog. The only model I had was how babies learn. So we played games on the floor, with me rolling marbles, and him having to catch them. Or we'd throw coins on the floor, and he'd have to try and pick them up with his weak right hand. Everything we tried involved turning normal life experiences into exercises.[3]

Each day, they practiced these exercises for hours. Slowly Pedro was able to crawl, then stand, then finally walk. After three months of working on his speech, Pedro was able to make some sounds. He forced himself to relearn how to write.

> He would sit in front of the typewriter, his middle finger over the desired key, then drop his whole arm to strike it. When he had mastered that, he would drop just the wrist, and finally the fingers, one at a time. Eventually he learned to type normally again.[4]

By the anniversary of his stroke, Pedro had progressed so that he could go back to teaching full time, which he did until he retired at the age of seventy. But he didn't slow down. He traveled widely and was an avid hiker.

At the age of seventy-two, during a mountain climbing expedition in the peaks near Bogata, Columbia, tragically, Pedro had a heart attack and passed away. Paul Bach-y-Rita requested an autopsy, and what the doctors found shocked them. Paul tells the story:

> What the slides showed was that my father had had a huge lesion from his stroke and that it had never healed, even though he recovered all those functions. I freaked out. I got numb. I was thinking, "Look at all this damage he has." . . . "How can you recover with all this damage?"
> When he looked closely, Paul saw that his father's seven-year-old lesion was mainly in the brain stem—the part of the brain closest to the spinal cord—and that other major brain centers in the cortex that control movement had been destroyed by the stroke as well. Ninety-seven percent of the nerves that

---

3. Ibid., 21.
4. Ibid., 22.

run from the cerebral cortex to the spine were destroyed—catastrophic damage that had caused his paralysis.

I knew that meant that somehow his brain had totally reorganized itself.[5]

What astonished Paul Bach-y-Rita and the other researchers were two basic things. The *first* was that the initial damage to the brain was "catastrophic," effectively destroying that region of the brain. *Second*, the brain has this amazing capacity to change—reorganize itself—through our actions and our thoughts. It was this discovery that led Paul Bach-y-Rita to switch his career and focus on brain research.

What do we learn from this story? Let's just note a few things:

- The brain is "plastic"—a term that indicates the brain is "changeable, malleable, modifiable."[6]

- Human transformation—real change—is possible. This is true in the physical realm, as this story illustrates, but we will see that it also holds true in the mental, psychological, and spiritual realms as well.

- That means none of us are "stuck" in patterns, habits, and lifestyles that can't be reversed—whether these habits relate to playing tennis or to sinful habits we have formed.

- No matter how old or how young we are, we can change.

- What we *do* with our *bodies* and what we *think* with our *minds* literally changes the structure of our brains—whether these actions and thoughts are what we label "spiritual" or "non-spiritual."

Vance Vanders

The neuroscientist, Dr. Helen Pilchers, recounts this unusual story of Vance Vanders.

> Late one night in a small Alabama cemetery, Vance Vanders had a run-in with the local witch doctor, who wafted a bottle of unpleasant-smelling liquid in front of his face, and told him he was about to die and that no one could save him.

5. Ibid., 23.
6. Ibid., xix.

Back home, Vanders took to his bed and began to deteriorate. Some weeks later, emaciated and near death, he was admitted to the local hospital, where doctors were unable to find a cause for his symptoms or slow his decline. Only then did his wife tell one of the doctors, Drayton Doherty, of the hex.

Doherty thought long and hard. The next morning, he called Vanders's family to his bedside. He told them that the previous night he had lured the witch doctor back to the cemetery, where he had choked him against a tree until he explained how the curse worked. The medicine man had, he said, rubbed lizard eggs into Vanders's stomach, which had hatched inside his body. One reptile remained, which was eating Vanders from the inside out.

Doherty then summoned a nurse who had, by prior arrangement, filled a large syringe with a powerful emetic [to induce vomiting]. With great ceremony, he inspected the instrument and injected its contents into Vanders' arm. A few minutes later, Vanders began to gag and vomit uncontrollably. In the midst of it all, unnoticed by everyone in the room, Doherty produced his pièce de résistance—a green lizard he had stashed in his black bag. "Look what has come out of you Vance," he cried. "The voodoo curse is lifted."

Vanders did a double take, lurched backwards to the head of the bed, then drifted into a deep sleep. When he woke next day he was alert and ravenous. He quickly regained his strength and was discharged a week later.[7]

Sam Shoeman

A similar story is told by Dr. Clifton Meador of the Vanderbilt School of Medicine in Nashville, Tennessee, who researched cases similar to that of Vanders. Dr. Meador describes the tragic case of Sam Shoeman, whom doctors had diagnosed as having terminal cancer. The doctors told Sam he only had a few months to live. True to what the doctors had predicted, Sam died right on schedule. The only problem was that the doctors had misdiagnosed Sam. The tumor remained small, and did not spread. Dr. Meador concluded that Shoeman "didn't die from cancer, but from *believing* he was dying of cancer."[8]

7. Pilcher, "The New Witch Doctors," 30. This story was related in the book by Jennings, *The God-Shaped Brain*, 9–10.

8. Pilcher, "The New Witch Doctors," 30.

Most people are familiar with the placebo effect: a person is given a fake pill and is told it will cure them—and their health improves. Careful clinical trials have been shown to demonstrate this time and again.[9] But there is also the flip-side phenomenon: The *nocebo* effect (as in the story of Vance Vanders) refers to the power of *negative* suggestion that can lead to declining health or death. This also has been solidly documented.[10]

What do we learn from these last two stories?

- What we think and believe has a direct impact on our physical and emotional health.
- Our beliefs have the power to change us.
- Optimistic thoughts and positive thought-patterns have the power to heal our mind, our body, and our relationships.
- Conversely, when our thoughts and thought-patterns are based on negative or damaging ideas or information, this has the power to destroy us psychologically, spiritually, and physically.
- In other words, your thoughts, beliefs, and expectations can heal you—but they can also kill you.

⚶

The stories of Pedro Bach-y-Rita, Vance Vanders, and Sam Shoeman highlight a number of aspects of how the brain and the body work. These findings hold tremendous potential in our desire to become more like Christ. They can help us avoid frustration and discouragement and help us *work with the way God designed us* as we seek to conform our lives to the pattern of Jesus.

Let's look more carefully at a number of key insights from neuroscience research that help us understand how the brain and the body work. Then we'll reflect on how these insights relate to our desire to grow spiritually.

9. Doidge, *The Brain that Changes Itself*, 191; Pilcher, "The New Witch Doctors," 30–31.

10. See the resources in the previous footnote.

Key Insights from Neuroscience

Although the study of the human brain has been going on for millennia, it was not until the 1990s that brain research exploded. Why? Technology! It was particularly the development of functional Magnetic Resonance Imaging (affectionately known as fMRI) that allowed researchers to see the inner workings of the brain in real time, helping them identify how blood flowed to certain regions of the brain when stimulated. This allowed them to draw conclusions about the way the brain actually works on a micro level.

Every day, the *Medical News Today*[11] website publishes the newest research detailing what neuroscientists continue to uncover about the workings of the brain. What they publish is just a snippet of the research going on now. Some of these discoveries simply confirm what we already sensed in our gut was true. Other discoveries completely overturn how we thought the mind and the body functioned. Still other discoveries give us, for the first time, a depth-perception into human behavior that was simply not possible before these technological breakthroughs. These new technologies enable us to study the human brain and the body in ways that scientists even a decade ago did not dream was possible. For example:

- Some research focuses on examining the mechanisms of our *thought*-processes and how *what we think about* actually changes our brain structure.

- Other discoveries help us understand what happens inside of us when we experience *emotions*.

- Still other research examines what happens to us as a result of *bodily experiences*—both what *we* do and what has been done *to us*. They identify how physical experiences lead to changes in every part of us: our bones, blood, muscles and tissue structure, as well as the structure of our brain.

- There is also research that focuses on the effects of human *relationships* on us. The effects of experiencing love or rejection or abuse in our relationships leave lasting imprints in our minds and bodies.

11. The website is http://www.medicalnewstoday.com/.

- Then there is still another area of research that examines the brain-body processes of how *habits* are formed and how habits can be changed.

Whenever we experience anything, in any dimension of who we are—our thoughts, emotions, actions, or relationships—this causes changes to occur in every part of us, from the shape of our brain all the way down to changing our individual blood cells and molecules.

Yes, these are exciting times![12]

And whenever I hear neuroscientists have discovered something new about how the mind and the body work, I can't help but do a little happy dance inside, lift up my heart to God, and say, "we truly are fearfully and wonderfully made!"[13]

⁂

In the rest of this chapter, we'll take a peek into how we have been fearfully and wonderfully made. This could get complex real fast, so I'll try to keep it as simple and focused as possible. Since I am not a neuroscientist, I will be leaning heavily upon those who are experts in the field.

To focus our attention, we'll highlight two kinds of insights from neuroscience I have found helpful to learn about for my own spiritual formation. Some of these insights help us understand how our mind and body work, and we will briefly point out how this information can help us in our desire to grow spiritually.

Other insights explain what goes on inside of us as a result of experiences we have encountered in our lives and the habits we have developed. I am especially concerned about the negative experiences and harmful habits not only because of the damage they cause us emotionally and spiritually, but also because of the barriers they create for our emotional and spiritual development. In order to explore pathways that can help us overcome these negative experiences and damaging habits, we will need

---

12. At the same time, we need to watch out for what neuroscientists Raymond Tallis and Paolo Legrenzi call "neuromaniacs." These are people who hold that everything about human beings can be explained in terms of biological processes and brain function. Tallis and Legrenzi argue that neuroscience is very helpful, but it doesn't explain everything about human beings. Tallis, *Aping Mankind*; Legrenzi and Umiltà, *Neuromania*.

13. Psalm 139:14. In fact this entire Psalm is one extended happy dance before God for how marvelously he has made us.

to include the concepts and resources that we will be covering in Parts 3 and 4 of the book, where we look at the transformation process directly.

Learning by Imitation

Have you ever seen another person yawning, and then found yourself yawning also? Have you seen someone crying, and it makes you sad? Or when someone smiles at you, you find yourself automatically smiling back? It's as if these things are contagious.[14]

While I was in graduate school, I went to visit my friend, Todd. It took a long time for him to answer the door. He was experiencing so much back pain, that he had to limp doubled-over and leaning to the left. His kids were playing in the back of the room and appeared not to notice us.

In the midst of our conversation, we watched Todd's three-year-old son limp across the room, doubled-over and leaning to the left. Without conscious reflection, he began doing exactly what he saw his dad doing.

Humans frequently find themselves spontaneously imitating others. The action of another person evokes an involuntary response within us to mirror what we have just observed.

Why do we do that? Neuroscientists have discovered what they call "mirror-neurons" in the brain that stimulate us unconsciously to imitate what we see.[15] When a person acts in a particular way, these mirror-neurons are activated in the same brain region as when we are performing it ourselves. Someone weeps and that stimulates the part of our brain that is associated with weeping.

Researchers from the University of Washington and Temple University conducted a study of fourteen month old babies watching an adult touch a toy with different body parts. When the babies watched an adult touch a toy with their hand, the region of the brain that directs hand movement lit up in the baby. When babies watched an adult touch a toy with their foot, the region of the baby's brain that directs foot movement lit up.[16]

Andrew Meltzoff, who co-authored the study, wrote:

14. These things are, in fact, "neurologically contagious." See Newberg and Waldman, *How God Changes Your Brain*, 157.

15. Iacoboni, "Neurobiology of Imitation," 661–65.

16. McElroy, " A First Step in Learning by Imitation."

> Babies are exquisitely careful people-watchers, and they're
> primed to learn from others. . . . And now we see that when
> babies watch someone else, it activates their own brains. This
> study is a first step in understanding the neuroscience of how
> babies learn through imitation.[17]

How does this relate to spiritual formation? Two observations stand
out: *First,* human learning, at its most fundamental level, is by imitation:
we learn by observing how others do things. *Second,* human learning is
social: in our learning, we are largely dependent on other humans.

We can use these insights from neuroscience for our spiritual formation by surrounding ourselves with positive role models of how to live
godly lives. As we do, the lifestyle of these godly role models will begin to
influence our thoughts and actions in godly ways and will play a significant role in our spiritual growth.

Learning by Imitation—Through Our Senses

Another closely related finding from neuroscience is that, yes, we learn
by imitation, but we learn by imitation directly by using our senses: what
we see, hear, taste, smell, and touch. All human learning is based on what
we take in from our environment through our senses that take the information from the external world and transfer it to our brains.

What researchers are discovering is that this process begins even
before birth. The German researcher Kathleen Wermke and her team
studied cry patterns of newborn babies in France and compared them to
those of new born babies from Germany. They discovered that the cries
a French baby made had a rising accent—just like their French-speaking
mothers. The cries of German babies, however, had a falling accent—just
like their German-speaking mothers had.[18] Even in the womb, children
are aware of the physical environment around them and "learn" from it
through their senses.[19]

17. Ibid.

18. Mampe et al., "Newborns' Cry Melody is Shaped by Their Native Language."
This research was related in Henderson, "Babies Pick Up Mothers' Accents in the
Womb."

19. Since our learning is based primarily on our senses, how does that relate to
"abstract reasoning"? It seems that any abstract reasoning we do is dependent upon
and mapped off of what we have experienced in the concrete world around us.

Beyond, this, however, there is a further dimension that is significant. Dr. Wermke comments on her research: "The dramatic finding of this study is that not only are human neonates capable of producing different cry melodies, but they prefer to produce those melody patterns that are typical for the ambient language they have heard during their [life in the womb]."[20]

Science writer Annie Murphy Paul, in her fascinating TED Talk, "What Babies Learn Before They're Born," explains how:

> [R]esearchers discovered that, after women repeatedly read aloud a section of Dr. Seuss' *The Cat in the Hat* while they were pregnant, their newborn babies recognized that passage when they hear it outside the womb. My favorite experiment of this kind is the one that showed that the babies of women who watched a certain soap opera every day during pregnancy recognized the theme song of that show once they were born. So fetuses are even learning about the particular language that's spoken in the world that they'll be born into.[21]

This indicates that from the very beginning of human life, we pattern what we do on what we take in from our immediate surroundings.

How does this finding relate to spiritual formation? From the very beginning of life, we have this innate drive to imitate what comes to us through our senses, what we see, hear, taste, etc., and automatically pattern our actions on those around us. The people we surround ourselves with and intentionally spend time with will impact our behavior and our thinking.

Pregnant mothers and their husbands can use this knowledge to begin setting down spiritual patterns for their children that will "predispose" them to their faith. If children can learn to recognize *The Cat in the Hat*, in the womb, then why not passages from Scripture and hymns and prayers?

Wired for Relationships

The fact that we learn by imitating others highlights another dimension of how the brain functions: the human brain is wired for relationships. This is the conclusion neuroscientist Matthew Lieberman documents

20. "Babies 'Cry in Mother's Tongue.'"
21. Murphy Paul, "What we Learn Before We're Born."

in his book, *Social: Why Our Brains Are Wired to Connect*. Lieberman, director of the Social Cognitive Neuroscience Lab at UCLA, writes that humans are "wired to be social. We are driven by deep motivations to stay connected with friends and family. We are naturally curious about what is going on in the minds of other people. And our identities are formed by the values lent to us from the groups we call our own."[22]

This drive to stay relationally connected with others is so powerful that Lieberman argues it "lead[s] to strange behaviors that violate our expectation of rational self-interest and make sense only if our social nature is taken as a starting point for who we are."[23]

By the way, this remarkable finding goes against the conclusions of Richard Dawkins in his influential book *The Selfish Gene*, in which he insistently promotes the idea that humans are wired to be selfish and need to be taught to act contrary to their selfishness. Lieberman's work, as well as the work of other neuroscientists,[24] are coming to the conclusion that the reverse is the case.

Lieberman illustrates this in his chapter entitled "Fairness Tastes like Chocolate" in which he explains that "the same brain regions that are associated with loving the taste of chocolate or any other physical pleasures respond [in the same way] to being treated fairly as well. In a sense, then, fairness tastes like chocolate."[25]

Lieberman tested humans' drive to connect relationally with others through a simple game in which two players have the choice either to cooperate together or reject cooperation in order to get something they saw as desirable for themselves. The game involved the possibility of getting ten dollars. If both cooperated, they would split the money. If Player A indicates he will cooperate, but Player B defects, then Player B would get all the money and Player A none. If both defected, then each player would get one dollar. Lieberman explains the challenge this way:

> Assume that you have never met the other player, do not get to discuss your decision with the other player, and will have no further interactions with that person after this one game. What do you do? If you want to make the most money and you assume the other person will cooperate, you should defect

22. Lieberman, *Social*, ix.

23. Ibid.

24. See the article that reviews this literature: Fishbane, "Wired to Connect," 395–412.

25. Lieberman, *Social*, 75.

(because you'll earn $10 instead of $5). If you assume the other person will defect, then you should still defect (because you'll earn $1 instead of nothing). Regardless of what the other person does, you make more money by defecting.[26]

What were the results of this experiment?

If player A is not told of B's decision beforehand, player A will cooperate 36% of the time—the fear of being taken advantage of wins the battle. Now suppose player A is told of B's decision before making a decision themselves. If B defects, Player A will always defect. *But if B cooperates then Player A also cooperates 61% of the time—despite the fact that they reduce their winnings by cooperating.* If Player A chooses to defect there is a guaranteed $10 payoff, but 61% of the time this player will choose to split the $10 with Player B by cooperating.[27]

The significant finding is that players preferred to cooperate even when the selfish choice would get them more money. This was further confirmed by examining the fMRI image, which showed the pleasurable reward-response parts of the brain light up when the players cooperate even when the money they would receive will be less.[28]

How does this finding relate to spiritual formation? This research indicates that we are fundamentally wired with both a need and a desire to be in relationship with others. In fact, the pleasure centers of our brain light up when we are in nurturing relationships.

When we bring together the earlier insight that we learn by imitating with this insight that we need relationships to thrive, we can combine both of these to stimulate our spiritual growth by seeking out relationships that nourish and strengthen us spiritually and in other ways. Still another way we can use this insight for our spiritual formation is by intentionally extending love and care to others in the name of Jesus. This can encourage spiritual growth in us as well as those to whom we are ministering.

26. Ibid., 82–83.

27. This summary comes from Scot McKnight's blog posted by RJS: "Fairness Tastes like Ice Cream." (My italics)

28. Lieberman, *Social*, 85–86.

Memory: Recalling the Past with Our Senses

We human beings are deeply influenced by our capacity to remember—to recall our past. Understanding *how we recall the past* can be a significant step to personal and spiritual transformation. When we recall something from the past, what is happening in our brains? Let me illustrate how we remember.

Recently, I was traveling with my wife on a road trip to visit family and felt a headache coming on. I remembered I had a little pill container in my computer bag directly in back of my seat—a bag with quite a number of zippered pockets all over it. My wife was sleeping so I didn't want to wake her. I knew the pill container was in one particular outside bottom zipper compartment, but that compartment had a slew of other little things in there as well. Without taking my eyes off the road, I felt back to the backpack, found the zipper compartment, and felt my way through until I found the pill container and pulled it out.

How could I do that? The reason I could do that was based on previous sensory experience: I had *seen* the computer bag and had *touched* it and the contents in it many times. In other words, I had *experienced* my computer bag in the past with all my *senses*.

I called that image out of the databank of images that have been stored away in my brain. Then I relived that experience in "my mind's eye" when I went to retrieve the pill.

From a neuroscience perspective, what happened was that the same neural pathways my body used when I previously had that experience were reactivated when I sought to recall how to find the pill container in my backpack.

This gives us an important insight into how we remember: we remember by recalling past *sensory* experiences. Our memory stores these experiences—sights (images, video clips), smells, sounds, and things we have touched—in a massive database that we have been building over a lifetime, and each of these become encoded in our brains.

This was documented in an experiment undertaken by Itzhak Fried, neuroscientist at University of California, Los Angeles (UCLA). Fried and his co-workers

> measured neural activity in the brains of 13 study participants as they watched short video clips of shows like *Seinfeld* and *The Simpsons*. Afterward, while their brains were still being monitored, subjects were asked to describe whichever of the video

clips came to mind. The same neurons that had fired as they watched a given clip fired again when they recalled that clip.[29]

What were these participants doing when they recalled these video clips? They were seeing these clips again—but this time internally. It was as if they were going into a movie theater in their minds and re-watching the episode.

It is important to note that these "video clips" are not encoded simply as thoughts or words running through our head. Rather, they are recorded as sensory experiences.

Researchers working with people who experienced PTSD (Post-Traumatic Stress Disorder) discovered that, regardless of what type of traumatic experience they've had, when patients had flashbacks of the traumatic events, they experienced "visual sensations . . . followed by other sensory impressions (bodily sensations, sounds, smells, and tastes)." These researchers went on to note that "it was not uncommon for intrusive memories to have several sensory components, but they were rarely described as thoughts."[30] Memory is not just about recalling words. *Remembering is itself an experience!*

In the *National Geographic* article, "Beyond the Brain," the author tells the story of the early neurosurgeon Wilder Penfield, who

> in the 1950s . . . used an electrode to directly stimulate spots on the brains of hundreds of epilepsy patients while they were awake during operations. Penfield discovered that each part of the body was clearly mapped out in a strip of cortex on the brain's opposite side. A person's right foot, for example, responded to a mild shock delivered to a point in the left motor cortex adjacent to one that would produce a similar response in the patient's right leg. *Stimulating other locations on the cortical surface might elicit a specific taste, a vivid childhood memory, or a fragment of a long-forgotten tune.*[31]

Our memory encodes and stores experiences such that when we call them to mind, we *re-experience* them.

In summary, three observations stand out as significant here: *First,* what we have experienced in our past becomes etched in our brains.

29. Interlandi, "Mysteries of Memory," 64.

30. Hackmann and Michael, "Intrusive Re-experiencing," 404.

31. Shreeve, "Beyond the Brain," 3. (My italics) This fascinating article is accessible online at http://science.nationalgeographic.com/science/health-and-human-body/human-body/mind-brain/.

Second, when we recall these experiences, we recall them with all of our senses. *Third*, when we remember past events, we do *not* recall them like a string of words running like a tape on the bottom of a news report. Recalling something means we are literally *experiencing* again what we had experienced at some earlier time in our lives.

How does this relate to spiritual formation? Since what we experience, whether for good or for ill, leaves an indelible impression on us physically in our brains, we will need to face those past experiences that have left a negative mark on us. These negative experiences shape us spiritually: they shape our understanding of God's character as well as our relationship to him. Since we cannot erase from our memory what has happened to us, we will need both to reexamine our understanding of God's character as well as find an approach to processing these memories in positive ways that lead to spiritual growth.

Memory, Past Experiences, and Emotions: The Past Is Present Today

We not only re-experience in the present what we experienced in the past; we also re-experience the same *emotions* in the present that came with original experience. The emotion of the original experience is stored with that original experience, and when that experience is recalled, we feel the same emotions all over again.

I recall talking with a friend a while ago. As my friend was speaking, his words triggered in me an early childhood memory of an event in second grade that had caused a sense of shame to come over me. At that moment, I *saw* that scene from second grade unfold in my mind. As this scene became vivid in my imagination, my friend stopped himself in mid-sentence and asked, "Why are you turning red right now? You look all embarrassed." Without realizing it, that scene from my early childhood in which I felt such shame, suddenly caused that same sense of shame to come over me in the middle of my conversation, and as a result I had turned beet-red and begun to sweat.

Why does this happen? Researchers working with people who experienced PTSD discovered that when patients experience a flashback, the individual

> literally appears to relive the experience. The sensory impres-
> sions are re-experienced as if they were features of something

happening right now, rather than being aspects of memories from the past. Also, the emotions (including physical reactions and motor responses) accompanying them are the same as those experienced at the time ("original" emotions).[32]

Although this is referring to deeply traumatic events people experience, the dynamics of what goes on inside us hold true for all types of experiences we recall. When a memory of some prior experience surfaces in our minds, we experience the same physical symptoms that we had when it first happened. If, for example, it is a negative experience, then the effects could be fear, heart racing, sweating, dilated pupils, skin becoming flush, etc. If we are recalling a positive experience, we may feel a sense of peace and joy, accompanied by our muscles relaxing and possibly a smile spreading across our faces.

How does this relate to spiritual formation? What we have physically experienced, positively and negatively, becomes imprinted within us as *emotion*-laden images that have affected our bodies as well. These experiences, along with the emotions attached to them, affect us spiritually. If the experiences and emotions are negative, they can hold us imprisoned in fear, guilt, shame, or anger. In order to grow spiritually, we will have to face them in a way that leads to freedom from this emotional scarring. (We will discuss breaking free from these traumatic images and experiences later.)

Learning and Our Imagination

Neuroscience research has also uncovered that simply thinking about (i.e., imagining) something changes our brain.

In a research experiment, Dr. Pascual-Leone of the National Institute of Neurological Disorders and Stroke, compared one group of individuals, who physically practiced playing the piano, with another group who just *imagined* playing the piano in their heads. Norman Doidge explains what Dr. Pascual-Leone did:

> Pascual-Leone taught two groups of people, who had never studied piano, a sequence of notes, showing them which fingers to move and letting them hear the notes as they were played. Then members of one group, the "mental practice" group, sat in front of an electric piano keyboard, two hours a day, for five

32. Hackmann and Michael, "Intrusive Re-experiencing," 404–5.

days, and imagined both playing the sequence and hearing it played. A second "physical practice" group actually played the music two hours a day for five days. Both groups had their brains mapped before the experiment, each day during it, and afterward. Then both groups were asked to play the sequence, and a computer measured the accuracy of their performances.

Pascual-Leone found that both groups learned to play the sequence, and both showed similar brain map changes. Remarkably, mental practice alone produced the same physical changes in the motor system as actually playing the piece. By the end of the fifth day, the changes in motor signals to the muscles were the same in both groups, and the imagining players were as accurate as the actual players were on their third day.

The level of improvement at five days in the mental practice group, however substantial, was not as great as in those who did physical practice.[33]

The reason this occurs is that our thoughts and what we imagine in our heads actually alters the arrangement of the neurons and nerve cells. In a real way, what we imagine changes how our brain is structured and how it works.[34]

Why is it that practicing something "in our heads" actually changes us? Again, Dr. Doidge explains it this way:

One reason we can change our brains simply by imagining is that, from a neuroscientific point of view, imagining an act and doing it are not as different as they sound. When people close their eyes and visualize a simple object, such as the letter *a*, the primary visual cortex lights up, just as it would if the subjects were actually looking at the letter a. Brain scans show that in action and imagination many of the same parts of the brain are activated. That is why visualizing can improve performance.[35]

How does this relate to spiritual formation? The intentional use of our minds—how we visualize things and "practice" them in our imagination—has the power to change us. This holds true for the "non-spiritual" dimension as it does for the overtly spiritual dimension. We can use this insight for our spiritual development by visualizing specific ways we desire to be conformed to the pattern and image of Jesus. We can practice

33. Doidge, *The Brain that Changes Itself,* 201–2.

34. Doidge, "On Neuroplasticity."

35. Doidge, *The Brain that Changes Itself,* 203–4.

in our minds, for example, being compassionate and loving to people that we have a hard time with.

Our Actions Influence Our Emotions

Neuroscience researchers have discovered that *what we do influences how we feel*—and conversely—*how we feel influences what we do*. In his book, *Thinking, Fast and Slow: On The Machinery of the Mind*, Daniel Kahneman, Nobel Laureate and Emeritus Professor of Psychology at Princeton University, recounts a number of studies that illustrate this connection between our actions and our emotional responses. He writes, "being amused tends to make you smile, and smiling tends to make you feel amused." He continues by challenging the reader:

> Go ahead and take a pencil, and hold it between your teeth for a few seconds with the eraser pointing to your right and the point to your left. Now hold the pencil so the point is aimed straight in front of you, by pursing your lips around the eraser end. You were probably unaware that one of these actions forced your face into a frown and the other into a smile. College students were asked to rate the humor of cartoons from Gary Larson's The Far Side while holding a pencil in their mouth. Those who were "smiling" (without any awareness of doing so) found the cartoons funnier than did those who were "frowning." In another experiment, people whose face was shaped into a frown (by squeezing their eyebrows together) reported an enhanced emotional response to upsetting pictures-starving children, people arguing, maimed accident victims.[36]

The facial expressions themselves lead us to feel the corresponding emotion of those facial expressions.

Kahneman also relates a similar experiment that shows that even very common movements we perform in our daily lives have an impact not only on what we think but also on our emotional state.

> In one demonstration, people were asked to listen to messages through new headphones. They were told that the purpose of the experiment was to test the quality of the audio equipment and were instructed to move their heads repeatedly to check for any distortions of sound. Half the participants were told to nod their head up and down while others were told to shake it side

36. Kahneman, *Thinking, Fast and Slow*, 54.

to side. The messages they heard were radio editorials. Those who nodded (a yes gesture) tended to accept the message they heard, but those who shook their head tended to reject it. Again, there was no awareness, just a habitual connection between an attitude of rejection or acceptance and its common physical expression.[37]

Kahneman then suggests that when we "act calm and kind regardless of how you feel," the natural result is that we will experience a feeling of calm.[38]

How does this relate to spiritual formation? The actions that we perform have a direct impact on our emotional state. Conversely, our emotional state influences our action. Both our actions and emotional state affect our spiritual state. When we want to grow spiritually and feel our emotional state is blocking us, knowing that we can influence our moods through our actions empowers us. Instead of remaining victims of our emotions, we can undertake practices for our spiritual growth that will influence our emotional state.

Brain Maps and Forming Habits

Neuroscientists have discovered that our brain forms maps that govern our behavior. A "brain map" is an interconnected network of processes that function together in the brain. For example, Dr. Norman Doidge describes how a sense of pleasure can get fused with something many would consider disgusting.

> Neurons that fire together wire together, and feeling pleasure in the presence of [something unappealing] causes it to get wired into the brain as a source of delight. A similar mechanism occurs when a "reformed" cocaine addict passes the seedy alleyway where he first took the drug and is overwhelmed with cravings so powerful that he goes back to it. The pleasure he felt during the high was so intense that it caused him to experience the ugly alleyway as enticing, by association.[39]

When we repeat an action over time, this interconnected network increases in strength and speed. It is this process of brain map forming

37. Ibid.
38. Ibid.
39. Doidge, *The Brain that Changes Itself*, 114–15.

that is at the heart of habit formation. Because of the brain's plasticity, it is able to form new brain maps. Once these brain maps are formed, they can be changed—though not without difficulty.

Norman Doidge explains that there is constant competition in our brains for skills we are using: what we don't use, we lose. He explains that

> there is an endless war of nerves going on inside each of our brains. If we stop exercising our mental skills, we do not just forget them: the brain map space for those skills is turned over to the skills we practice instead.[40]

Once a brain map has established itself, however, it doesn't want to give up that territory easily and marginalizes the development of other, rival brain maps. He explains the way competition works through the example of learning a second language:

> Think of the difficulty most adults have in learning a second language. . . . As we age, the more we use our native language, the more it comes to dominate our linguistic map space. Thus it is also because our brain is plastic—and because plasticity is competitive—that it is so hard to learn a new language and end the tyranny of the mother tongue.[41]

Doidge then goes on to relate this to the difficulty of learning new habits:

> Competitive plasticity also explains why our bad habits are so difficult to break or "unlearn." Most of us think of the brain as a container and learning as putting something in it. When we try to break a bad habit, we think the solution is to put something new into the container. But when we learn a bad habit, it takes over a brain map, and each time we repeat it, it claims more control of that map and prevents the use of that space for "good" habits. That is why "unlearning" is often a lot harder than learning, and why early childhood education is so important—it's best to get it right early, before the "bad habit" gets a competitive advantage.[42]

An initial habit that we develop, once established, will create a brain map that reinforces itself—which then prevents other habits from being formed.

40. Ibid., 59.
41. Ibid., 59–60.
42. Ibid., 60.

How does this relate to spiritual formation? Since virtually all that we do, the helpful and the harmful, is habitual in nature, it is possible to identify those habits that are helpful in our spiritual lives and strengthen them. On the flip side, we have to realize that the sins we commit are also habitual in nature. It is crucial to recognize that we have trained ourselves to sin in regularly recurring behavior patterns—patterns which have etched themselves into our brain.

Since our brains are malleable, we can develop new brain maps that allow us to engage in godly behaviors habitually just as we engaged in sinful behaviors habitually. We can establish brain maps that are marked by loving and doing what Jesus himself loved and did. If we know that acting against a well-entrenched brain map will be challenging but not impossible, this will encourage us to keep on working on it until that godly oriented brain map is established.[43] (We will also talk about this later on.)

Our Surroundings Have the Potential to Heal or to Harm Us

There is mounting evidence that our immediate environment has a negative or positive impact on our thinking and our emotional state. Dr. Esther Sternberg, among her other numerous accomplishments, has been recognized for her research on brain-immune interactions as well as mind-body interactions. In her book, *Healing Spaces: The Science of Place and Well-Being*, she relates the remarkable, carefully controlled 1984 study by Roger Ulrich, an environmental psychologist, entitled "Room with a View." In this study, gallbladder patients were placed in the same ward as they awaited surgery. After surgery, some patients were randomly assigned beds with a window view of an adjacent brick building. Other patients were assigned a bed with a window view of a tree landscape.

Ulrich measured the amount of pain medication that patients needed in their recovery and noted how long they stayed in the hospital. He made sure that the single variable differentiating the patients was having, or not having, a "room with a view." What Ulrich documented was that

> patients whose beds were located beside windows with views of a small stand of trees left the hospital almost a full day sooner than those with a view of a brick wall. Not only that, but the

43. That is the point that Michael Ginnis makes in his book, *Signature Sins: Taming Our Wayward Hearts.* Just as the way we live our lives reveals patterns of behavior, so our sins display a pattern of behavior. We will come back to this a bit later.

patients with nature views required fewer doses of moderate and strong pain medication. The results were dramatic and statistically significant.[44]

This study by Ulrich launched Dr. Sternberg into a study of how the space around us affects us. She found that the brain responds positively to sights, sounds, and smells the person perceives as pleasing.[45] People particularly responded to nature in general, and to views of natural landscapes. Such positive sensory experiences release hormones into the blood stream that activate the healing and restorative processes of the body.

How does this relate to spiritual formation? Even our surroundings have an impact on us, for good or for ill. God has wired us to enjoy the beauty of the natural world. He has designed us to be healed and soothed by it. In our desire to grow spiritually, we can intentionally order our lives so that we experience the goodness of God's creation as a means of restoring us, opening us up to the presence of God, increasing our trust in God's goodness, and as a means of bringing a sense of peace and joy into our lives.

Thinking Our Way to Healing

The physical body has an amazing ability to heal itself. One of the ways this has been documented is through research on "placebos"—pills individuals take, thinking they are medicine, but which have no medicinal value at all.

Dr. Sternberg relates a study of "the placebo effect" undertaken by Dr. Jon-Kar Zubieta of the University of Michigan:

> [Dr. Zubieta] gave healthy people a painful stimulus and then treated them with a placebo that they believed was an active painkiller. Their brain images showed that the greater the pain relief they experienced when given the placebo, the more of the brain's morphine-like molecules were released in those parts of the brain that control pain. This proved once again that the brain's own morphine-like molecules can be as effective in relieving pain as morphine itself, while avoiding the drug's terrible

44. Sternberg, *Healing Spaces*, 3.

45. Dr. Sternberg goes on to discuss the reasons why the brain responds so positively to seeing nature and natural light.

addictive side-effects. Besides activating [the body's own] opioid anti-pain pathways, the placebo stimulated other brain regions [as well].[46]

The placebo effect demonstrates another way that our thoughts influence our health and well-being. Positive thoughts release the body's own pharmaceutical supplies to begin the healing process. Negative thoughts, in contrast, release the body's toxins into our blood stream, and over time these can cause severe damage to a number of brain and bodily functions.[47] So severe, in fact, that it is not an overstatement to say, as I mentioned earlier, that our thoughts can kill us.

Jon Kabat-Zinn recounts a story that cardiologist Bernard Lown of Harvard Medical School told him.

> Some thirty years ago I had a postdoctorate fellowship with Dr. S. A. Levine, Professor of Cardiology at the Harvard Medical School. . . . He was a keen observer of the human scene, had an awesome presence, was precise in formulation, and was blessed with a prodigious memory. . . . Dr. Levine conducted a weekly outpatient cardiac clinic at the hospital. With patients, he was invariably reassuring and convincing, and they venerated his every word.
>
> In one of my first clinics, I had as a patient Mrs. S., a well-preserved middle-aged librarian who had a narrowing of one of the valves on the right side of her heart, the tricuspid valve. She had been in low-grade congestive heart failure . . . but was able to maintain her job and attend efficiently to household chores. She was receiving digitalis and weekly injections of a mercurial diuretic. Dr. Levine, who had followed her in the clinic for more than a decade, greeted Mrs. S. warmly, and then turned to the large entourage of visiting physicians and said, "This woman has TS," and abruptly left.
>
> No sooner was Dr. Levine out of the door than Mrs. S.'s demeanor abruptly changed. She appeared anxious and frightened and was now breathing rapidly, clearly hyperventilating. Her skin was drenched with perspiration, and her pulse had accelerated to more than 150 a minute. In reexamining her, I found it astonishing that the lungs, which a few minutes earlier had been quite clear, now had moist crackles at the bases. This was extraordinary, for with obstruction of the right heart valve, the lungs are spared the accumulation of excess fluid.

46. Sternberg, *Healing Spaces*, 195.
47. Edsall, et al., "Childhood Trauma," 279–81.

> I questioned Mrs. S. as to the reasons for her sudden up-set. Her response was that Dr. Levine had said that she had TS, which she knew meant "terminal situation." I was initially amused at this misinterpretation of the medical acronym for "tricuspid stenosis." My amusement, however, rapidly yielded to apprehension, as my words failed to reassure and as her congestion continued to worsen. Shortly thereafter she was in massive pulmonary edema. Heroic measures did not reverse the frothing congestion. I tried to reach Dr. Levine, but he was nowhere to be located. Later that same day she died from intractable heart failure. To this day the recollection of this tragic happening causes me to tremble at the awesome power of the physician's word.[48]

Notice what happened: Mrs. S.'s condition had not changed one bit. She misunderstood the information that she received and interpreted them as a death pronouncement. Her brain processed this as truth and this triggered a shut-down in her body. It seems Mrs. S. was killed by her own thoughts.

How does this relate to spiritual formation? Since much of what we experience in life is determined by *what* we think about and *how* we think, it is important to pay attention to our thoughts as they relate to God, ourselves, and others and to guard against negative patterns of thinking that can hinder our experience of the full life that Jesus promised us. We can do this by intentionally "feeding" ourselves those thoughts that lead us toward God and toward the life he desires for us.

Meditation

There have been numerous studies of the effects of meditation on the brain and body that indicate many positive overall benefits of the practice.[49]

In one study, Tonya Jacobs (University of California-Davis) compared thirty individuals who had been on a meditation retreat with a control group of thirty others waiting to go on the meditation retreat. The participants meditated six hours a day for three months.

The researchers found that at the end of the three months, there was "30% more activity of the enzyme telomerase than the [control group

---

48. Kabat-Zinn, *Full Catastrophe Living*, 226–27.

49. This has been well-documented by Andrew Newberg in his book *How God Changes Your Brain.*

had]."[50] This is a key ingredient for slowing the aging process and is connected to clear and positive psychological development.

Other studies indicate that practicing meditation decreases stress hormones, can shorten recovery time from depression, has positive effects on managing pain, and speeds recovery from addictions.[51]

In meditation, it is all-important what you meditate on. Dr. Andrew Newberg observes that

> what you choose to meditate upon, or pray for, can do more than change your brain. You can damage it, especially if you choose to focus on something that makes you frightened or angry. . . . . In a Stanford brain-scan study, people who focused on negative aspects of themselves, or on a negative interpretation of life, had increased activity in their amygdala. This generated waves of fear, releasing a torrent of destructive neurochemicals into the brain.[52]

How does this relate to spiritual formation? When meditation is focused on the right object—God himself—and conducted well, the practice of meditation will open a person up to reaping the benefits mentioned here. Christian meditation has even more benefits than other types of meditation for our spiritual growth since we can allow our minds to dwell on all the spiritual truths found in Scripture. This practice will re-shape our thinking and deepen our trust in God that will influence all areas of our life.

Healing of Painful Experiences

When a person desires to be healed from painful experiences, it is important to distinguish between two closely related elements: (1) the traumatic experience itself and (2) a person's emotional response to it.

Susan, a friend of mine, was playing with friends at a farm when she was three years old. In a game of tag, she ran around the corner of a barn—and found herself face-to-face with a huge dog! The dog, also startled, barked aggressively at her. She was traumatized! Ever since, whenever she sees a dog, fear grips her. In fact, every time she even hears

50. Szalavitz, "Explaining Why Meditators May Live Longer."

51. Ibid.

52. Newberg and Waldman, *How God Changes Your Brain*, 39.

the word "dog," fear overcomes her. For Susan, dogs and fear have become fused together in her brain.

Have you ever wondered why, when you are in pain, it feels so good to express that pain to someone who empathizes with you? For example, when Susan talks about her experience with others and they respond in a caring way, she feels better, calmer, less fearful. Why is that? The neuropsychologist, Rick Hanson, addresses this question from the standpoint of activity inside the brain. He writes that

> positive experiences can . . . be used to soothe, balance, and even replace negative ones. When two things are held in mind at the same time, they start to connect with each other. That's one reason why talking about hard things with someone who's supportive can be so healing: painful feelings and memories get infused with the comfort, encouragement, and closeness you experience with the other person.[53]

Hanson goes on to explain how this works. It is a longer explanation, but what he writes is significant:

> Rutgers University neuroscientist Denis Paré has found that if other things are in your mind at the same time—and particularly if they're strongly pleasant or unpleasant—your amygdala and hippocampus will automatically associate them with that neural pattern. Then, when the memory leaves awareness, it will be reconsolidated in storage along with those other associations.
>
> The next time the memory is activated, it will tend to bring those associations with it. Thus, if you repeatedly bring to mind negative feelings and thoughts while a memory is active, then that memory will be increasingly shaded in a negative direction. For example, recalling an old failure while simultaneously lambasting yourself will make that failure seem increasingly awful. On the other hand, if you call up positive emotions and perspectives while an implicit or explicit memory is active, these wholesome influences will slowly be woven into the fabric of that memory.
>
> Every time you do this—every time you sift positive feelings and views into painful, limiting states of mind—you build a little bit of neural structure. Over time, the accumulating impact of this positive material will literally, synapse by synapse, change your brain.[54]

53. Hanson, "Taking In the Good."
54. Ibid.

This is a hope-giving insight. We can, over time, re-frame negative experiences we may have encountered and transform the way we feel about them. It may take a long time, but change is possible.

This is in no way denying the reality of the pain. Nor is it denying the wrongness of abuses that may have taken place. People who abuse should be confronted and held accountable for that abuse. That reality does not change or go away. What can change, however, is the negative emotional charge we feel that is associated with the experience.

How does this relate to spiritual formation? For many, the painful experiences they have gone through often directly block their spiritual growth. They form an insurmountable wall in their minds that they cannot climb over. In addition, what makes this wall even higher at this point is the sense that God abandoned them in this traumatic situation—or even worse—thinking that God caused it to happen.

Knowing it is possible to reframe our negative experiences will enable us to begin the process of transforming the shame, fear, or hopelessness we feel associated with those experiences, but this process will need to be accompanied by re-examining our understanding of God's love for us. We will discuss this process in more detail in chapter 15.

What Can We do with These Insights?

Although there are other insights from neuroscience that connect to spiritual formation, I have found the insights above particularly helpful to keep in mind as we consider how to grow spiritually. In Part 3 of this book, I will build on and incorporate these insights as we look at transforming each dimension of our being: our heart, thoughts, emotions, actions, and our relationships.

In the last section of the book (Part 4), I suggest steps you can take to develop your own unique pathway to spiritual growth, targeting those areas you sense the need to grow in. You may find it helpful at that point to review the insights from this section, looking for connections with your own personal journey. Then you can reflect on how to integrate these insights into your own personalized plan for spiritual growth.

9

The Bible and Neuroscience: Friends or Foes?

What are mere mortals that you are mindful of them,
human beings that you care for them? (Psalm 8:4)

IMAGINE SOMEONE FROM A stone-age tribe suddenly being transported to New York City. They have never seen a car before, and suddenly are interested in what it is and how it works. How would they figure it out? They might want to find out where the car came from and why someone made it—the history and purpose of cars. They need to identify parts of the car essential for it to run, understand what each part does, and figure out how each part relates to the others in a way that makes it run smoothly.

If you are interested in learning how spiritual formation works and how you go about it, you would proceed in basically the same way as that person would to understand a car.

To understand spiritual formation, we need to first look at what the Bible tells us about the nature of humanity. Second, we must identify the major parts of what it means to be human. Third, we need to understand what each of those parts are and how they function. Then, we should consider how each individual part relates to the other parts to allow a person to function well spiritually. This is what we will do in the coming chapters.

An additional challenge that we must consider is this: Do the findings of neuroscience about how human beings function mesh with the Bible's understanding? Is there conflict and contradiction, or can we bring these into a harmonious conversation with each other?

This chapter will

- examine the Bible's view of human beings and the dimensions that comprise them;
- look at how neuroscience views human beings and the dimensions that comprise them; and
- wrestle with whether we can relate these two views together in a meaningful way.

I need to warn you that parts of this chapter get a bit technical. Some people—like mechanics—love to figure out how things work, down to the smallest nuts and bolts; while other people just want to drive the car.

If you are in the latter category, feel free to skim this chapter, just reading the bits that catch your eye. Or you can skip the chapter altogether and move on to Part 3 that describes the dimensions of who we are and how these dimensions are changed and transformed.

The Bible's Understanding of Human Beings: "What are . . . human beings that you care for them?" (Psalm 8:4)

In Ps 8:4, David asks what seems to be a simple question, "What are mere mortals?" If we were to put it in language we use today, we would ask, "What are human beings?" The answer might seem obvious since we are one and have been surrounded by humans since birth! Of course we know what we are! However, it is important not to get ahead of ourselves by assuming we know the answer. It is particularly important to look at Scripture to see how the Bible understands who human beings are. The answer just might surprise us.

Let's turn, first, to look at the foundational passages that describe what human beings are; then we'll look at the key terms that the Bible uses to describe the various dimensions that comprise human beings.[1]

---

1. I gladly acknowledge my debt to the writings of and correspondence with Dr. Malcolm Jeeves, Emeritus Professor of Psychology at the University of St. Andrews in Scotland, one of the leading figures in the field of neuropsychology. Dr. Jeeves has sought to integrate his research with his personal faith in Christ through numerous books, articles, and public lectures. These have been particularly helpful in this chapter.

What are Human Beings? The Key Passages

The Old Testament scholar Lawson Stone writes, "the encounter with neuroscience should inspire a closer reading of the [biblical] text, wherever that might lead."[2] Inspired by neuroscience, let's take a closer look at two foundational passages in the creation narrative of Genesis that play a central role in shaping our understanding of what it means to be human:

- *"So God created human beings in his own image,* in the image of God he created them; male and female he created them." (Gen 1:27)

- "Then the LORD God formed a man from the dust of the ground and *breathed into his nostrils the breath of life,* and the man became *a living being."* (Gen 2:7)

Genesis 1:27

Although we touched on this passage earlier, we need to build on what we said in order to understand more fully what this passage communicates about who we are as human beings.

To recap briefly: In the ancient world, kings were understood as the image of the god their people worshiped; only kings were their god's representative on earth; only kings ruled their nation on behalf of their god; and only kings had a special relationship with their god that noone else had.

Genesis 1:27 intentionally contradicts this assumption of the ancient world by telling us that *all humanity*—not just kings—are made in the image of God! In other words, *all human beings* are God's representatives on earth; *every human being* is to participate in ruling the entire world on behalf of God—reflecting the loving care and creative order of God himself; (3) and *all human beings* were created to have a unique relationship with God that no other living creature has.

These three dimensions comprise the meaning of "being made in the image of God."

2. Stone, "The Soul," 48–49.

Genesis 2:7

Three key expressions in this verse are significant to understanding the nature of human beings.[3]

(1) "God formed man from the dust of the ground." It is interesting that it is not only man who is formed from the dust of the ground. Identical language is used a few verses later to refer to animals: "Now the LORD God had *formed out of the ground* all the wild animals and all the birds in the sky" (Gen 2:19).

This expression "formed from the dust/out of the ground" indicates that humans, like the animals, were made of earthy, physical stuff. Part of what made the first man and woman human is that they partook of the physicality of the created world, and were shaped, limited, and in part defined by that.

In the next chapter of Genesis, the word "dust" is associated with weakness, pain, struggle, and mortality: "By the sweat of your brow you will eat your food until you return *to the ground*, since from it you were taken; for *dust you are* and *to dust you will return*" (Gen 3:19).

(2) "The breath of life." The second thing that strikes us about the nature of humanity in this passage is that God himself breathed into human beings "the breath of life." To determine what this means, it helps to observe how the phrase "breath of life" is used in these other passages.

- "I am going to bring floodwaters on the earth to destroy all life under the heavens, every creature that has *the breath of life* in it." (Gen 6:17)

- "Pairs of all creatures that have *the breath of life* in them came to Noah and entered the ark." (Gen 7:15)

- "Everything on dry land that had *the breath of life* in its nostrils died. Every living thing on the face of the earth was wiped out; human beings and animals and the creatures that move along the ground and the birds were wiped from the earth." (Gen 7:22–23)

From these passages, it is clear that both animals and humans have the breath of life. This seems to indicate that this expression, "breath of life," simply refers to having physical life, whether that be animal life or

---

3. In what follows, I am indebted to Lawson Stone's article "The Soul: Possession, Part, or Person? The Genesis of Human Nature in Genesis 2:7," for his significant insights. I was directed to this article by Malcolm Jeeves.

human life. What makes humans special—different from the animals—is not the breath of life, but that humans are made in the image of God and animals are not.

(1) *"And the man became a living being."* The Hebrew phrase for "a living being," is *nefesh hayyam*. Although a number of versions translate it this way (NRS, NAB, NASB, NET, etc.), other translations render it as "a living soul" (ASV, KJV, etc.), "a living creature" (ESV), or "a living person" (NIRV).

This phrase, *nefesh hayyam*, is used three other times in Gen 1. The words in italics below are the English rendering of the Hebrew expression *nefesh hayyah*.

- "So God created the great creatures of the sea and *every living thing."* (Gen 1:21)
- "And God said, "Let the land produce *living creatures* according to their kinds." (Gen 1:24)
- "And to all the beasts of the earth and all the birds in the sky and all the creatures that move on the ground—everything that has the *breath of life* in it—I have given every green plant for food." (Gen 1:30)

It is significant that all three of these passages refer to animals as *nefesh hayyah*—living beings. When we compare these passages with Gen 2:7, this phrase seems to indicate that God gave both humans and animals *physical life*.

Genesis 1–2

The third text provides us with the cinematic backdrop within which the two previous texts are found. In Gen 1–2—with chapter 3 filling in some details through the negative image it draws. In these chapters we are given the broader picture of creation, which, in turn, provides us also with a fuller presentation of humanity.

From these chapters, the original creation is described in terms of an ideal state of harmony. All of creation—every aspect—reflects a relational harmony that can best be captured by the word *shalom*—the notion that everything on earth is as it should be. Cornelius Plantinga explains that

In the Bible, shalom means *universal flourishing, wholeness, and delight*—a rich state of affairs in which natural needs are satisfied and natural gifts fruitfully employed, a state of affairs that inspires joyful wonder as its Creator and Savior opens doors and welcomes the creatures in whom he delights. Shalom, in other words, is the way things ought to be.[4]

All of creation in Gen 1–2 is viewed as "good"—indeed, "very good." The creation narratives of Gen 1–2 are marked by *shalom* in five sets of relationships. There is harmony and relational oneness:

- between God and humanity,
- between Adam and Eve,
- between Adam with Eve as they relate to the rest of creation,
- within the created order itself,
- within Adam and Eve themselves.[5]

The act of human disobedience in Gen 3 led to, in Paul's words, "the whole of creation . . . groaning in labor pains until now." Not only creation, writes Paul, "but *we ourselves* [humanity] . . . groan inwardly while we wait for adoption, the redemption of our bodies" (Rom 8:22–23 NRS).

The prophetic vision of the end of time that we see particularly in Isaiah and Revelation envisions the restoration of all creation, including restoration of humanity into the image of his Son (Rom 8:29), the new Adam (1 Cor 15:45), where we will again reflect the image of God in how we "rule" the earth and embody his character and values in our lives.

Summary

So, what do we learn about human beings from these three passages? We learn that

1. The "image of God" indicates that human beings are God's representatives on earth, they participate with him in ruling the entire world on his behalf, and that they were created to have a unique

---

4. Plantinga, *Not the Way It's Supposed to Be*, 10.

5. This observation is evoked by the line, "and they were both naked and unashamed" (Gen 2:25).

relationship with God that no other living creature has. As his image bearers, we are to reflect the character qualities and values of God.

2. Humans were fashioned by God out of the dust of the earth. This has several significant implications:

   a. Human beings are mortal.

   b. Human beings are physical beings, made up of the "dust" of the earth.

   c. Humans are defined and limited by the way their physical bodies function.

   d. How these physical bodies function leads either to human flourishing or to harm.

Although Gen 1 and 2 contribute to our understanding of what it means to be human, this account does not seem to include an understanding of human beings having an immortal soul. In fact, Paul emphasizes that it is God "who alone is immortal" (1 Tim 6:16). Thus, two major emphases in the teachings of Jesus—and the rest of the New Testament—gain heightened importance.

First: When we examine the message of Jesus and the apostles, we see clearly that God's plan for human beings was that he would take up residence inside of us. Notice the theme that emerges from these verses:

- "I am the vine; you are the branches. If you *remain in me* and I in you, you will bear much fruit; apart from me you can do nothing." (John 15:5)

- "I pray also for those who will believe in me through their message, that all of them may be one, Father, just as you are in me and I am in you . . . *I in them and you in me*—so that they may be brought to complete unity." (John 17:20–23)

- "But if *Christ is in you*, then even though your body is subject to death because of sin, the Spirit gives life because of righteousness." (Rom 8:10)

- "I pray that out of his glorious riches he may strengthen you with power *through his Spirit in your inner being, so that Christ may dwell in your hearts* through faith." (Eph 3:16)

- "To them God has chosen to make known among the Gentiles the glorious riches of this mystery, which is *Christ in you*, the hope of glory." (Col 1:27)

The message of the New Testament is that God wants to take up residence inside our mortal, flesh-and-blood bodies. He wants to *in-carnate* himself in us. The Latin root of the term incarnation is *caro*, which means "flesh." To incarnate means "to be made flesh." God, in other words, wants to take on flesh *in us*. That desire of his shows up repeatedly throughout the entire New Testament.

Second: Going hand-in-hand with this idea of God dwelling in us is the theme of eternal life. It works like this: since God created us as mortal human beings, we can only experience eternal life through him. This explains why there is so much discussion in the New Testament of God granting us the gift of eternal life.

- "...that everyone who believes may *have eternal life* in him. For God so loved the world that he gave his one and only Son, that whoever believes in him shall not perish but *have eternal life*." (John 3:15–16)

- "Whoever believes in the Son has *eternal life*, but whoever rejects the Son will not see life." (John 3:36)

- "I give them *eternal life*, and they shall never perish; no one will snatch them out of my hand." (John 10:28)

- "For you granted him authority over all people that he might give *eternal life* to all those you have given him." (John 17:2)

- "For the wages of sin is death, but the gift of God is *eternal life* in Christ Jesus our Lord." (Rom 3:23)[6]

Notice three things about these verses: *First*, it is Jesus who "brings" and "gives" eternal life. *Second*, eternal life is described as a "gift" that is given to us. And *third*, it is through putting our full trust in Jesus that we "have" eternal life. Eternal life, in other words, is not something that human beings intrinsically have. Humans are *mortal beings* who must face death. The only way they can escape death is to be given the gift of eternal life by God through Jesus.

Paul explains this idea most clearly in 1 Cor 15:47–54.

---

6. For example: John 4:14; 6:45; Rom 5:21.

The first man was of the dust of the earth; the second man is of heaven. As was the earthly man, so are those who are of the earth; and as is the heavenly man, so also are those who are of heaven. . . . . [T]he dead will be raised imperishable, and we will be changed. For the perishable must clothe itself with the imperishable, and the mortal with immortality. When the perishable has been clothed with the imperishable, and the mortal with immortality, then the saying that is written will come true: "Death has been swallowed up in victory."

Given this overall understanding of what it means to be a human being created in the image of God, we can now look at the key terms the Bible uses to describe the various dimensions that comprise human beings.

Biblical Language Relating to What It Means to be a Human Being

The Bible speaks of human beings having particular "aspects" or "dimensions" (not "parts"). In this section, we'll give an overview of the key terms Scripture uses and then seek to understand more precisely what these terms refer to. Why is this important? Because all of who we are—in all our "aspects"—needs to experience spiritual transformation.

Soul

The broadest term in the Old Testament used to refer to a human being is the term we encountered in Gen 2:7, *nefesh*.[7] This term, used 755 times in the Old Testament, is normally translated as "soul," but is also rendered as "being," "person," "one," "he," "self," "I/me," as well as "appetite" or "desire."[8]

The basic concept of the soul (*nefesh*) in the Old Testament refers to the *totality* of the person, not simply a distinct part of the person. The word "soul," in other words, stands for the person themselves. For example, Abraham tells Sarah, "Say you are my sister, so that I will be treated well for your sake and *my life* (*nefesh*) will be spared because of you" (Gen 12:13). When Abraham uses the word *nefesh*, which the TNIV translates as "my life," he is referring to himself, the *sum total of*

7. I am indebted to Bruce Waltke's analysis of the term in "*Nefesh*," 587.
8. Ibid.

who he is. It is not simply his physical life, though that is included. It "denotes the living self with all its drives."[9] It is the entire person that is made up of all their passions and desires that are localized in their physical being. That is why, Waltke can make this observation, "It comes as no surprise, then, that in some contexts [*nefesh*] is best rendered by 'person,' 'self,' or more simply by the personal pronoun ['he/she,' 'I,' 'me,' etc.]."[10]

The corresponding Greek term in the New Testament and Septuagint (the Greek Old Testament) that corresponds to *nefesh* is *psychē*.[11] Anthony Thiselton remarks that the understanding of the human person in Paul's writings is "fully in accord with the Old Testament."[12]

Note the following examples:

- "for those who were trying to take the child's *life (psychē)* are dead." (Matt 2:21)

- "For even the Son of Man did not come to be served, but to serve, and to give his *life (psychē)* as a ransom for many." (Mark 10:45)

- "Let *everyone (psychē)* be subject to the governing authorities." (Rom 13:1)

- "Priscilla and Aquila . . . risked their necks for my *life (psychē)*." (Rom 16:3–4)

All of these references indicate that the Greek term *psychē* refers to the entire person, just as the Hebrew term *nefesh* does.

If we follow the lead of the Old and New Testament usage of the term soul, it would then be more accurate to say that we *are* a soul rather than that we *have* a soul. When God's Spirit takes up residence within us, he takes up residence not just in a place within us that some people call our "soul". Rather, he takes up residence in the totality of our being.

9. Ibid., 589.

10. Ibid., 590.

11. In case it's not blindingly obvious, it's from this term that we get all the English words beginning with "psych": psychology, psychiatry, "psyche," and even "psycho."

12. Thiselton, *The Living Paul*, 69.

Internal Aspects of the Person

The New Testament uses four major terms to speak of various internal aspects or dimensions of the person.[13]

MIND

There are two Greek words for mind: *nous* and *dianoia*. The word *nous*, has two basic usages. *First*, it can refer to thinking, comprehending, and understanding: "Then he opened their *minds* so they could understand" (Luke 24:45). *Second*, it can also indicate a mindset or attitude: "But we have the *mind* of Christ" (1 Cor 2:16).

Paul sees that our minds can become depraved (2 Tim 3:8) or unfruitful (1 Cor 14:14), and because of that, our minds need to be transformed (Rom 12:2) and renewed (Eph 4:23).

The second word, *dianoia,* is used in one of three ways in the Bible:

1. the seat of perception and thinking mind, understanding, intellect;

2. an inner disposition of mind and heart attitude, thought, way of thinking;

3. a function of the intellect resulting in insight, comprehension, [and] understanding.[14]

This is the word Jesus uses in Luke 10:27: "Love the Lord your God with all your . . . *mind.*" In short, the word *dianoia* refers to everything we do with our mind cognitively.[15]

---

13. We will skip a review of the Old Testament language for the various aspects of the person and concentrate only on the New Testament. This section is informed by Anthony Thiselton's helpful summary of "Paul's view of humanity" in ibid., 67–78. For a more thorough discussion of these terms, see Jewett, *Paul's Anthropological Terms.*

14. Friberg, et al., *Analytical Lexicon to the Greek New Testament,* 111.

15. I am aware of the current discussion/debate on what the mind is, but much of it does not directly relate to our concerns here. For an extended discussion of the mind, the brain, and consciousness, see Schwartz and Begley, *The Mind and the Brain.* In addition, the Wikipedia page has an informative (and quite comprehensive) discussion on the understanding of the mind in philosophy, the different branches of sciences, and religion: http://en.wikipedia.org/wiki/Mind.

HEART

The New Testament's understanding of heart (in Greek, *kardia*) and the Old Testament's (in Hebrew, *lēb*) are both used to "denote deep human feelings, an obstinate or determined will, or the core of one's being."[16] In addition, the heart, in the OT, is viewed as the center of thought. Whereas Westerners link heart with emotions, the OT links heart with thinking too.

Paul describes God as pouring his love into our *hearts* (Rom 5:5), a way of indicating God's desire for his love to thoroughly fill us, "including reaching aspects of the self of which we may be unaware."[17]

The most pervasive way Paul uses the term *kardia* is referring to "the core of one's being" as reflected in Gal 4:6, "God sent the Spirit of his Son *into our hearts*," and Rom 10:8, "The word is near you; it is . . . *in your heart.*"

SPIRIT

When Paul uses the term spirit—*pneuma* in Greek—referring to the "human spirit," it often has the basic meaning of "you." This comes out in some of the endings of Paul's letters in expressions such as, "The grace of our Lord Jesus Christ be with your spirit" (Gal 6:18). When it is used this way, it is virtually identical with the word *psychē*. This comes out in the words of Mary in Luke 1:46–47: "And Mary said: 'My *soul* glorifies the Lord and my *spirit* rejoices in God my Savior.'"

But even though soul and spirit are often synonyms for each other, at times they are marked off as distinct from each other. Though, as McDonald explains

> this distinction and contrast is always with reference to two specific functions of man's psychical nature, not to two separate substances. From different points of view, soul and spirit appear as two aspects of man's inner nature. Spirit denotes life as having its origin in God; and soul denotes life as constituted in man . . . . The *pneuma* is man's non-material nature looking

16. Although this is particularly referring to how Paul uses it, this holds true for the rest of the New Testament. Thiselton, *The Living Paul*, 68.

17. Ibid.

Godward; and *psyché* is the same nature looking earthward and touching the things of sense.[18]

The New Testament uses the term spirit to refer to the Holy Spirit and often connects it to the human spirit. Humans can receive the Spirit of God (1 Cor 2:12), and God's "*Spirit* himself joins with our *spirit*" (Rom 8:16 NJB). When this happens, we receive an inner confirmation and assurance that we are children of God, and we are able to communicate with him and he with us in the depth of our being (Rom 8:26).

Since the Spirit dwells inside of us, our responsibility is to "live according to the Spirit" (Rom 8:4), to have our "minds set on what the Spirit desires" (Rom 8:5), and to "keep in step with the Spirit" (Gal 5:25) in all we do. And as we do these things, we become "spiritual people . . . who are animated and characterized by the Holy Spirit."[19]

CONSCIENCE

At times, Paul uses the word conscience—*syneidēsis* in Greek—to refer to the awareness of the moral appropriateness of our actions. The New Testament speaks of people having a good, clear, or blameless conscience (Acts 23:1; 24:16) or "an evil conscience" (Heb 10:22). The conscience can be wounded (1 Cor 8:12) and can even become seared (1 Tim 4:2).

In other passages, Paul speaks of his conscience bearing witness to him (Rom 9:1 NASB), describing it almost as a separate entity that communicates with him, "as if another quality of the self considers the action of the self."[20] At other times, the word conscience "verges on the meaning *self-awareness*, stressing a security of conviction rather than necessarily a moral capacity."[21]

⚓

These four terms—mind, heart, spirit, conscience—describe the internal aspects or capacities of the human being identified in the New Testament. The question must be raised: are these each separate parts or

18. McDonald, *Christian View of Man*, 79. Cited in Jeeves, *Minds, Brains, Souls, and Gods*, 78.

19. Thiselton, *The Living Paul*, 72.

20. Ibid., 71.

21. Ibid.

compartments within the individual? If so, where are they located? We will come back to this question after we look at the external aspects of the person.

External Aspects of the Person

The New Testament uses three major terms to refer to the external aspects of a person.

FLESH

Although Paul uses this term flesh—in Greek, *sarx*—in a number of places in a more theological sense (especially in Romans 7–8),[22] there are at least fifty-six "value-neutral" uses in Paul,[23] that either denote "neutral, creaturely, or vulnerable, human existence," or "the physical substance from which we are made."[24] In other words, the term *sarx* can refer simply to our physical bodies, which are weak and vulnerable. Other uses of the term *sarx* are interchangeable with *psychē*: "And all *flesh* shall see the salvation of God" (Luke 3:6 NRS).

BODY

The Greek term for body—in Greek, *sōma*—is often used to refer to the physical body, which other people see and experience. It is the "public" and tangible you (Matt 26:12).

Paul stresses the proper sexual use of the physical body (1 Cor 6:16). Since our "*bodies* are temples of the Holy Spirit?" (6:19), we should also "glorify God in your *body*" (1 Cor 6:20).

Paul makes clear that the body is something we have power over: "All who take part in the [athletic] games train hard. . . . I train my body and bring it under control" (1 Cor 9:25–27 NIRV). We can bring our physical bodies into alignment with the ways of God.

At times, the words flesh (*sarx*) and body (*sōma*) overlap in meaning: "Do you not know that he who unites himself with a prostitute is one

22 The word *sarx* is used in a theological sense to refer to living life apart from the Holy Spirit and being controlled by sinful passions and desires.

23. Ibid., 76.

24. Ibid., 6.

with her in *body* (*sōma*)? For it is said, 'The two will become one *flesh* (*sarx*)'" (1 Cor 6:16).

MEMBERS

The New Testament gets more detailed about the physical body (*sōma*) and speaks of the body having "parts" or "members" (in Greek, *melē*).

Jesus identifies various body parts in Matt 5:29, "If your right eye causes you to stumble, gouge it out and throw it away. It is better for you to lose one part (*melē*) of your body than for your whole body to be thrown into hell," which is a figure of speech for "take temptation and sin seriously and act decisively to avoid them."

Paul at times connects our body parts with sinful passions. For instance, in Rom 7:5, "While we were living in the flesh, our sinful passions . . . were at work in our members (*melē*) to bear fruit for death." Paul gives concrete instructions on what we are *to do* and *not do* with the parts of our body when he writes "No longer present your *members* (*melē*) to sin as instruments of wickedness, but present yourselves to God as those who have been brought from death to life, and present your *members* (*melē*) to God as instruments of righteousness" (Rom 6:13).

These terms—flesh, body, and members—are the three external aspects of the person that are identified in the New Testament. Together with the internal aspects, they comprise the entire human being—the complete *psychē* of a person.

Putting the Pieces Together

Now, let's circle back to the question I raised earlier: are all of these internal and external aspects of the human being separate parts or compartments within the individual that we can locate in a certain part of our bodies? It's clear that the external "members"—the eyes, the hands, etc.—can be individually identified. But what about the internal aspects—the mind, heart, spirit, and conscience? Are they separate parts? If so, where are they located?

Anthony Thiselton concludes these internal aspects do not "denote 'parts' of people at all, [but are] rather aspects or capacities of the whole human person" and argues that "Paul believes in what today we call the psychosomatic unity of the whole person."[25]

But what do we make of passages like the following, which clearly identify the various dimensions?

- "Jesus replied: 'Love the Lord your God with all your *heart* and with all your *soul* and with all your *mind.*'" (Matt 22:37)

- "May God himself, the God of peace, sanctify you through and through. May your whole *spirit, soul* and *body* be kept blameless at the coming of our Lord Jesus Christ." (1 Thess 5:23)

- "For the word of God is alive and active. Sharper than any double-edged sword, it penetrates even to dividing *soul* and *spirit, joints* and *marrow*; it judges the *thoughts* and *attitudes* of the *heart.*" (Heb 4:12)

In each of these passages, the series of items are mentioned together in order to convey that *the whole person in their entirety* is in view. The purpose of these three passages is not to provide a scientific understanding of all the individual dimensions of what comprises a person. Rather, the purpose is to indicate the *totality* of the person, as if the authors/speakers were saying, *every last bit of the person.*

⚜

So far in this chapter, we have looked at what the first chapters of Genesis add to our understanding of what human beings are, and we have looked at the biblical terminology relating to the various dimensions of the human being. Before we go on to explore these dimensions in more detail, it is important to relate the Bible's understanding of the human person with what we are learning from neuroscience about the human person. How do we connect the two in a meaningful way, and how can this conversation inform our spiritual formation? Let's explore this next.

Neuroscience's Understanding of Human Beings

In this section, I want to push beyond the "key insights from neuroscience" we highlighted above and now sketch out how the body and the brain work together as seen from a neuroscience perspective. For this, I

25. Ibid., 69.

will be drawing on Anthony Damasio's works.[26] Anthony Damasio is one of the world's leading neuroscientists and has focused his research on understanding the formation of human consciousness, and in particular, on what feelings are.

There is a danger, again, when it comes to explanations of how the body works, of going into too much detail. My goal here is always guided by how the body functions as it relates directly to spiritual formation.

Maintaining Life and Ensuring Well-Being:
The Basic Systems of the Body

In order to sustain human life, God has embedded processes into the design of the human body at the most basic levels in order to help it survive and thrive. Everything else about human life—the "higher functions" of creativity; namely art, poetry, self-expression, etc.—are built on top of these processes and are connected to them in both direct and indirect ways.[27]

AWARENESS OF THE WELL-BEING OF THE BODY
—MAKING SURE THE BODY IS FUNCTIONING WELL

When something goes outside the "survive and thrive" norm, the body continually sends out monitoring signals alerting us to our state of being.

These signals function much like the control lights on the dashboard of a car. The green lights on the dashboard indicate that everything is functioning just fine and tell you, "Keep on driving the way you are. Everything is running the way it should." The red lights on the dashboard alert you that something is going wrong. They tell you, "Something is not functioning right. You need to take a careful look at this. If you keep on going, you might cause some significant damage. Check this out right away!"

The body is equipped with a similar signaling system. If everything is functioning in the "green zone," the body sends positive signals, such as a pervading sense of well-being. If we are attentive to them, we become

26. Damasio, *The Feeling of What Happens*; Damasio, *Self Comes to Mind*.

27. It would require another entire book to relate spiritual formation and neuroscience to those who have genetic and/or acquired limitations of normal brain functioning. Such a work, though, goes beyond my competency.

aware that we feel alert, energized, and alive! Interestingly, just like the green lights on a car dashboard stay on all the time, we may not notice that sense of well-being until we intentionally attend to it.

Similarly, when something in the body begins to malfunction, it sends out warning signals to alert us. These negative signals register more strongly to us because negative changes could threaten your life. The bigger the sense of threat is, the stronger the signal that is sent to your consciousness, in order to compel you to act quickly.

Once your brain gets these warning signals from your body, they serve as a trigger to consider the various options of how to bring the body back to the place where it is functioning properly again. When you decide the best plan of action, you can take the necessary steps to hopefully bring the body back into the normal range.

Awareness of Our External Environment for Our Well-Being

In its desire to ensure its own thriving, the body not only has to be aware of internal processes and how they are functioning, it also has to be aware of the world outside of it. The body examines its external environment to make sure it has what it needs to sustain its own life, looking for sources of food and registering any potential danger.

For both the internal and external processes, the body sends out different positive and negative signals to get you to act accordingly in order for you to survive and thrive.

Explaining How It All Works: An Overview

We now have the necessary building blocks in place to explain how the body functions at the most basic level. The chart below indicates how the body itself works to maintain life in the face of "threats"—that is, anything that the body perceives as threatening the flourishing of our lives.[28]

Let's work our way through this chart so that we can understand it. *First*, there is some sort of stimulus that our body experiences as negative, either from within our bodies themselves (internal), or from what our senses—what we see, hear, smell, taste, or touch—tell us about our external environment.

28. This chart is adapted from Damasio and Carvalho, "Nature of Feelings," 144.

Second, this stimulus causes a response from the body, which we cannot control since they occur as part of the automatic threat response mechanism the body has to ensure its survival.

Stimulus:	Internal		External	
	Loss of water	Sharp object against a limb	Sight of a bear	Receiving bad news
Signals of the Body:	• Dry mouth • Decreased water elimination • Irritability • Tiredness	• Retraction of affected limb • Facial muscles form expression of pain • Attention focused on affected body part	• Increased heart and respiratory rates • Secretion of adrenaline • Redistribution of blood flow • Facial muscles form expression of fear • Attention focused on perceived threat	• Increased blood pressure • Irregular heart rhythm • Decreased respiratory rate • Facial muscles form expression of sadness
Feeling:	Thirst	Pain	Fear	Sadness
Thinking: (Developing an Action Plan)	"I need water, so I will get it from the tap."	"I should move my hand away."	"I need to run far away to get out of danger."	"I need to be with someone who cares for me so they can console me."
Acting: (Engaging the Body)	I get a glass and get water from the kitchen sink.	I move my hand and begin rubbing it to make it feel better.	I run as fast as I can.	I call my best friend and ask him/her to come visit me.

Third, when we become aware of what the body is doing, we experience a feeling that is directly connected to what our body is doing.

Fourth, this feeling leads us to think about what is happening and search for solutions for why we are feeling the way we are.

Fifth and finally, once our minds have settled on an action plan, it engages the body to act on that plan so that the problem can be dealt with.

To make this clearer, let's walk through one example from this chart based on an external stimulus. When we hear a loved one was suddenly killed in a car accident (stimulus), our heart automatically starts beating rapidly, our face goes white, and we might even faint (the body's signal that something is wrong). As a result, we feel grief, pain, and sadness (feeling). Our mind begins to race as we try to think about what will help us deal with our grief (thinking), and so we call our best friend and ask them to come be with us (acting).

This is how life works on its most fundamental level. All of our natural drives—hunger, thirst, sex, safety/shelter, and relationships, etc.—are maintained according to this system and it is these that in large part generate human behavior on a day-to-day basis.

How Our Body Works (from the Perspective of Neuroscience) and Spiritual Formation

Based on the above description, we are able to draw a direct line from the way our bodies work to our spiritual formation. Think, for example, about how our basic drives connect to the "seven deadly sins" of lust, gluttony, sloth, pride, greed, envy, and wrath.

Our bodies have processes designed to ensure our well-being, with a drive toward *safety and secure shelter.* This natural desire, however, can become distorted and turn to *greed*—hoarding all we can and building luxuriant homes far beyond what we need. We have a physical drive to *eat* in order to sustain ourselves. This drive can become excessive and lead to *gluttony.* We have a physical drive to *procreate* so that the human race doesn't die out. This drive, however, can become inordinate, leading to lust and sexual perversions.

In the article "The Neuroscience of the Seven Deadly Sins: Brain Researchers Are Finding the Sources of Our Nastiest Temptations," research consultant Adam Safron argues that we can view a number of the seven deadly sins actually "as virtues taken to the extreme." He explains, "you want the organism to eat, to procreate, so you make them rewarding. But there's a potential for that process to go beyond the bounds."[29] The body is created with these natural desires, but they can become "ill-regulated affections" or "inordinate desires," as Thomas a Kempis writes.[30]

Spiritual formation is about dealing with these dis-ordered desires, which are rooted in how the body is made, bringing them into alignment with the way of Jesus.

Creating Meaning in Life: Some Secondary Systems of the Body

Building on top of these basic systems are some secondary systems that are designed to create meaning for us out of what we experience with our senses. I would like to highlight a few of those that have a direct bearing on spiritual formation. Understanding them will help us be aware of the way these systems affect us as persons and as spiritual beings.

We are Image-Making, Map-Making Beings

One of the most significant insights in how we function as human beings that neuroscience has documented is that human beings are driven by what we experience through our senses—what we see, hear, taste, touch, and smell. This creates images in our brains. The brain then takes this sensory experience and turns it into what neuroscientists refer to as "neural maps." We perceive these maps as composite images—much like individual puzzle pieces joining together to make a completed jigsaw puzzle picture. These maps are used by the mind to makes sense of the world and guide our behavior. Damasio explains it this way:

> The distinctive feature of brains such as the one we own is their uncanny ability to create maps. . . . When the brain makes maps, it informs itself. The information contained in the maps can be used nonconsciously to guide motor behavior [effectively]. . . . But when brains make maps, they are also creating images, the main currency of our minds. Ultimately consciousness allows us to experience maps as images, to manipulate those images, and to apply reasoning to them.[31]

29. McGowan, "The Neuroscience of the Seven Deadly Sins."
30. A Kempis, *The Imitation of Christ*, 115.
31. Damasio, *Self Comes to Mind*, 63.

The maps of the things we experience early on in life begin to shape what we see as good or bad, right or wrong, normal or abnormal.

When a child grows up seeing their parents constantly fighting, that will become a map telling them, "this is normal behavior for parents."

When a child sees his parents acting in hateful ways toward those whose skin color is different from their own, they are constructing a map that tells them it is normal and proper to judge someone on the basis of race. This process culminates in and generates particular *feelings*.[32] If the brain maps that I have been developing from my childhood tell me "racism is good," that will conjure up good feelings toward people who share my skin pigment and negative feelings toward those who don't. (Thankfully, our brain maps are malleable and changeable, so we are not slaves to those maps and can develop new ones.)

That the brain stores things we experience as images and as series of images leads to an important insight that has relevance for spiritual formation: human thinking is generated by images. *We are image-driven beings.* In a real sense, these images live in us and shape us, at times in ways we are conscious of, but most often they are driving and shaping us subconsciously.[33] We will come back to this in a moment.

Images Evoke Feelings

A further dimension of images is that they are associated with feelings we have toward them. If a person has done us harm in the past, when we see them walk into the room, or when we think of them, the feeling of anger, rage, fear, or panic comes over us.

Emotions are created in one of two ways. First, through our senses: we perceive something through sight, hearing, feeling, etc. The second way is "when the mind . . . conjures up from memory certain objects and situations and represents them as images in the thought process—for instance, remembering the face of a friend and the fact she has just died."[34]

So, with each map that our mind creates, it creates a corresponding emotional response with it. The people and objects we experience and

32. Damasio, *The Feeling of What Happens*, 169f.

33. Damasio, *Self Comes to Mind*, 10.

34. Damasio, *The Feeling of What Happens*, 56. Damasio makes a strong distinction between "emotions" and "feelings." Emotions are the automatic bodily responses to experiences. Feelings are the awareness of these bodily responses. The distinction is (for our purposes) slight and can be confusing, and so I will use the terms interchangeably.

their corresponding emotions become mapped in our brains.[35] When we encounter analogous situations in the future, those maps are used to help us determine how to respond.

In other words, all of the images that we experienced and then downloaded in our brains are tagged with particular emotions. Damasio writes, "[an] important consequence of the pervasiveness of emotions is that virtually every image, actually perceived or recalled, is accompanied by some reaction from the apparatus of emotion."[36]

How Emotions Work and How They Change Us

When we experience an emotion, instructions are then given to other parts of the brain and then passed on to the rest of the body by using the two major highways of the body. First, chemicals are shot into the bloodstream and distributed throughout the body. Second, electrochemical signals are sent via the central nervous system to particular muscles, organs, and limbs. When those signals arrive at their destination, they also release chemicals that make their way into the bloodstream, leading to physical changes in us. Emotions physically change us!

Experiencing an emotion, however, not only changes us; it also changes our brains in two ways: it causes various substances to be released into the brain and it causes neural connections to be formed, strengthened, or weakened. "In other words," Damasio writes, "both the brain and the body proper are largely and profoundly affected by the set of commands [initiated by the experience of an emotion]."[37]

Images, Feelings, and Storytelling

As the mind generates an image and a subsequent feeling attaches to it, it continues processing that feeling-laden image by creating a story about it in order to makes sense of it.

Damasio explains that "knowing springs to life in the story," which is embedded in the neural pattern of that image that was created.[38] He goes on to explain that we are barely aware of the storytelling dimension

35. Ibid.
36. Ibid., 58.
37. Ibid., 68.
38. Ibid., 172.

because the images dominate our mind. Nonetheless, the mind weaves what we encounter through our senses into a unified narrative that places all we experience into relationship with each other. "Storytelling," Damasio argues, "is something brains do, naturally and implicitly . . . and it should be no surprise that it pervades the entire fabric of human societies and cultures."[39] Lisa Cron explains this a little more simply in her book, *Wired for Story: The Writer's Guide to Using Brain Science to Hook Readers from the Very First Sentence*:

> We think in story. It's hardwired in our brain. It's how we make strategic sense of the otherwise overwhelming world around us. Simply put, the brain constantly seeks meaning from all the input thrown at it, yanks out what's important for our survival on a need-to-know basis, and tells us a story about it, based on what it knows of our past experience with it, how we feel about it, and how it might affect us.[40]

Let's put the elements we have looked at so far together: (1) Human knowledge is based on what we take in and experience through our senses. (2) Multi-sensory images form out of our experience that are then placed on maps that our mind has been continually creating throughout our lives, as a way to make sense of those experiences and images.[41] (3) Our feelings arise out of the interplay of our experiences/images as they are understood on the backdrop of those maps. (4) Finally, all of this is woven together into a story that our minds create out of these elements.

There are three significant things to notice about these elements. *First*, anchored into the very nature of how the brain functions is that we are storytelling creatures. In order to think, we need to construct a story that fits all the bits of information together in a way that makes sense. At first, in our minds it is a wordless story (think of it as a movie in your head). When we want to convey that wordless story, we need to use words to do it.

Second, the story we tell ourselves might be right or wrong, accurate or inaccurate. The person you are speaking to right now may be a loving and kind person, but the story you could be telling yourself is that

---

39. Damasio, *Self Comes to Mind*, 293.

40. Cron, *Wired for Story*, 8.

41. These are not just visual images, but are imprints that are made from input of all of our senses.

they are evil and repulsive. More importantly, the stories we tell ourselves about God may not be true stories of his character and his ways.

Third, the stories we tell ourselves have real-world consequences, affecting what we do and how we think. One story many people carry within them is that everything that happens on this earth occurs because "it is God's will." The Interstate 35W Bridge in Minneapolis is the busiest bridge in Minnesota. It collapsed in the middle of rush hour in August 2007, killing thirteen people. Right after that event, one prominent pastor blogged, "God had a purpose for not holding up that bridge."

The question I want to ask is: did God do it? There is a different way to tell this story. When Jesus prays "your will be done on earth as it is in heaven" (Matt 6:10), he indicates that God's will is not always being done. There is someone else who is "ruler of this world" (John 12:31 NRS). As a result "the whole world is under the control of the evil one" (1 John 5:19), who is now at work in people (Eph 2:2).

This pastor's story makes God ultimately responsible for all the events that take place—the good and the bad. A different possible story is that other forces are ultimately responsible for evil things happening.

If we adopt the first story, what does that do to our trust in God and our love for him? Can we truly and fully open our hearts to trust him, when we don't know if he will cause a bridge to collapse under us? Adopting the second story will not keep us from avoiding suffering ("in this world you will have trouble," John 16:33), but we can trust in a good God who will never leave us or forsake us.[42]

The stories we tell ourselves matter.

This brief sketch of how the human body works and how it creates meaning was intended to give us an awareness of the processes that are running in the background of our lives. We can use this knowledge to more purposefully shape our lives in a God-ward direction and avoid things that block our progress toward the goal of Christ-likeness. At the same time, it also raises some important questions.

---

42. Obviously this is a complex issue that I have drastically (over)simplified. To explore this further see Jowers, ed., *Four Views on Divine Providence*; Beilby and Eddy, eds., *Divine Foreknowledge: Four Views*.

Human Beings: The Bible, Neuroscience, and Spiritual Formation

You might, at this point, be asking, "with all that neuroscience is uncovering about the process of personal change, what role is left for the Holy Spirit in our lives, since, it seems, that we can do it all by ourselves?" In addition, these observations also raise the question, "what is the difference between Christian spiritual formation, personal transformation, and—to pick just one example—transformation that occurs through Buddhist practices?"

Those are valid and significant questions that need to be addressed. To address them, we will first place the discussion into a broader context and then draw on some observations we made earlier and build an answer based on them.

The Spirit is Always Active

It is helpful to take a step back from such questions in order to ask the broader question: *what is God, through his Spirit, doing in the world?*[43] Unfortunately, attempts at answering this question tend to narrow down the activities of the Spirit to convicting the world of sin, righteousness, and judgment, etc.[44] In doing this, however, we can overlook the activities of the Spirit in the cosmos.

When we look through a wider lens at what the Spirit does, we see that from the very beginning he was active in creation. In the second verse of the Bible, we see that the Spirit was "moving over the surface of waters" (Gen 1:2 NET), birthing creation out of chaos.

Soon after creation was pronounced "very good" (Gen 1:31), humanity turned away from God, plunging all of creation into a state of "groaning" (Rom 8:23). Yet, the Bible insists that God, through his Spirit, is still active in creation and human history.[45]

Christ's life, death, and resurrection led to a profound cosmic change, which was the decisive step toward restoring creation and humanity back

43. This is an insight that comes from McGarry, "Formed by the Spirit," 5.

44. John 16:13. In addition to these, McGarry mentions that the Spirit "guides us into all truth (John 16:13); regenerates us (John 3:5–8; Titus 3:5); glorifies and testifies of Christ (John 15:26; 16:14); reveals Christ to us and in us (John 16:14–15); etc." Ibid.

45. For example, Pss 19:1–6; 104:24–30; 147:18; Isa 42:1; 63:14; Joel 2:28; Acts 17:22–29.

to God's original intent—which is where the role of the Spirit comes in: the Spirit continues the work of Jesus in restoring all of creation. Joseph McGarry explains that it is the Spirit's job to be "always at work conforming creation to reality in Christ . . . and it is the ongoing and perpetual task of the Holy Spirit to make this reality [in Christ] actual in the world now . . . through the life of God's people."[46]

It is in the nature and "job description" of the Spirit for him to be— on a cosmic scale—active in re-creating this world in order to conform all of it to the reality that God intended it to be Christ. Joseph McGarry suggests that "formation in Christ is the process by which the Holy Spirit makes Christ truly present on Earth through the church as she lives her faithful life of obedient discipleship."[47]

If the Spirit is active in conforming all of reality to be all it was meant to be, that surely includes the way that the Spirit is active inside our bodies. Not only is he at work in the wider world, but he is also at work within us—in our neurons and sinews, we could say—guiding, shaping, and empowering us to become conformed to the image of Christ.[48]

Recalling the Role Scripture Gives Us in Our Spiritual Formation

As we wrestle with the role of the Spirit and the findings of neuroscience, it is important to factor in two basic truths that we mentioned earlier.

First, there are certain things God has placed in our hands to do. He won't do them for us. It is our job to do these things, and if we do not do these things, Christian spiritual formation will not happen. Two passages we looked at earlier underscore this. In Phil 2:12–13, Paul tells the Philippians to *work out their salvation because God was at work in them.* It is their job to bring their lives (desires, thoughts, emotions, actions, and relationships) into alignment with the life of Jesus and the values of his kingdom. In 2 Pet 1:5, Peter tells his readers to *make every effort* to add to your faith. We need to exert ourselves by intentionally developing the character qualities Peter lists in that passage. It is clear, then, that you and I have a role to play in our own spiritual transformation. It is

46. McGarry, "Short, 5–6.

47. Ibid., 10.

48. For more on this, see Johnston, *God's Wider Presence*, especially his chapter, "Moved by the Spirit," 160–87.

this dimension of who we are that connects to what neuroscience has uncovered about how we function and grow as human beings.

Second, at the same time, however, *it is also clear that there are certain things that only God can do.* And it is these specific things that we humans are simply powerless to do. We cannot get rid of our sinfulness. We need God to deal with that. We cannot get rid of our guilt by ourselves. We need God's forgiveness for that. We cannot heal people or deliver them from demonic oppression. Only God can do that. We do not naturally have the Spirit living inside of us. We need to ask God for that. And on our own, we cannot produce love, joy, peace, patience, or kindness.[49] These are the fruit *of the Spirit*, who develops these things within us. These things go beyond what our brain and biology can accomplish. It is clear, then, that the true change agent—the true power for transformation—does not come from us. It comes through God's Spirit dwelling in us.

The picture Jesus uses to explain the dynamic of these two points comes out most clearly in the imagery of the vine and the branches in John 15. Notice how this passage describes our role—or task—and Jesus' role:

> I am the true vine . . . . Remain in me, as I also remain in you. No branch can bear fruit by itself; it must remain in the vine. Neither can you bear fruit unless you remain in me. I am the vine; you are the branches. If you remain in me and I in you, you will bear much fruit; apart from me you can do nothing. (John 15:1, 4–5)

Jesus is described here as the vine—the source of power, the source of life that courses through us.[50] We are pictured as branches that are attached to the vine.

There is a difference, however, between a literal vine-and-branches and our relationship with Jesus. Literal branches don't have a choice to remain connected to the vine. We, however, do. We can choose to remain connected to the vine—or not. It's *our task* is to remain connected to the vine. It's *Jesus' task* to supply the power that will lead to our transformation.

49. Gal 5:22.

50. The New Testament seems fairly free to talk of God (Eph 3:19), God's Spirit (Rom 8:11), Jesus (Eph 3:17), or the Spirit of Jesus (Acts 16:7) dwelling in us. They are all interchangeable expressions for the reality of God himself living inside of us.

So, when we make every effort to bring our lives into alignment with the life of Jesus, and when we seek to learn all we can about how God designed us to live, and when we are abiding in Jesus and his life is flowing through us, then the Spirit of God has room to do his work of spiritual transformation.

Recalling the Bible's Understanding of Human Beings from Genesis 1:27, 2:7, and Genesis 1–3

In our examination of what human beings are, the texts we examined—Gen 1:27, 2:7, and Gen 1–3—indicated that we are a soul, and that when we say "yes" to Jesus, his Spirit takes up residence within in the totality of our being. Jesus, in a sense, becomes incarnated in us. Paul talks about Christ being born in us (Gal 4:19).

The aim of spiritual formation is that we shape our entire lives toward God. The aim is for us—in every dimension of our lives—to take on the life and the character qualities of Jesus, who is the image and exact representation of God.

Since that is the case, I would suggest that, for the Christian, it makes little sense to speak about "spiritual transformation" as distinct from and opposed to their "personal transformation." For the follower of Jesus, spiritual transformation and personal transformation can—and should—share the same goals. Joel Green explains it this way:

> To speak of "conversion" or . . . of "religious or moral formation," is always to speak of persons and not parts of persons. Transformation of "my inner person" can be nothing more or less than transformation of "me," understood wholistically. For our purposes, this "learning" [i.e., this transformation] is particularly focused on the practices that shape our lives and on interpersonal experiences, which directly shape the ongoing development of the brain's structure and function.[51]

Any transformation of the person, then, whether we focus on our spiritual growth or whether we focus on what some might call "personal growth," both of these use the same physical, biological, and neural networks. For the Christian, these converge.

In other words, for the Christian, "spiritual transformation" = "personal transformation." Neither Jesus, Paul, nor Peter make any distinction

---

51. Green, *Body, Soul, and Human Life*, 115–16.

or disjunction between the two in any of the texts we examined. Spiritual transformation is for them the transformation of the entire person.

The Difference between Christian Spiritual Formation, Atheistic Personal Transformation, and Transformation through Buddhist Practices

So, what then is the difference between the *Christian*, who is desirous of spiritual transformation, the *atheist*, who wants to better themselves personally, and the *Buddhist* who desires human transformation? I would suggest there are at least three significant differences marking Christian spiritual formation as separate and distinct.

The *first* and most significant difference is that the Spirit of God dwells in believers and imparts his divine life to our physical bodies, as Paul explains in Rom 8:11,[52] much like "the glory of God had dwelt in the Temple."[53] As a result of the Spirit's presence in us, we have abilities we did not have before. We can now resist participating in destructive activities and are empowered to live a life pleasing to God.[54]

The *second* difference between Christian spiritual transformation and other types of transformation is that Christian spiritual transformation focuses fully and exclusively on the person of Jesus in a way that changes virtually everything about a person, making them distinct in many ways from the atheist and the Buddhist. This holistic *christocentric* orientation would include the following elements.

1. taking on the worldview of Jesus as it unfolds in the narrative of Scripture, looking particularly at how Jesus viewed God the Father, humanity, and the world;

2. adopting this story of what God was doing in the world and taking it on as my own story that defines my thinking and my lifestyle;

3. taking in the life of Jesus through his Spirit into the core of our being;

4. taking on Jesus' character qualities and his values; and

52. "If the Spirit of him who raised Jesus from the dead dwells in you, he who raised Christ from the dead will give life to your mortal bodies also through his Spirit that dwells in you." (Compare this with Rom 8:2; John 6:63; 2 Cor 3:6.) For an extensive discussion of what the Spirit does, see Fee, *God's Empowering Presence*.

53. Wright, *Romans: Part One*, 143.

54. In Paul's words, we are able to "put to death the misdeeds of the body."

5. taking on practices, like Jesus did, that nurtured his relationship with God and with others.

The *third* difference between Christian spiritual transformation and other types of transformation is that it is embedded in a Christian social context of life together with others, who share in the life of Jesus, and who are also equally oriented toward him. This common life together includes both a shared set of symbols and symbolic acts that express our common understanding of our faith in Jesus as well as a shared set of regular corporate practices that shape us collectively into living into that Jesus-oriented life as described in the previous point.

These three differences mean that in some cases Christian spiritual transformation is going to look similar to other faith traditions sharing approximately similar outlooks on God, and who hold similar values and engage in approximately similar practices. In other cases, Christian spiritual transformation is going to look increasingly different than other faith traditions as the outlook on God and as the worldview, values, and practices increasingly diverge from the Christian tradition.

However, for anyone practicing any form of human transformation, they will be using the same types of neurological, mental, and physical processes that all human beings use.

Bringing the Chapter to a Close

We have covered a lot of territory in this chapter. We began by looking at how the Bible understands what it means to be human and how it views the various "aspects" or "dimensions" of the human being. Then we looked at how neuroscience understands the way the human body works. Finally we wrestled with how Scripture, neuroscience, and spiritual formation relate to each other.

Next, we will turn to look at each of the dimensions of human life and then examine what they are, and finally explore how they can be transformed. We'll begin first with an overview of the dimensions. Then, we'll analyze them more carefully, looking particularly at how transformation can take place in that dimension.

PART 3

Changing from the Inside Out

Transforming Every Dimension of Our Being

10

The Dimensions of Human Life: An Overview

"So use your whole body as an instrument to do what is right
for the glory of God." (Rom 6:13 NLT)

THIS BRIEF CHAPTER WILL compare how neuroscience understands the
human dimensions, how the Bible talks about them, and how we talk
about them today. Then I will give an overview of the six dimensions of
who we are as humans. This chapter will close with addressing a major
challenge in our quest for spiritual transformation of each of these dimensions: the challenge of changing habits that are unhealthy, damaging,
and/or sinful.

The Dimensions of Human Life:
Neuroscience, Jesus, and Dallas Willard

As we, in the last chapter, reviewed how the Bible views human beings
and how the neuroscientist Anthony Damasio describes what a human
being is, I found no fundamental conflict between them. This makes
perfect sense, since God is the ultimate "engineer" of the human body.
Though the focus and the language each uses is different, they can be
brought nicely into harmony with each other.

Using this neurobiological description of human consciousness laid
out by Damasio, and supplementing a missing dimension of this description of human life to include the social dimension, which neuroscientist
Matthew Lieberman outlines in his book *Social: Why Our Brains Are*

Wired to Connect, we can compare the language of neuroscience to the language of the New Testament in general, to that of Jesus in particular, and to the terminology of Dallas Willard in their respective descriptions of the human dimensions:

Damasio (Neuroscience)	New Testament	Jesus	Willard
The Body's processes for life regulation			
Feeling			Feeling (sensation, emotions)
Thinking	Mind (*nous*)	Mind	Thoughts (images, concepts, judgments, inferences)
	Spirit (*pneuma*) Heart (*kardia*) Conscience (*syneidēsis*)?	Heart	Choice (heart/ spirit/will, decision, character)
Action	Flesh (*sarx*) Body (*sōma*) Members (*melē*)	Strength	Body (action, interaction with the physical world)
Social (Lieberman)	"one another" language (*allēlous*)	Neighbor	Social context (personal and structural relations to others)
The entire human being	Soul (*psychē*)	Soul	Soul (the factor that integrates all of the above to form one life)

Though each use different terms, the concepts clearly overlap—but whereas the New Testament, Jesus, and Dallas Willard are describing capacities humans have, in contrast, neuroscience (Damasio) focuses on describing the physical properties of the brain and body.

Since we, in our everyday language, normally think in and use descriptive terms about ourselves, we will use the terminology and categories suggested by Dallas Willard. However, while we are using these descriptive terms, it will be important to keep in mind that the physical processes of the functioning body and mind that we have described above are all humming along and operating in the background—influencing our feelings, thoughts, choices, and actions.

Overview of Dimensions

Dallas Willard claims that life has six basic dimensions.

1. Thought (images, concepts, judgments, inferences)

2. Feeling (sensations, emotions)

3. Choice (will, decision, character)

4. Body (action, interaction with the physical world)

5. Social context (personal and structural relations to others)

6. Soul (the factor that integrates all of the above to form one life)[1]

Dallas Willard explains the six dimensions as follows:

> Simply put every human being thinks (has a thought life), feels, chooses, interacts with his or her body and its social context, and (more or less) integrates all of the forgoing as parts of one life. These are the essential factors in a human being, and nothing essential to human life falls outside of them.[2]

The aim of spiritual formation is to have "all of the essential parts of the human self . . . effectively organized around God as they are restored and sustained by him."[3]

The relationship between these dimensions can be envisioned as a series of concentric circles.[4]

---

1. Willard, *Renovation*, 30. I have changed the order to begin with the core of the individual and working out from there.

2. Ibid., 31. (Willard's italics)

3. Ibid., 31. (Willard's italics)

4. Ibid., 38

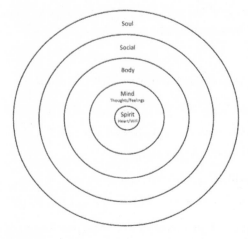

All of who we are emanates from our center—our *spirit* (also referred to in the Bible as our *heart* or our *will*)—which influences all of the rest of these dimensions in succession. Think of a throwing a pebble into a still pond. From the place it enters the water, it has a ripple effect that flows out of that center. The same is true of the heart: what goes on in the heart directly influences the mind (thoughts, feelings), which then influences what we do with our body, and how we relate to others. The soul, the outermost ring, encompasses all the other dimensions and comprises the sum total of who we are and who we have become.

The phrase "human nature" refers to the interplay between these dimensions as they function together *to accomplish things*. God has designed all these dimensions in such a way that, together, they drive us to action.

The Power of Habits and the Transformation of the Six Dimensions

Not only are all these dimensions intended to drive us to action, but God has designed us with built-in mechanisms that assist us in our actions. Those mechanisms are called "habits."

Habits are learned behaviors of the mind and body that help us accomplish something without having to actively think about doing them. They are actions we have trained ourselves to do by repeatedly engaging in them so that they have become ingrained in our brains ("neural pathways") and our body ("muscle memory").

Because of this, for example, when you tie your shoes—something that you have probably done since you were about four years old—you can at the same time use your active thinking capacity to solve a math problem, deal with a relational problem, or give detailed instructions on writing computer code. While you are using your active thinking capacity to do those things, your brain and body are silently, almost automatically, tying your shoes without you having to expend mental energy thinking about how to do it.

Why is this relevant for spiritual formation? To get at that, think about this question: *Why do New Year's resolutions fail?* It boils down to one primary culprit: our habits. We have trained ourselves over a long period of time in all of our dimensions to move and think and feel and act in a certain direction. Think of it like this: Look at all the human dimensions:

> Soul
> Social
> Body
> Mind
> Heart

Let's take these dimensions and indicate the habits we have developed over time through the symbol of an arrow facing left:

> ← Soul
> ← Social
> ← Body
> ← Mind
> ← Heart

Throughout the course of our lives, all of who we have come to be in all of our dimensions has been shaping us to desire, think, feel, act, and relate to others in specific ways. This causes my entire self to develop a particular "default" setting. We say of people, "he's always negative," "she's a jealous person," or "I've never heard her say an unkind word." (This is a bit of an exaggeration, but I hope you get the point.) These dimensions have been trained to travel relatively effortlessly down that path—together—to make us who we are today.

But suppose you realize you have not been living the way you want. What happens? A desire forms in your spirit to go in a new direction. We can map it out this way:

← Soul
← Social
← Body
← Mind
Heart →

Notice, however, that the rest of your dimensions are still being pulled by the habits that you had developed up to that time. It will take more than will-power to stop the gravitational pull of the habits of all those other dimensions. Our default settings are conditioned to move left, and it is only your will alone that wants to move right.

A similar dynamic occurs when a person comes to faith. Their spirit receives the divine life in seed form, and they begin desiring to move in a new direction. But they will be held back by the other dimensions of their being if they do not undertake specific actions to transform those other dimensions. This is why, even after coming to faith, many *still* struggle with the same addictions and patterns of behavior that they had prior to conversion.

In a sense, you could say that spiritual transformation is the process of "converting" all those arrows that are going in the wrong direction so they become aligned with our will and are all working and functioning together.

Soul →
Social →
Body →
Mind →
Spirit →

Dallas Willard explains it this way: "spiritual transformation only happens as each essential dimension of the human being is transformed to Christlikeness under the direction of a regenerate will interacting with constant overtures of grace from God."[5]

In the coming chapters, we'll describe each dimension, starting with the innermost dimension and working our way out.

5. Ibid., 41–42.

11

Our Heart (Will and Spirit)

"Above all else, guard your heart, for everything you do flows from it."
(Prov 4:23)

THE BIBLE USES THREE terms to refer to the core or center of our lives: *heart, will, and spirit.*[1] Each word emphasizes a different aspect of that center.

- *Heart* refers to the center of the human being that "controls" the other dimensions of the human being.

- *Will* refers to the power to initiate and create—to determine to do something.

- *Spirit* refers to the intangible, "non-physical" dimension that is often identified as the person him- or herself.

King Solomon identifies the significance of the heart for human life in Prov 4:23: *"Above all else, guard your heart, for everything you do flows from it."* It's a brilliant, yet somewhat disturbing insight: your heart is the well-spring of every aspect of your life. Everything you are flows from this center. Should this center somehow become damaged or polluted, then everything about you will suffer.

1. This is something Dallas Willard notes in ibid., 33.

How Our Heart Influences the Rest of the Dimensions

Jesus gets at this idea of how our heart influences the rest of our lives through a word-picture about how trees produce fruit:[2]

> No good tree bears bad fruit, nor again does a bad tree bear good fruit; for each tree is known by its own fruit. Figs are not gathered from thorns, nor are grapes picked from a bramble bush. The good person out of the good treasure of the heart produces good, and the evil person out of evil treasure produces evil; for it is *out of the abundance of the heart* that the mouth speaks. (Luke 6:43–45, NRS)

Let's think about this passage for a moment and ask a few questions relating to spiritual formation:

What are the "good treasures of the heart"?

The good treasures are composed of the good things in our heart: positive thoughts, good desires, and positive intentions to do things that are helpful and God-honoring.

What are the "evil treasures of the heart"?

These are the flipside of the good treasures: destructive things such as harmful thoughts, self-seeking desires, and negative intentions to advance ourselves and cause harm to others.

How do the good and the evil treasures get into your heart?

You *put it in there.*

How do you put it in there?

Through what you think, see, and do.

What results from storing up good or evil treasures in your heart?

What you put inside of yourself will come out. Whether good or bad, it will eventually "leak" out. We can't stop it from coming out in some form.

How does this passage relate to spiritual formation? As followers of Jesus, we need to ask how we can order our lives in such a way that we are regularly and consistently bringing good into our hearts so that good will naturally flow out of us.

We need to guard our heart, being careful to only allow that which is good into it, because the heart is the source of the rest of our lives.

---

2. This is another key spiritual formation passage in the NT.

The Dark Side of the Heart: Sin

One clear theme throughout the Bible is that all is not right with our hearts:

- "The heart is deceitful above all things and beyond cure. Who can understand it?" (Jer 17:9)

- "The hearts of people, moreover, are full of evil and there is madness in their hearts while they live, and afterward they join the dead." (Eccl 9:3)

- "For from within, out of your hearts, come evil thoughts, sexual immorality, theft, murder, adultery, greed, malice, deceit, lewdness, envy, slander, arrogance and folly. All these evils come from inside and defile you." (Mark 7:21–23)

The Bible calls this bent toward evil "sin." "Sin" is a badly mistreated word that we've probably heard used to refer to a wide variety of things. We say, "That chocolate was sinfully delicious!" A nail polish color or a clothing line might be called "sinful" because it is supposed to make the wearer sexy and attractive. On the other hand, some people consider playing cards, movies, magic shows, Halloween, and Harry Potter to be sinful.

Some of the ways we use the term "sin" are meant to be funny, while some are damaging, and most are plain off-base. And if we've absorbed this mishmash of meanings throughout our lives, it may have had a harmful effect on us both psychologically and spiritually. It's worth clearing the fog on this topic.

So what is sin? That is the task that Cornelius Plantinga Jr. set for himself in his book, *Not the Way It's Supposed to Be: A Breviary of Sin.* He clears away much of the nonsense about how we use the word sin and seeks to help us recapture how the Bible actually understands it.

In a brilliant move, Plantinga doesn't begin by defining sin. He begins by talking about the vision the Old Testament prophets painted of the future, when God will restore all things back to how he intended them to be in the beginning. This vision is captured in the word *shalom.*

> The webbing together of God, humans, and all creation in justice, fulfillment, and delight is what the Hebrew prophets call *shalom.* We call it peace, but it means far more than mere peace of mind or a cease-fire between enemies. In the Bible, shalom

means *universal flourishing, wholeness, and delight*—a rich state
of affairs in which natural needs are satisfied and natural gifts
fruitfully employed, a state of affairs that inspires joyful wonder
as its Creator and Savior opens doors and welcomes the creatures in whom he delights. Shalom, in other words, is the way
things ought to be.[3]

This backdrop helps us understand the biblical concept of sin: "Sin"
is everything that damages the *shalom* God intended for all human relationships: whether with God, with others, or with the world. *Anything
that damages or breaks those relationships is sin.*

This way of viewing sin takes it out of the "you've got to follow the
rules" category and puts it in its proper context: sin is, in its essence,
about broken relationships. That is the Bible's understanding of sin, and
it is captured well in Isa 59:1, "But your iniquities have separated you
from your God; your sins have hidden his face from you, so that he will
not hear." It is in the nature of sin to "separate" us from God, breaking the
relationship.

Modifying Plantinga's definition slightly, I would say that sin is any
act or disposition of the heart—any thought, desire, emotion, word, or
deed—or any absence of them—that breaks our relationship with God
or with others.[4]

⚖

For our own spiritual growth, we have to take sin seriously or we will end
up deceiving ourselves, thinking, "I'm not really *that* bad. I might need
a little bit of therapy or a little more spiritual insight, but I'm not *that*
bad." This way of thinking will never move us into true, deep spiritual
transformation.

It's not by chance that the first step of Alcoholics Anonymous'
twelve steps toward recovery is to admit "we were powerless over our
addiction, that our lives had become unmanageable." Ask anyone in AA
and they will tell you that it is only when you get to that point—usually
only possible after you've hit rock bottom—that you can actually begin
the road to recovery.

3. Plantinga, *Not the Way It's Supposed to Be*, 10. (Plantinga's emphasis)

4. The original is "*a* sin is any act—any thought, desire, emotion, word, or
deed—or its particular absence, that displeases God and deserves blame." Ibid., 13.

Why is this point the beginning of recovery? Because it opens you up to the second step, "we came to believe that a Power greater than ourselves could restore us to sanity."[5] Only when we come face-to-face with our own brokenness before God—that Power greater than ourselves—and release the things we are clutching onto, can we receive the healing, forgiveness, and power God longs to give us.

The Heart as the Choosing Center ("the Human Will")

When we use the word *will* as in "the human will," we are focusing on our ability to choose, decide, and initiate. Our *will* refers to the capacity to make decisions of any kind:[6]

- To decide to go to Hawaii on vacation—or to Europe;
- To choose a business major—or a music major;
- To watch TV and eat junk food—or to get off the couch and go jogging;
- To surf the internet for hours—or to invest in a friendship through conversation;
- To fudge on your income tax—or to be honest but end up paying more;
- To cheat on your spouse—or to remain faithful.

This ability to choose between different options is simply a property of how God made us. This holds for morally inconsequential choices (going to Hawaii or Europe for vacation) as well as for moral choices (cheating on your spouse or not). This is something that God puts in our hands.

- "I have set before you life and death, blessings and curses. Now *choose* life." (Deut 30:19)
- "*Choose* for yourselves this day whom you will serve." (Josh 24:15)

5. Many don't realize that the origins of Alcoholics Anonymous were solidly Christian, and that the twelve steps have deep roots in the teachings of Jesus. For Bill Wilson, that Power greater than ourselves was Jesus.

6. Whether your theology leads you to a deterministic understanding of human action or not, I would imagine most of us operate on the assumption that we are choosing to do things. If you want to pursue this topic in more detail, this would be a good place to start: Feinberg, Basinger, and Basinger, *Predestination & Free Will: Four Views.*

If it is the case that God has put *choice* into our hands, that means that every time we sin, on some level, we are actually *choosing* to sin.

The Heart as Choosing to Sin

So, what happens when we don't *choose* to sin? It's not a trick question, but the answer seems blindingly obvious: *we won't sin!*

If that's the case, then why don't we choose *not to sin*? That's a question worthy of a solid answer. Let's explore the mechanics of how sin works—which also happens to be the mechanics of how virtually everything we do works.[7]

Sin, Habits, and Making Choices

Have you noticed that when you sin, you don't sin randomly? You (almost) always sin in the same ways again and again. Why is that? Michael Mangis explores this question in his book, *Signature Sins*. He writes:

> My life, like my home, carries unique markers of my own experiences, relationships, likes, dislikes, gifts and vices. My life displays patterns, consistencies and habits . . . .
> My sin is similarly patterned. I can predict my temptations by the choices that have enticed me before. Other temptations may afflict my neighbor but cause me no struggle at all. My patterns of sin are unique to me.
> Most of us are not tossed about by temptations like winds from every direction. Few people are tempted one day by drunkenness and the next day by sexual immorality and the next day by stealing or violence or sloth. We do not sin at random. Our sin takes a consistent and predictable course.[8]

Normally we don't even think about our choices, whether they are sinful choices or otherwise. They seem to happen automatically. They

7. I am speaking here of "sins of commission" as they are often called. What I am saying here may not apply to "sins of omission." Since it would lead to quite a lengthy discussion, I will avoid getting into a discussion of these types of sins as well as the notion of "original sin." There has been a renewed debate the nature of sin, particularly what has been called "original sin". I have found these three books to be helpful on this topic: Toews, *The Story of Original Sin*; Lamoureux et al., *Four Views on the Historical Adam*; Osborn, *Death Before the Fall*.

8. Mangis, *Signature Sins*, 10–11.

feel automatic because of our past experiences and the habits we have developed as a result.

Through these past experiences we have amassed over a lifetime, we have developed standard responses, which then have become habits of the heart, the mind, and the body. They become such a part of us, we are no longer aware of them.

We are also not aware of how the past is present in the present. Let me explain what I mean. Imagine you grew up in a home marked by explosive anger and yelling. Your parents or older siblings were constantly at it. Growing up in this, you lived with the fear that this could happen any moment. Your response was fear, shame, and withdrawing.

Then imagine that you are now in college, and you have just begun your first relationship. You are head over heels in love. Things go fine for a few weeks or months. You seem to think the same about everything. But then you have your first disagreement. What happens inside of you in that moment? Most likely fear, shame, and withdrawing. Why? Any experience we face in the present automatically evokes associations or parallels with past experiences. Those past experiences triggered certain emotional reactions that developed into patterned reactions that we use today when we encounter people who are angry with us. Just as we developed the pattern of reacting with fear, shame, and withdrawing in the past—so are likely to respond the same way in the present when we perceive someone disapproving of something we said or did. Our repeated responses, sinful or otherwise, become ingrained in us—as habits.

Now, even though our reactions *seem* automatic, there is still an element of choice at play. We still choose to react in those ways, even though this takes place at the margins of our awareness. With all normal human action, there is an element of our *will* that is involved.

It is both the beauty—and the curse—of habits that we become only peripherally aware we are making choices at all. Good habits lead us to "automatically" doing good. Negative habits lead us to "automatically" damaging ourselves and others.

An Aside: The Effects of Choosing to Sin

Since we don't like thinking about sin, we may not realize the toll it takes on us—in every dimension of who we are. Let's think about this for a moment by exploring Ps 38.

David wrote this Psalm after he had committed some sin. David doesn't divulge what the sin was—but that doesn't matter since most sin has the same general dynamic and effect.

This Psalm describes how sin affects all the dimensions of the human person. Notice what it does to his heart, his thoughts and emotions, his actions, and his relationships.

> LORD, do not rebuke me in your anger or discipline me in your wrath.
> Your arrows have pierced me, and your hand has come down on me.
> Because of your wrath there is no health in my body; there is no soundness in my bones because of my sin.
> My guilt has overwhelmed me like a burden too heavy to bear.
> My wounds fester and are loathsome because of my sinful folly.
> I am bowed down and brought very low; all day long I go about mourning.
> My back is filled with searing pain; there is no health in my body.
> I am feeble and utterly crushed; I groan in anguish of heart . . . my sighing is not hidden from you.
> My heart pounds, my strength fails me; even the light has gone from my eyes.
> My friends and companions avoid me because of my wounds; my neighbors stay far away . . .
> I am like the deaf, who cannot hear, like the mute, who cannot speak; I have become like one who does not hear, whose mouth can offer no reply.
> LORD, I wait for you; you will answer, Lord my God . . .
> LORD, do not forsake me; do not be far from me, my God.
> Come quickly to help me, my Lord and my Savior.

In a remarkable way, David describes how sin, willfully committed, has had a direct impact on every dimension of his life:

- It affects how he thinks and feels.
- It has a direct impact on his physical condition, on his physical energy level.
- It has alienated him from his social relationships.
- It has distanced him from God.

Those are the effects on us of choosing to sin. If we are doing things that we know are not right—or if we are trying to rationalize a behavior we know is wrong—living on an ongoing basis in that state of willful wrong cannot help but directly impact us physically, emotionally, psychologically, and spiritually. Sin can kill you.

Breaking the Action-Reaction Cycle

If we want to break out of this "action-reaction" cycle of damaging responses, how do we do this?

Think about the difference between a child learning how to tie their shoes for the first time and an adult who ties their shoes without thinking about it. For the child it is a slow, awkward, unfamiliar, and frustrating process because they have to concentrate on every step. For the adult, it's easy, effortless, and "automatic." The only difference is training. Repeated practice over time leads to effortless action. This also holds true for the spiritual realm.

With this in mind, I would suggest there are a few steps to breaking the action-reaction cycle of destructive responses.

Step 1: Creating space by developing self-awareness. The first step in breaking this "action-reaction" response is to create a space between the action and our reaction to it. We begin creating that distance by developing self-awareness in the present moment. It is a matter of training ourselves to become aware of our thoughts, emotions, actions, and motives as we go about our day. We start paying attention to what is going on inside of us in the moment.

This is a particular challenge in our contemporary culture. Our sophisticated electronic gadgetry (smart phones, tablets, mobile internet, etc.) leave us no space in our minds for creating self-awareness in order to think deeply about why we do what we do. These modern inventions, for all the good they do, block our ability to engage in personal reflection.

Only when we become aware of what is going on inside us, can we actively make a choice to break from habits that hold us in bondage and begin new ways of living that lead us to life as Jesus came to give it.

Step 2: Activate our will. After we begin the work of self-awareness, we need to intentionally exert our *will* into the equation. We can exercise our power to *choose* in order to move in a life-giving direction.

Step 3: Envision situations beforehand. When we become aware of this pattern of action-reaction and desire to choose a new way of reacting, it is helpful to *envision beforehand* the way we want to respond.

In other words, we identify situations we have encountered in the past, where we have "blown it." We then imagine ourselves encountering similar situations again in the future—but this time we envision ourselves responding in ways that are in line with the life and teaching of Jesus.

The more "real" we make this envisioning process and the more we rehearse it in our minds, the more power it will give us to choose the right way of responding.

Step 4: Practice in advance how we intend to respond. Perhaps the one thing most effective in helping us respond in a "Jesus way" in the moment of choice is if we *practice* in advance how we intend to respond. When an actor rehearses, they memorize their lines and walk through what they will say, where they will stand, how they will act and react. All this is practiced before the actual performance. We can apply the same dynamics when we think about the areas that need to change in our lives.

An Aside: The Choices We Make and Our Brain Structure

In this whole process of changing our will, it is important to know what happens in our brain as we make choices: The decisions we make change the actual structure of our brains.

William Newsome, Professor of Neurobiology at Stanford (and also a Christian), was asked in an interview, "Does my brain shape me or do I shape my brain?" to which he answered, "Yes!" Here's his explanation.

> You are shaped by your brain. You can't do things that your brain won't allow you to do. You have certain emotional make-ups, and you have certain emotional history and background that's embodied in the current structure of your brain, and that lays constraints on how you're going to act in the future.
>
> But ... you can shape your brain! And one of the ways you shape your brain is what you choose to do when you get out of bed in the morning. The fact you've chosen to be here talking with me today will shape your brain.
>
> If you remember anything tomorrow from this conversation today, and if I remember anything tomorrow from this conversation today, it will be because our brains have changed. . . . [Your actions and choices] really do change the physical structure of your brain.

And when you choose to [do something] . . . that choice shapes your brain, and it has real implications for what behavior you're capable of in the future.[9]

Newsome's words dovetail with our earlier discussion of how the brain works: since the brain is plastic, we have the ability to change our brain by *choosing* carefully what we engage in. Do you see the potential this has for our spiritual transformation?

9. Newsome, "Does My Brain Shape Me, or Do I Shape My Brain?"

12

Our Thoughts

"The mind is a terrible thing to waste."

WHEN I WAS A kid, I remember a commercial that ended with the words, "the mind is a terrible thing to waste."[1] At the time, I had no idea what the commercial was about, but the idea that what I do with my mind as important has stuck with me ever since. Your mind—and what you do with it—matters.

In this chapter we begin by exploring what thoughts actually are, then look at various aspects of how we think, and end by looking at the things we can do to transform our thinking.

What Thoughts Are

I find helpful (for our purposes here) Dallas Willard's understanding of what "thoughts" are:

> By "thoughts" we mean *all of the ways in which we are conscious of things.* That includes our memories, perceptions, and beliefs, as well as what we would ordinarily refer to when we say "I thought of you yesterday," or "I was just thinking of our meeting tomorrow."[2]

Thoughts have two components. The *first* component identifies the raw material of our thoughts. It refers to the information we receive

1. It was sponsored by the United Negro College Fund.
2. Willard, *Renovation*, 96.

through our sense organs—what we see, hear, touch, taste, and smell. Once this raw material comes through our sense organs and reaches our brain, the *second* component is activated: the brain begins to process that information and integrate it into the brain's vast storehouse of processed information we have been accumulating over a lifetime. These two components together make up the process we call "thinking."

Our Thinking Is Based on the Map of Our Past Experience

This thinking doesn't happen in a vacuum but is triggered by and based on concrete experiences coming at us through our senses. However, what we see, taste, touch, and feel *today* only makes sense to us because we connect it to things we have seen, tasted, touched, etc. *in the past*.

In other words, we only understand our present experiences because our brain connects them to past experiences that in some way resemble what we experience today. This is how "brain maps" work: they map each present experience onto the larger map of past experiences.

When we go through our day, our brain is taking everything we experience and running it through our internal archives of past experiences in order to match it with a map of parallel experiences. When it finds the map (usually in a nano-second), we "understand" our present experience. This match helps us know how to respond in the present based on the patterns of responses we have developed in the past—the maps our brains create.

We face some challenges regarding these maps in our spiritual formation. *First*, our maps may be flawed and in need of change. For example, let's say that the map of my past experiences was based on the thinking, "The way to get the love I am craving is to give myself to others sexually." That map needs to be dislodged, modified, and replaced—or else any present experiences that correlate to that map will lead that person to give themselves sexually to others today.

A *second* challenge comes when a person develops inadequate responses based on those inaccurate maps. We will come back to remapping our maps and retooling our responses later in the chapter.

Our Thinking is Based on Ideas and Idea Systems

Our brain not only has the ability to draw a map of how we respond in individual situations, it also has the ability to draw even larger maps by stitching the smaller maps together into a comprehensive system that forms our foundation for understanding all of life. We might call that larger map a belief system, a metanarrative, or an "idea system."[3]

It may help us understand what an idea system is if we look at a person who developed an extremely unhealthy idea system. The movie *A Beautiful Mind* is based on the life of a brilliant, Nobel Prize-winning mathematician, John Nash. In the film you can see how an idea system has taken control of his mind. John Nash's brilliant mind was obsessed with numbers, and he developed this idea that the numbers he encountered in his daily life were all interconnected and full of clues about the meaning of life.

This theory—this *idea system*—began to dominate his thinking. The more he thought about it, the more these numbers began to control him. It was as if he was possessed by these number-patterns, and the film portrays this brilliantly.

The problem was that this idea system did not match up with reality but was something he created in his brilliant mind. Since it did not match up with reality, it began to ruin his life, and destroy his relationships.

In the same way, we develop ideas and idea systems about life. We develop a particular way of seeing ourselves and God. This then begins to *govern* and *direct* the way we think and act. These ideas and systems are normally not present to us consciously, but are operating on the subconscious level, influencing us.

If these idea systems are in sync with the reality of the way God designed life, it leads to freedom and flourishing. If they are out of sync with reality, they can become strongholds that enslave us.

How Do Idea Systems Develop?

How do idea systems develop? They develop through individual experiences that we have throughout our lives that we then associate together. For example, if we have a number of negative encounters with others that

---

3. Ibid., 101.

terrify us, an "idea system" can begin to form that the world is a dangerous place.

We can also create destructive theological idea systems based on our
experiences that warp our image of God. Consider this example: imagine
Johnny as a four-year-old in children's church, hearing the Bible story of
Noah's Ark. The teacher tells the children, "God is angry at people who
disobey him and will punish them." While at church, Johnny encounters
a number of adults, who are constantly critical and always pouncing on
him when he acts out. And then at home, Johnny experiences a father,
who regularly goes to church, but whips him for the slightest infraction.

Now think about these questions:

- What idea system might be developing within Johnny's mind?

- How does that impact how Johnny views God?

- How will this impact Johnny's prayer and his behavior?

Fast-forward to Johnny as an adult (he goes by "John" now). He has
left his religious upbringing behind. He avoids church. When he meets
religious types, he has an instinctive perception that they are judging
him. If he ever thinks about God (he tries not to) a sense of shame, guilt,
and anger comes over him. John has no idea where his negative view of
God came from. The source of it is buried so deep in his childhood that
he is not aware of it.

Two important points here relate to our spiritual formation. *First*, it
is important to recognize, identify, and root out false idea systems. This
is perhaps one of the most challenging tasks we face in our own personal
spiritual formation, because every dimension of our lives has been integrated around this false idea system. Changing this fundamental idea will
often require complete upheaval of everything else in our lives.

Second, since the information we take into ourselves directly influences us, and since it is the nature of ideas/idea systems to govern or
control us, it is extremely important to monitor carefully what kind of
information we are putting inside our heads.

Information and Thinking as Brain Food

In light of that, I find it helpful to think of information we take in through
what we see and hear as *food* for the brain. Rick Hanson describes it this

way when he writes, "Much as your body is built from the foods you eat, your mind is built from the experiences you have. The flow of experience gradually sculpts your brain, thus shaping your mind."[4]

You know what happens over time, when you eat junk food: it eventually ruins your health and affects every part of your body. The same happens with the "food" we feed our brains: it can literally harm our brains.

Rick Hanson explains that

> the brain takes its shape from what the mind rests upon. If you keep resting your mind on self-criticism, worries, grumbling about others, hurts, and stress, then your brain will be shaped into greater reactivity, vulnerability to anxiety and depressed mood, a narrow focus on threats and losses, and inclinations toward anger, sadness, and guilt. On the other hand, if you keep resting your mind on good events and conditions (someone was nice to you, there's a roof over your head), pleasant feelings, the things you do get done, physical pleasures, and your good intentions and qualities, then over time your brain will take a different shape, one with strength and resilience hardwired into it, as well as a realistically optimistic outlook, a positive mood, and a sense of worth.[5]

If the pattern of our thinking "rests on" what is negative, it will shape the brain according to the negative way we think. If, happily, we guide our thinking to feed on what is positive, then that will shape our brain in positive ways that will produce a pattern of thinking that rejuvenates us.

The Power of Choice: Choosing Your Thoughts

Implicit in what we have been talking about in this chapter is our fundamental human capacity to *choose*: we can choose what we do, and we can also choose what we think about. Dallas Willard expresses it this way: "The ultimate freedom we have as human beings is the power to select what we will allow or require our minds to dwell upon."[6]

4. Hanson, "Taking in the Good."
5. Ibid.
6. Willard, *Renovation*, 95.

I would suggest that the truth of this statement provides the possibility for any change to take place in our lives. If this were not true, the whole enterprise of spiritual transformation would not be possible.

That is why in 2 Cor 10:5 Paul tells us that we must "demolish *arguments* and every *pretension* that sets itself up against the *knowledge* of God, and we take captive every *thought* to make it obedient to Christ."

Notice all the italicized words refer to a variety of thoughts that the mind is able to "think." Paul indicates that we have power over our thoughts and are able to bring them into alignment with the teachings and lifestyle of Jesus.

Can We Force Our Minds to Think Certain Things?

You might be thinking to yourself, "Can we really *force* our minds to think certain things?" We actually do it all the time. What do college students find themselves doing the night before an exam? We call it *cramming!* Cramming is nothing more than forcing your mind to think certain things. You are directing your mind to focus on the material and pound it into your head. Even when you are studying and you get distracted— a thought flits through our head—you are generally able through sheer willpower to turn your mind back to the material you need to study.

This holds true not just for studying for exams. We do this in many other area of human life. The biggest problem we face, however, is actually in our down time, when we're not actively giving our mind something to think about. It is in these times when we are not compelled by external forces to think on certain things that our minds go on autopilot and begin to travel down the default thought pathways we have developed throughout our lives.

But, just like a mind on autopilot might drift toward ingrained unhealthy thought patterns, it is possible to develop new patterns of thinking so that when our minds go on autopilot, our thoughts drift toward the good.

The challenge we have as followers of Jesus is to lay down a new set of default pathways that lead us naturally to think on that which is good, right, pure, and lovely (Phil 4:8) from a Jesus-centered perspective. And whenever we stray off of that path, it is possible—like someone cramming for an exam—to turn our mind back toward what is good, right, pure, and lovely.

Are There Any Exceptions to Being Able to Force Our Mind to Think Certain Things?

We also need to ask the question, are there any exceptions to this? Are there certain circumstances in a person's life where they are powerless to control what their mind does with respect to what they think about?

There seem to be two exceptions. The first is when there has been damage done to the brain in some way, or when the brain is not working as it should. With the second area, we need to tread cautiously: there are situations where people may have come under demonic influence. Dr. Henry Virkler, professor of counseling at Palm Beach Atlantic University, explains it this way:

> Sometimes people who are demonically possessed may not be free to choose their behavior. I would see sin on a continuum, from sin that is committed because of our sin nature (no demons necessary), to sin committed in response to demonic temptation, to sin committed because of demonic oppression, to sin committed because of demonic possession (the latter being cases where people may not be capable of choosing how they will behave).[7]

There is much confusion in this area. Some see a "demon behind every bush." Others discount there is such a thing at all.

A woman we had come to know had, since her teenage years, struggled with depression. Since her family was involved in a church that emphasized the power of the Spirit, she was told that she had the "demon of depression." This demon was "cast out" numerous times over two decades, yet the depression never lifted. It was only in her later adult years, after she was encouraged to have a complete physical checkup that the doctors discovered a chemical imbalance her body was producing that generated the depression.

While utmost care, wisdom, and sensitivity are needed here, there may be situations in which a person can come under demonic influence.[8] In such cases, the ministry of deliverance may be necessary. Tackling this challenging topic adequately would require another book, but thankfully several helpful resources are available.[9]

7. Henry Virkler, email message to author, July 22, 2014.

8. See the discussion in Richards, *But Deliver Us from Evil.* For different approaches to this topic, see Beilby and Eddy, *Understanding Spiritual Warfare.*

9. I have found the writings of Neil Anderson to be particularly insightful and

Taking In the Good

Although we will talk more about strategies for transforming all of our dimensions in the next section of the book, I want to camp out on the mind a bit longer, because the transformation of the mind is perhaps the most crucial of all the dimensions for spiritual formation, since it influences all the other dimensions.

Notice how Prov 23:7 makes this connection between our thinking and the rest of who we are: "For the way a person thinks, so, in fact, are they."[10] In other words, the totality of who we are is dependent upon our thoughts. We *become* what our mind dwells on.

For this reason, a major part of the transformation process must concern itself with actively taking in what is good, right, and true—about God, about ourselves, and about how God designed us to live our lives. We need to seek out this information, bring it inside of us, and then internalize it so that it can transform us.

You can see the critical role Scripture needs to play in our live at this point. It is *the primary source* of information about the character of God, about who we really are, and about how we are to live.

Remember, however, that this information is not primarily about amassing and mastering Bible facts. Simply taking in "raw data" will not transform us. An atheist could memorize the Bible without it changing them in the least. Spiritual transformation requires taking this truth into us in such a way that it leads to transformation in the depths of who we are.

The words of Scripture are rooted in a reality that is conveyed as images and stories. For our reading of Scripture to be transformative, it has to be visualized by our minds in such a way that we enter into the reality to which Scripture points. In so doing, the Bible becomes the *living* and *experienced* word of God *to* and *in* us!

Life-transforming encounters with Scripture have four characteristics: they must be *sustained, regular, experiential,* and must *engage our senses.*

Sustained refers to the duration of an individual reading. It must be of sufficient length for us to enter into the text—and for the text to enter

---

practical in helping people become free from demonic oppression, especially his books *The Bondage Breaker; Victory Over the Darkness; Steps to Freedom in Christ.*

10. This is my translation. Although the verse speaks of someone who is a "begrudging host," the principle holds true in general for life.

into us—in a way that touches, moves, and reshapes our inner being. A quick, unconcentrated, check-it-off-the-list kind of devotional reading in the midst of a busy day is not likely to be transformative.

Regular has to do with a consistent, habitual reading of Scripture that becomes part of our daily routine. Just as you won't notice a significant change in your physical health by jogging only every once in a while, so it is the cumulative effect of a habit of daily Scripture reading that begins to impact our entire life in deep ways.

Experiential has to do with our approach to the text: we want to enter into the text so that it becomes an encounter with God. If we approach our daily time of Bible reading as if it were a homework assignment, its effect in our lives will be minimal.

Engaging the senses drills down into the last characteristic of seeking to experience the text as much like real life as possible: with all of our senses. This type of reading is the means to greater levels of spiritual transformation.

Let me give two examples of this approach to make clear what I mean.

Guigo II: The Ladder to Heaven

In the twelfth century AD, a French monk, Guigo II, described how, when he was reflecting on the spiritual vocation of a monk one day, all of a sudden "four stages of spiritual exercise" presented themselves to him.[11] These stages appeared to him as a ladder that would, rung by rung, allow a person to ascend—like Jacob's ladder—to paradise. These four rungs of the ladder are reading, meditation, prayer, and contemplation.[12]

- *Reading* has to do with a slow and thorough examination of a passage of Scripture that calls for the soul's full attention.
- *Meditation* enters more deeply with the heart into the text, seeking for spiritual treasures. This seeking for the spiritual meaning of the text leads the soul naturally to desire and possess what it has been seeking.

11. This also goes by the name *lectio divina*.

12. Many people, however, prefer using the Latin terms for these four steps: *lectio, meditatio, oratio,* and *contemplatio.*

- *Prayer* is the turning of the heart to God, begging him for the treasure they are longing for.
- *Contemplation* is the stage where the soul experiences God himself and "tastes the joys of everlasting sweetness."[13]

Guigo then goes on to describe the process of reading using a couple of analogies.

> Reading seeks for the sweetness of a blessed life,
> meditation perceives it,
> prayer asks for it,
> contemplation tastes it
> Reading, as it were, puts food whole in the mouth,
> meditation chews it and breaks it up,
> prayer extracts its flavor,
> contemplation is the sweetness itself which gladdens and refreshes.[14]

Notice how sensory this Scripture reading is. It involves entering into Scripture through our capacity to *attend, perceive*, and *taste* what we read—and thereby *experience* it.

Saint Ignatius of Loyola: Reading Scripture with the Senses

An even more experiential method of reading was suggested by St. Ignatius of Loyola in his book *The Spiritual Exercises*, written in 1524 AD. St. Ignatius intended this work to be used as a guide for a four-week spiritual retreat for monks pursuing a holy life and desiring to discern the will of God for their lives.

To get a fuller idea of how St. Ignatius instructed his fellow monks to read Scripture, I will quote two passages at length.

The first passage is a contemplation of Christ's birth, which begins with a few "preludes" (to set the context for the reading) followed by three points to focus on as they read. The emphasis on experiencing the text with our senses is striking:

---

13. Guigo II, *The Ladder of Monks*, 82.
14. Ibid. I have set these out like the rungs of a ladder.

FIRST PRELUDE. This is the history of the mystery. Here it will be that our Lady [referring to the virgin Mary], about nine months with child, and, as may be piously believed, seated on [a donkey], set out from Nazareth. She is accompanied by Joseph and a maid, who was leading an ox. They are going to Bethlehem to pay the tribute that Caesar imposed on those lands.

SECOND PRELUDE. This is a mental representation of the place. It will consist here in seeing in imagination the way from Nazareth to Bethlehem. Consider its length, its breadth; whether level, or through valleys and over hills. Observe also the place or cave where Christ is born, whether big or little; whether high or low; and how it is arranged.

. . .

FIRST POINT. This will consist in seeing the persons, namely, our Lady, St. Joseph, the maid, and the Child Jesus after His birth. I will make myself a poor little unworthy slave, and as though present, look upon them, contemplate them, and serve them in their needs with all possible homage and reverence.

Then I will reflect on myself that I may reap some fruit.

SECOND POINT. This is to consider, observe, and contemplate what the persons are saying, and then to reflect on myself and draw some fruit from it.

THIRD POINT. This will be to see and consider what they are doing, for example, making the journey and laboring that our Lord might be born in extreme poverty, and that after many labors, after hunger, thirst, heat, and cold, after insults and outrages, He might die on the cross, and all this for me.

Then I will reflect and draw some spiritual fruit from what I have seen.[15]

A few days later, the person on this spiritual retreat is to contemplate a second passage. St. Ignatius instructs them to take the scene from the nativity again, but this time the reading "will consist in applying the five senses" to the contemplation of the birth of Jesus:

15. Ignatius of Loyola, *Spiritual Exercises*, 43.

After the preparatory prayer . . . it will be profitable with the aid of the imagination to apply the five senses to the subject matter . . .

FIRST POINT. This consists in *seeing* in imagination the persons, and in contemplating and meditating in detail on the circumstances in which they are, and then in drawing some fruit from what has been seen.

SECOND POINT. This is to *hear* what they are saying, or what they might say, and then by reflecting on oneself to draw some profit from what has been heard.

THIRD POINT. This is to *smell* the infinite fragrance, and taste the infinite sweetness of the divinity. Likewise to apply these senses to the soul and its virtues, and to all according to the person we are contemplating, and to draw fruit from this.

FOURTH POINT. This is to *apply* the sense of touch, for example, by embracing and kissing the place where the persons stand or are seated, always taking care to draw some fruit from this.[16]

St. Ignatius's aim in reading Scripture this way is to make it so real that the person experiences the text of Scripture as if they were part of the events themselves. Engaging in this type of reading has real transformative power. This is not only the experience of St. Ignatius but of many others, including myself.[17]

Taking in the Good, Imaginative Scripture Reading, and Neuroscience

What is fascinating is that brain research today is confirming the power of the process that Guigo II and St. Ignatius described, since reading this way rewires the brain and changes the neural networks. Though the spiritual dimension of individuals is not the focus of neuroscience, it is exciting that current findings in neuroscience support the fact that this way of reading can lead to real change, physically and spiritually.

16. Ibid., 44–45. (My italics)

17. For an updated discussion of using the senses in reading the Bible, I would suggest Smith, *The Word is Very Near You*; Peterson, *Eat this Book*; Foster, *Life With God*.

Notice, for example, the parallels between the steps that Guigo II describes and Rick Hanson's description of "taking in the good." Hanson defines taking in the good as "the deliberate internalization of positive experiences in implicit memory"[18] (that is, memory that operates more on the subconscious level). He argues that when we deliberately internalize a desirable experience, it will then reshape how we subconsciously think, act, and feel in the future.

The same thing occurs when we deliberately internalize Scripture and the realities contained in it. For the follower of Jesus, taking in Scripture is a positive experience that will reshape our inner world, so that we will find ourselves naturally thinking God's thoughts after him and living the way he wants us to live without consciously thinking about it.

From a neuroscience perspective, Hanson suggests the following steps to "taking in the good" in ways that change our brain-structure:[19]

1. Have a positive experience.

2. Enrich it.

3. Absorb it.

Hanson explains that step 1, having a positive experience, "*activates* a positive mental state, and steps 2 and 3 *install* it in your brain."[20] Although Hanson (as far as I am aware) is not a Christian and although he is speaking about positive experiences in general, the same processes are taking place in the brain of a person who desires spiritual transformation through reading Scripture. I would encourage you, as you read this, to think about the experience of reading your Bible in this way. It could have a revolutionary impact!

Step 1: Have a positive experience. Notice some positive experience you are having—or intentionally create a positive experience. You can do this by bringing to mind something that has lifted you up in the past, encouraged you, etc. Then, seek to make these things you bring to your mind an "emotionally rewarding experience." Otherwise, explains Hanson, this will be an exercise in positive thinking, with little lasting impact.

Step 2: Enrich it. Remain in this emotionally rewarding experience for a while (he suggests ten seconds or longer). He explains how and why:

18. Hanson, *Hardwiring Happiness*, 60.

19. Ibid. Hanson lists an optional fourth step if you want to re-wire negative experiences you have had: link positive and negative material.

20. Ibid. (Hanson's italics)

Open [yourself] to the feelings in it and try to sense it in your body; let it fill your mind. Enjoy it. Gently encourage the experience to be more intense. Find something fresh or novel about it. Recognize how it's personally relevant, how it could nourish or help you, or make a difference in your life. *Get those neurons really firing together, so they'll really wire together.*[21]

Step 3: Absorb it. This step is actually an extension and intensification of the previous one.

Intend and sense that the experience is sinking into you as you sink into it. Let it really land in your mind. Perhaps visualize it sifting down into you. . . . Know that the experience is becoming part of you, a resource inside that you can take with you wherever you go.[22]

Hanson argues that from the perspective of neuroscience, these three steps literally begin to rewire the brain.

How do we look at what Hanson says from a Christian standpoint? When a follower of Jesus desires to transform their thinking by meditating on Scripture in this way, two things are happening. On a *physical* level, our brains are *physically* transformed when we engage in Scripture reading through the use of our imagination. What happens in the *spiritual* dimension when we open ourselves up to the Jesus we encounter in the text is that we are *spiritually* transformed. This spiritual transformation happens as we open ourselves up to the work of the Spirit, who draws closer to us, and as a result, we experience his presence and his power.

21. Ibid., 61. (My italics)
22. Ibid., 61–62.

13

Our Feelings

"For the love of Christ overwhelms us." (2 Cor 5:14, NJB)

IT IS NOT ONLY our thoughts that need to experience transformation. Many of our feelings—which are ever so tightly associated with our thoughts—also need to be transformed.

In this chapter, we want to focus on three questions: What exactly are emotions or feelings?[1] How do they relate to our thoughts? And how can they be transformed?

Let's begin by briefly looking at what feelings are and how they work.

What Feelings Are

Feelings have three major characteristics. *First,* feelings are *how we perceive* the experiences we have with people, places, and things. *Second,* feelings are internal and personal *value judgments* of those experiences. *Third,* feelings are *learned responses* we experience that are based on the

---

1. As I mentioned earlier, for simplicity's sake, I am using the words "emotions" and "feelings" interchangeably. Antonio Damasio's distinction between these two terms are not uninteresting, however. He uses the term "emotion" to refer to the body's automatic "action plan," which alerts us to threat or danger: our heart involuntarily starts to race or we begin to sweat. Damasio uses the word "feeling" when he refers to our perception or awareness of the body's action plan: we become fearful, nervous, etc. He explains the distinction in this way: "Emotions are complex, largely automated programs of *actions* carried out in our bodies," and "feelings . . . are composite *perceptions* of what happens in our body and mind." Damasio, *Self Comes to Mind,* 109–10.

brain maps we have developed over a lifetime. These maps determine for us what we perceive as good and pleasing or bad and disgusting.

When we have an experience today, our brain automatically takes a snapshot of what we see and finds the maps in our head that in some way correspond to what we are now experiencing. The closer that the experience we are having connects to our map of what we think is good, the more we perceive that experience as pleasant. The further away our present experience is from our map of what is good, the more we will have a feeling of disgust or revulsion.

One simple illustration of this might suffice: I recall once watching a documentary of a Stone Age tribe. In one scene, they showed children and adults looking through the hair of other members in the tribe and eating the bugs that they found in the hair. For that Stone Age tribe, this was apparently a tasty treat. That is what their brain map told them. For me—not so much! My brain map told me that hair bugs should not be on anyone's food pyramid.

Anthony Damasio, in his study of emotions, identifies three different types of emotions, which I find helpful. *Primary emotions* (also called *universal emotions*) are happiness, sadness, fear, anger, surprise, or disgust. *Secondary emotions*, which he also labels *social emotions,* are embarrassment, jealousy, guilt, or pride. *Background emotions* are a sense of well-being or malaise, calm or tension.[2] Though not a complete catalog, these form the basis for all the other emotions we experience.

How Feelings Work

There are various dimensions to how our emotions function. Let me briefly highlight what we mentioned earlier, and then build on these insights.

Feelings as Dashboard Signals

In chapter 9 I explained that, like the green lights and red lights on the dashboard of a car, emotions alert us to our state of being. Positive emotions—green lights—tell us that everything is going ok, and we don't need to do anything. Painful emotions or feelings—red lights—alert us

2. Damasio, *The Feeling of What Happens,* 50–51.

that something is not as it should be and that we need to become active to deal with the source of that pain.

Because of how emotions function as a warning system, they are absolutely essential to life. Without them, we couldn't survive.[3]

Feelings Draw Us Toward or Repel Us Away

Feelings also have another function. Like the two sides of a magnet, feelings draw us toward certain things and push us away from other things. Positive feelings we have—love, empathy, etc.—create the desire to move toward people and situations where we experience things we sense will enhance our lives. Negative feelings—fear, shame, harm, etc.—create the desire to avoid those people, situations, or objects we sense are harmful for our lives.

Feelings Attach Themselves to and Are Driven by Images

Feelings also attach themselves to our images and thoughts. Every experience we have in our day-to-day life is experienced by us *emotionally*.

The brain links particular experiences with a particular emotion. These become wired together,[4] get downloaded, and stored in our brain's memory bank. Recalling a past experience from our memory also recalls the feeling attached to that experience—and we feel the same emotions all over again.

Try this: bring to mind your favorite vacation right now. As you visualize it, how do you feel? When I bring to mind last year's vacation, I automatically smile because it was such a glorious time. On the other hand, when I bring to mind my doctoral exams, I experience that same feeling of dread I had when I was taking them years ago!

When an experience has wounded us deeply, the images associated with that particular experience—along with the emotions we experienced—can create a mood or tone in our lives that mark us from then on.

Dallas Willard explains it this way,

> Feelings and emotions are fostered and sustained by ideas and images. . . . Hopelessness and rejection (or worthlessness and

3. Ibid., 54.

4. Damasio observes that, "virtually every image, actually perceived or recalled, is accompanied by some reaction from the apparatus of emotion." Ibid., 58.

"not belonging") live on images—often of some specific scene or scenes of unkindness, brutality, or abuse—that have become a permanent fixture within the mind, radiating negativity and leaving a background of deadly ideas that take over how we think and structure our whole world.

Such images also foster and sustain moods. What we call "moods" are simply feeling qualities that *pervade* our selves and everything around us.[5]

Feelings Are Learned and Can Be Miswired and Confused

It is important to realize that feelings are learned responses. We have learned certain feelings through the experiences we have had. We have, in essence, *trained* ourselves to feel in certain ways.

Because of this, it is possible that our feelings may actually be inappropriate responses to what we experience. A friend of mine had a dog that he had gotten from a pet shelter. The person working at the shelter explained that the dog had been beaten and abused. When I visited my friend, I noticed that "Rusty" almost never left his kennel, and when he did, he made sure no humans were around. When I tried to be friendly to Rusty, he perceived me as a threat.

The same happens in humans. We may feel like a person is dangerous, because they in some way resemble someone in our past who had done us harm, even though, in fact, that person is actually good, kind, and caring. For a healthy relationship to be possible, such feelings will need to be reshaped.

Feelings Are Complex and Sometimes Impossible to Figure Out

Have you ever found yourself in a weird or "down" emotional state and asked yourself, "Why am I feeling this way? What is causing me to feel so sad or alone?" At times, you might be able to pinpoint the reason, but at other times it seems impossible to figure out. Why is that?

Anthony Damasio explains there are a lot of factors that go into the emotions we feel.

> You may find yourself in a sad or happy state, and yet you may be at a loss as to why you are in that particular state now. A careful

5. Willard, *Renovation*, 127.

search may disclose possible causes, and one cause or another may be more likely, but often you cannot be certain. The actual cause may have been the image of an event, an image that had the potential to be conscious but just was not because you did not attend to it while you were attending to another. Or it may have been no image at all, but rather a . . . change in the chemical profile [inside your body], brought about by factors as diverse as your state of health, diet, weather, hormonal cycle, how much or how little you exercised that day, or even how much you had been worrying about a certain matter. The change would be substantial enough to engender some responses and alter your body state, but it would not be imageable in the sense that a person or relationship is imageable, i.e., it would not produce a sensory pattern of which you would ever become aware in your mind.[6]

How does knowing this help us? I think it helps us be ok with not knowing why we are feeling the way we do at a given moment when a particular feeling comes over us for a time. We might not figure it out, and we shouldn't beat ourselves up about it. We can feel what we feel, acknowledge it, and move forward without getting stuck, knowing that this feeling will pass. In those times we can use our ability to focus our attention on thoughts that bring healing, comfort, and encouragement. This is the strategy that Paul himself suggests when he tells us to "set our mind on what the Spirit desires" because eventually "the mind governed by the Spirit is life and peace" (Rom 8:5–6).

Of course, if you are feeling down, you should ask why that is and get to the root of it, if possible. If you can't figure it out after you tried, then it is helpful to acknowledge that is how you are feeling without panicking about it.

Some Feelings Are Trying to Get Our Attention

But what happens if the feelings are not momentary? What happens if they persist and just won't go away? It may very well be that our feelings are indicating that something is wrong in our lives.

Remember what we said about our emotions functioning as a warning system alerting us to something wrong in our physical bodies? Our feelings have the same function when it comes to the well-being of our

---

6. Damasio, *The Feeling of What Happens*, 47–48.

person: our feelings may be telling us that something is not as it should be. Getting to the root of it may take some time.

Parker Palmer, in his book *Let Your Life Speak*, describes his journey through depression. Before the depression set in, he felt something in his life wanting to get his attention. He describes it this way:

> Imagine that from early in my life, a friendly figure, standing a block away, was trying to get my attention by shouting my name, wanting to teach me some hard but healing truths about myself. But I—fearful of what I might hear or arrogantly trying to live without help or simply too busy with my ideas and ego and ethics to bother—ignored the shouts and walked away.
>
> So this figure, still with friendly intent, came closer and shouted more loudly, but I kept walking. Ever closer it came, close enough to tap me on the shoulder, but I walked on. Frustrated by my unresponsiveness, the figure threw stones at my back, then struck me with a stick, still wanting simply to get my attention. But despite the pain, I kept walking away.
>
> . . . Since shouts and taps, stones and sticks had failed to do the trick, there was only one thing left: drop the nuclear bomb called depression on me, not with the intent to kill but as a last-ditch effort to get me to turn and ask the simple question, "What do you want?" When I was finally able to make that turn—and start to absorb and act on the self-knowledge that then became available to me—I began to get well.[7]

I like how Parker Palmer describes our feelings as "a friendly figure" that is trying to alert us to something being off-kilter in our lives. It may take some time (and maybe even counseling) for us to figure out what God is trying to point out in our lives through those feelings. It is important to listen to what that friendly figure is trying to tell us.

Emotions and Feelings Change Us Physically

Another dimension of feelings that is helpful to be aware of is that they literally change us physically. When we experience an emotion, instructions are given to other parts of the brain, then to the rest of the body. These instructions are sent using the two major highways of the body. First, chemicals are shot into the bloodstream and distributed throughout the body. Second, "electrochemical signals" are sent via the central

7. Palmer, *Let Your Life Speak*, 68.

nervous system to particular muscles, organs, and limbs. When those signals arrive at their destination, they also release chemicals that make their way into the bloodstream to prepare us to respond in certain ways.

For example, when we dwell on thoughts that evoke anxiety and stress in our lives, this releases the chemical cortisol that the body produces into our bloodstream, which is designed for the "fight or flight" mechanism of the body to respond to danger. However, stress induced by our thoughts—with no actual danger being present—has a damaging effect on the body. Randall explains:

> High levels of stress, even over relatively short periods and in vastly different contexts, tend to produce similar results: prolonged healing times, reduction in ability to cope with vaccinations, and heightened vulnerability to viral infection. The long-term, constant cortisol exposure associated with chronic stress produces further symptoms, including impaired cognition, decreased thyroid function, and accumulation of abdominal fat, which itself has implications for cardiovascular health.[8]

When we experience an emotion, it changes our body! Randall goes on to say that "the good news is that stress levels rest largely on our own behavior and decisions and . . . we can optimize our bodies' responses to stress based on how we live our daily lives."[9]

But experiencing an emotion not only changes the body; it also changes our brain—as neural connections are formed, strengthened, or weakened. Damasio writes, "both the brain and the body proper are largely and profoundly affected by the set of commands [initiated by the experience of an emotion]."[10]

When it comes to allowing ourselves to think certain thoughts that produce certain feelings within us, the longer we do this, the more of an imprint it leaves on both our mind and body.

Transformation of Feelings

In the rest of the chapter I will (1) make a few observations about feelings, (2) identify the specific feelings that we should cultivate, (3) explain how we can go about transforming damaged or falsely wired feelings,

8. Randall, "Physiology of Stress."
9. Ibid.
10. Damasio, *The Feeling of What Happens*, 68.

and finally, (4) synthesize the ideas from this chapter into a pathway for transforming our feelings.

1. Some Observations about the Nature of Feelings

Three observations about our feelings will help us understand them and transform feelings that are damaging.

You Can't Directly Control Your Feelings.

The first observation is that, you can't directly control your feelings. It is not possible by a sheer act of the will, to control or change your feelings. But although we don't have *direct* control of our feelings, we do have *indirect* control.[11]

To understand this better, although it is not the most pleasant image, think of feelings as *parasites*. Parasites are creatures that live off of and feed off of other things. Feelings "feed off" of our *thoughts*. They are dependent upon and kept alive by the thoughts we focus on, attend to, and keep at the center of our attention.

To change your feelings, then, you have to change what you allow your mind to dwell on. If you change the thoughts and images your mind dwells on, then over time your feelings will also change.

Developing a Perspective and Strategy for Dealing with Our Feelings

In a brilliant passage, Dallas Willard points the way forward toward developing a better perspective on disordered feelings and gives a strategy for transforming them. I would suggest reading it slowly and carefully to absorb what he is saying. (I have broken his one paragraph into two sections.)

> By contrast [to the one who is enslaved to their feelings], the person who happily lets God be God does have a place to stand in dealing with feelings—even in extreme cases such as despair over loved ones or excruciating pain or voluptuous pleasure. They have the resources to do what they don't want to do and not do what they want. They know and deeply accept the fact

11. Willard, *Renovation*, 118.

that their feelings, of whatever kind, do *not* have to be fulfilled. They spend little time grieving over non-fulfillment.

And with respect to feelings that are inherently injurious and wrong, their strategy is not one of resisting them in the moment of choice but of living in such a way that they do not have such feeling at all, or at least do not have them in a degree that makes it hard to decide against them when appropriate.[12]

There are three significant points that come out here.

The *first* is that for the follower of Jesus, with a new perspective on life and with the Holy Spirit living within us, we need no longer remain slaves to our fallen selves—including our fallen emotions. The Spirit empowers us to say "no" to unhealthy thoughts that produce unhealthy emotions when they begin to form in us.

Second, because we have a new place to stand, we know that feelings do not have to be fulfilled. We can "simply" choose to turn away from that. OK, it's not as easy as the word "simply" might suggest, but this new place we stand in our relationship with God creates a new starting point to turn away from damaging thoughts that produce damaging feelings in the present.

Third, our strategy in dealing with potentially harmful feelings is less about dealing with them "in the moment of choice" and more about developing a lifestyle that nurtures positive feelings and starves out negative ones before they actually arise.

That is the core strategy of the spiritual transformation of our feelings.

Our Image of Ourselves and Transforming Our Feelings

One challenge we have in dealing with falsely wired feelings is that *we identify ourselves with those feelings*. In other words, we don't just *have* those feelings; we think we *are* those feelings! Our identity—our image of ourselves—is wrapped up so tightly with our feelings that we cannot *imagine* who we are without them being part of us. This image of ourselves keeps us in bondage.

If this false way of seeing ourselves is present, then it will be a stronghold that will keep us enslaved. The follower of Jesus has to realize that our identity as a person is not bound up with our feelings.

12. Ibid., 119.

In order to dislodge this way of thinking, we have to envision a new identity for ourselves. This will require, in many cases, a long journey toward laying down a false identity that has become entrenched over time and then progressively "clothing ourselves" with a new one.

In C. S. Lewis's *The Great Divorce*, he tells a powerful allegorical story about a ghost of a man on a visit to heaven. This man has a red lizard—symbolizing lust—sitting on his shoulder. As you read, notice how this man identifies with his lust.

> Sitting on his shoulder is a little red lizard, twitching its tail like a whip and whispering things in his ear. The man turns his head to the reptile and snarls, "Shut up, I tell you!"
>
> Just then one of heaven's radiant angels sees the man. "Off so soon?" he calls.
>
> "Well, yes," says the man. "I'd stay, you know, if it weren't for *him*," indicating the lizard. "I told him he'd have to be quiet if he came. His kind of stuff won't do here. But he won't stop. So I'll just have to go home."
>
> "Would you like me to make him quiet?" asks the angel.
>
> "Of course I would," says the man.
>
> "Then I will kill him," says the angel, stepping forward.
>
> The man panics at the thought of permanently losing the lizard and the sweet fantasies the creature whispers in his ear. But he *is* tired of carrying him around. He dithers back and forth between the two choices. Solemnly, the angel reminds him he cannot kill the lizard without his consent. And yes, it will be painful for the man; the angel refuses to soften the truth. Finally, in anguish, the man gives his consent, then screams in agony as the angel's burning hands close around the lizard and crush it.
>
> "Ow! That's done for me," gasps the man, reeling back.
>
> But then, gradually but unmistakably, the man begins to be transformed. Bright and strong he grows, into the shape of an immense man, not much smaller than the angel. And even more surprisingly, something is happening to the lizard, too. He grows, rippling with swells of flesh and muscle, until standing beside the man is a great white stallion with mane and tail of gold. . . .
>
> In joyous haste the young man leaps upon the horse's back . . . . And then they are off across the green plain.[13]

---

13. Lewis, *The Great Divorce*, 98–103. The version used here is the condensation by Patrick Means found in *Men's Secret Wars*, 220–21.

Just like this man, many cannot imagine life without that disordered desire they struggle with. This feeling has become such a part of us, we cannot imagine how life could be fulfilling if that craving—and the fulfillment of that craving—were not a central part of that picture.

It is brilliant how Lewis ends the story: when we allow God to "kill" the lizard—by our giving that lust to him, and by choosing to detach ourselves from it—God can transform that lizard into something in our lives that is even more glorious than we could have imagined.

That is the hope that we have, and that is what many have experienced when they have done this.

2. What Are the Feelings We Should Be Developing?

If we desire our feelings to be transformed, we should take our cue from the feelings Jesus and the New Testament authors emphasized.

When we scan the New Testament to look for emotions, we see them blend in with character qualities and virtues. This makes sense in the Greek-dominated culture in the New Testament era, where such virtue lists were common.

Two things stand out in the virtue lists from Paul and Peter in the New Testament when compared to the other Greco-Roman virtue lists from that time.[14]

Gal. 5:22–23	1 Cor. 13	2 Cor. 6:6	Col. 3:12-14	1 Tim. 4:12	1 Tim. 6:11	2 Tim. 2:22	2 Pet. 1:5–7
love	love	love	love	love	love	love	love
joy							
peace							
patience		patience	patience		steadfastness	peace	steadfastness
kindness		kindness	kindness				
goodness			compassion				
faith	faith			faith	faith	faith	faith
gentleness			gentleness		gentleness		self-control
self-control							
		purity		purity			knowledge
		knowledge					
					righteousness	righteousness	godliness
					godliness		virtue
							brotherly-love
			humility				
	hope						

14. Except for the addition of 1 Cor 13 and Col 3, the remainder of the list was compiled by James Dunn. *Galatians*, 309.

The *first* difference is the prominence of *love* as the constant in every list. This tells you something. One commentator expressed it this way: "love is not one virtue among a list of virtues, but the sum and substance of what it means to be a Christian."[15] Love, it seems, is the overarching virtue that encompasses all of the others. Think of love like a diamond with many facets. All of the items in the lists are facets of what love is.

The *second* difference is more subtle. When Paul and Peter wrote these lists, they had Jesus in mind. James Dunn, speaking particularly of the list in Gal 5, suggests that "Paul had in mind here a kind of 'character-sketch' of Christ."[16] So, when Paul lists patience and peace as virtues on his list, he is thinking of a Jesus-kind-of-patience and a Jesus-kind-of-peace that we are to cultivate.

How do these emotions compare with the basic set of emotions that neuroscientists and psychologists have identified? In a major study of human emotions that took into account the research on this topic, the neuroscientist David Robinson has identified eleven basic positive emotions,[17] many of which we can correlate with the emotions in the virtue lists from the New Testament.

15. Charles Cousar, cited in ibid.

16. Ibid., 310.

17. Robinson, "Brain Function, Mental Experience and Personality," 155. Robinson uses the term "cathected" instead of "invested."

Kind of Emotion	Positive Emotions	Negative Emotions
EMOTIONS RELATED TO OBJECT PROPERTIES	**Interest**, curiosity	**Alarm**, terror, panic
	Attraction, desire, admiration	**Aversion**, disgust, revulsion
	Surprise, amusement	**Indifference**, familiarity, habituation
FUTURE-APPRAISAL EMOTIONS	**Hope**	**Fear**
EVENT-RELATED EMOTIONS	**Gratitude**, thankfulness	**Anger**, rage
	Joy, elation, triumph, jubilation	**Sorrow**, grief
	Relief	**Frustration**, disappointment
SELF-APPRAISAL EMOTIONS	**Pride** in achievement, self-confidence, sociability	**Embarrassment**, shame, guilt, remorse
SOCIAL EMOTIONS	**Generosity**	**Avarice**, greed, miserliness, envy, jealousy
	Sympathy	**Cruelty**
INVESTED* EMOTIONS (in persons, objects, ideas)	**Love**	**Hate**

Where Do We Begin?

Although the list from the New Testament is a relatively short list, its length still poses a problem of where to begin in the transformation of our feelings. Dallas Willard, however, whittles the list down to three emotions we should focus on. He writes,

> Now the realm of feelings may appear on first approach to be an area of total chaos. But this is not so. There is also order among feelings, and it is a much simpler one than most people think.

When we properly cultivate with divine assistance those few feelings that should be prominent in our lives, the remainder will fall into place.

What then are the feelings that will dominate in a life that has been inwardly transformed to be like Christ's? There are the feelings associated with love, joy, and peace . . . though . . . love, joy, and peace are *not* mere feelings but conditions of the whole person that are accompanied by characteristic positive feelings.[18]

These three—love, joy, and peace—Dallas Willard suggests, "inform one another and naturally express themselves in the remainder of that *one* fruit: '. . . patience, kindness, goodness, faithfulness, gentleness, self-control.'"[19] His suggestion is to concentrate on developing love, joy, and peace—the first three of the virtues listed in Gal 5:22–23—and the rest will come with it.

I would suggest, however, that undergirding these virtues of love, joy, and peace are two others, which Paul emphasizes when discussing the greatest virtues in 1 Cor 13:13. Alongside love, Paul emphasizes faith and hope. These appear to be the pillars upon which all the other virtues rest.

Hope is that sure confidence of a *future* that is secure in God (Heb 11:6). We have something to look forward to that will make the challenges and pain we face now pale in comparison (Rom 8:20–25). It is this type of hope that sustains us, motivates us, produces joy, and keeps us going.

This hope also generates *faith* in us—a faith that is grounded in the *past*, in what Jesus has done for us. If it weren't for the life, death, and resurrection of Jesus, there would be no hope, and our faith would be pointless. Jesus gives us *hope* for the *future* because of what he did in the *past*. And because of that, we can have *faith*. This faith is aimed at the *future* hope that Jesus has promised to us, and it preserves and sustains us in the *present*, no matter what we are experiencing.

When we blend Paul's ideas from Gal 5:22–23 and 1 Cor 13:13, we see five virtues/emotions—faith, hope, love, joy, and peace—that are the foundation and gateway to all of the positive feelings we can experience.

18. Willard, *Renovation*, 128.
19. Ibid.

How Do We Cultivate These Feelings?

How do we cultivate these positive feelings? Again, it is important to remind ourselves that we cannot directly change our feelings. We change our feelings as we fill our mind and senses with things that are good and true that have the power to change how we feel. Paul expresses it this way: "Finally, brothers and sisters, whatever is true, whatever is noble, whatever is right, whatever is pure, whatever is lovely, whatever is admirable —if anything is excellent or praiseworthy—think about such things" (Phil 4:8).

The phrase "think about these things" is critical. Other translations render this as

- "focus your thoughts on" (CEB, CJB),

- "keep your thoughts on" (GWN),

- "concentrate your attention on" (MIT), and

- "let your mind dwell on" (NASB).

Filling of our mind with all the good things that God has created evokes positive emotions. This includes the wonder of creation, those things that are beautiful and good in art, culture, society, and the people and things that surround us—as well as, of course, the images and stories of the Bible.

If you gaze at something good and beautiful, and if you open yourself to it, then you will feel pleasure. Sustained attention on anything over time begins to rewire the synapses in your brain so that you *literally* become a more joyful person. Joy will become embedded in your brain.

When we talked earlier about "taking in the good," we mentioned Rick Hanson's three-step process of "hardwiring happiness" into our brains: have a positive experience, enrich it, and absorb it. However, in order for this process to be *Christian* spiritual formation, it cannot simply be just any positive experience, as good as that may be. For the follower of Jesus, who is seeking a Jesus-oriented transformation of their entire being, the positive experiences would need to be marked by at least the following things. They must be

- shaped by the story of God,

- driven and informed by the values of Jesus,

- undertaken with a dependence on Jesus and awareness of his presence in us through his empowering Spirit, and

- experienced in a way that is in harmony with the ethics of Jesus.

When these ingredients are in place, those positive experiences will transform the entire person in all its dimensions more into the image of Christ.

3. Transforming Our Damaging Feelings

We have spoken about cultivating positive feelings. But what about the feelings that we have developed in our lives that are harmful or damaged—that tend to draw us away from God and toward sinful, destructive desires? How can we unlearn these feelings? How can we shed them so that we are not driven by them and held in their grip?

Rick Hanson has addressed this topic of dealing with damaged emotions from the standpoint of neurobiology in his book, *Hardwiring Happiness*. We mentioned earlier his three steps to hardwiring happiness, but he suggests a fourth step that particularly targets destructive or negative emotions:

1. Have a positive experience.

2. Enrich it.

3. Absorb it.

4. *Link positive and negative material.*

What does he mean by "link positive and negative material"?

Bringing the Negative into the Light of the Positive

Linking positive and negative material means bringing something positive into your focus of attention; then, without letting that slip out of your main focus, bringing to your background awareness some pain or difficulty you have experienced. But—and this is critical—don't let it take over the center of your focus. He explains it this way:

> While having a vivid and stable sense of a positive experience in the foreground of awareness, also be aware of something negative in the background. For example, when you feel included

and liked these days, you could sense this experience making contact with feelings of loneliness from your past. If the negative material hijacks your attention, drop it and focus only on the positive; when you feel recentered in the positive, you can let the negative also be present in awareness if you like. Whenever you want, let go of all negative material and rest only in the positive. Then, to continue uprooting the negative material, a few times over the next hour be aware of only neutral or positive material while also bringing to mind neutral things (e.g., people, situations, ideas) that have become associated with the negative material.[20]

Although Hanson goes on to give some examples that are quite helpful for how this works, there are also many examples in Scripture that illustrate this. The Psalms are filled with David bringing his burdens to God and finding peace and contentment.[21] In Ps 27:4–5, David centers his gaze on the Lord and then, as he remains focused on the Lord, he brings his awareness of "negative material."

> One thing I ask from the LORD, this only do I seek: that I may dwell in the house of the LORD all the days of my life, to gaze on the beauty of the LORD and to seek him in his temple. For in the day of trouble he will keep me safe in his dwelling; he will hide me in the shelter of his sacred tent and set me high upon a rock.

Similarly, Paul's description of prayer in Phil 4:6–7 illustrates this principle of keeping the focus of our attention on the positive (God) while bringing the negative into the periphery of our awareness: "Do not be anxious about anything, but in every situation, by prayer and petition, with thanksgiving, present your requests to God. And the peace of God, which transcends all understanding, will guard your hearts and your minds in Christ Jesus."

Let me illustrate the way this linking works with an experience my wife recently had. My wife, Kathy, was responsible for a major new project in her job at our church. There were many problems to solve and details to consider, and it was causing her sleepless nights and not a little worry! In her Bible reading one morning, she was reading the story in Isa 37 about Hezekiah receiving a frightening letter, in which King Sennacherib threatened Israel with death and destruction. It said, either surrender or face invasion and destruction.

20. Hanson, *Hardwiring Happiness*, 63.

21. For example, Pss 27; 37; 40; 62.

Isaiah records Hezekiah's response: "Hezekiah received the letter from the messengers and read it. *Then he went up to the temple of the* LORD *and spread it out before the* LORD" (v. 14).

That scripture hit Kathy in a powerful way. She decided to do the same. She sat in the chair she often prays in and positioned it in front of our large sliding glass doors so that she could see the beautiful landscape: the sun shimmering on the river, the wild birds flying by, the colorful plants. She took the beauty in. She took the truths of this passage in. She focused her awareness on the presence of God with her in that moment and rested in his goodness and his care for her. Then she spread out her problem before God and talked with him about it. She didn't let the problem dominate. She allowed God and the joy of his presence and the beauty of his creation to remain the focus of her attention. She asked God for his help and his wisdom. As she remained in that posture, she felt the burden lift. She put her full trust in God that he would supply all that she needed. She got out of that chair filled with peace and a renewed sense of love for God and trust in him.

Kathy did what Rick Hanson suggests: First, remain centered and focused on a positive experience—in Kathy's case, the goodness and care of God. Second, bring the negative experience into the picture, but not as a dominant focus—in Kathy's case, she brought her concerns into the periphery of her positive focus; never taking her main attention off of God.

Dealing with Deep Wounds and Deep Emotions

The situation that Kathy faced was, relatively speaking, a small challenge. Does this work, however, for people who have suffered from traumatic experiences that have left them with deep emotional scars?

I believe this approach holds true even for more devastating trauma that people experience, but we need to factor in a general principle here: *the depth of the traumatic experience will require a corresponding depth of engagement in dealing with that trauma.*

Though there are different depths and durations of challenging or painful experiences, I would suggest that the process of steps outlined above can be used to deal with any difficult situation. Some situations will certainly require more focused attention and working through them with the guidance of another person, but these basic tools are powerful ones that we can use in the healing process.

Dr. Bessel van der Kolk has specialized in working with PTSD patients as well as children who have been severely traumatized. His findings dovetail with what we have been suggesting here. He writes:

> Traumatized children must be helped actively to overcome their habitual fight/flight/freeze reactions by engaging their attention in actions that (1) are not related to trauma triggers and (2) provide them with a sense of mastery and pleasure . . . . Children must learn to know what they feel, put those feelings into words, or find some other symbolic expression (drawing, play acting) that can allow them to gain distance from the traumatic events and help them imagine alternative outcomes.[22]

Dr. van der Kolk's suggestion goes beyond what Rick Hanson suggests in that he not only suggests *thinking* about something pleasant, but also *doing* something that provides the feeling of accomplishment and pleasure.

Dr. Norman Doidge recounts the work of Dr. Jeffrey Schwartz with individuals with severe cases of Obsessive Compulsive Disorder (OCD) and describes the therapies Dr. Schwartz used to help them face and ultimately overcome these compulsions. Dr. Schwartz discovered that compulsions could become unstuck from their *brain-lock* "by paying constant, effortful attention and actively focusing on something besides the worry, such as a new, pleasurable activity."[23]

Dr. Schwartz identified two key steps in the therapy. The *first* step was relabeling what was happening to them:[24] "Yes, I do have a real problem right now. But it is not germs, it is my OCD." By doing this, the person is able to begin distancing themselves from the obsession and view it as a symptom of their compulsion. The *second* step was for the individual to "*refocus* on a positive, wholesome, ideally pleasure-giving activity the moment he becomes aware he is having an OCD attack."[25]

Dr. Schwartz's therapy also dovetails with Rick Hanson's suggestion to link positive and negative material, and like Dr. van der Kolk, takes it a step further, when he recommends focusing on "pleasure-giving activities."

22. Kolk, "The Neurobiology of Childhood Trauma and Abuse," 310. Van der Kolk's article suggests other things that aid in dealing with trauma, but what is mentioned here is central to the healing process.

23. Doidge, *The Brain that Changes Itself*, 170.

24. Ibid., 171.

25. Ibid., 173.

From a neurobiological standpoint, what happens in this process is that the individual is developing new neural pathways that help circumvent the compulsion. When a person practices this therapy repeatedly, the new circuitry in the brain fuses more strongly together, paving the way to lasting change.[26]

In a summary of research on neurology and trauma, the researchers highlight three forms of therapy that are particularly effective. *Cognitive Behavioral Therapy* helps individuals relabel their memories in ways that help them to "gain a sense of meaning and control" over the trauma. *Imagery Rescripting Therapy* allows individuals to replace traumatic images with ones that are positive. *Narrative Therapy* enables someone to retell the event in a way that allows them to "reconceptualize" the event.[27]

All these approaches confirm Rick Hanson's suggestion that linking negative experiences with something positive (both in our thoughts and actions) leads to significant changes in the neural pathways of the brain.

Gregory Boyd has written some helpful Christian resources for dealing with deeply traumatic experiences and the negative memories and feelings they evoke. As a young child, Greg experienced abuse at the hands of a step-mother. He describes a process of dealing with those traumatic childhood experiences in his book *Seeing is Believing: Experience Jesus through Imaginative Prayer*. In this book, he outlines a way to bring Jesus into those painful experiences—or rather—to bring those painful experiences into the light of the presence of God.

A second book that Greg Boyd co-wrote with Al Larson goes into greater depth on this topic: *Escaping the Matrix: Setting Your Mind Free to Experience Real Life in Christ*. Both of these books are informed by neuroscience research, Scripture, and Greg's own personal experiences; and I recommend them highly![28]

26. The same types of discoveries are being made in work with individuals who have suffered from emotional and/or physical traumatic experiences (both short term and long term).

27. Dowd and Proulx, "Neurology and Trauma."

28. Some Christians have raised warning flags about the danger of imagination. While their intention is good, the argumentation is often skewed. From a neurobiological standpoint, human beings can't help but imagine things. That is simply how the mind works. The issue is not whether imagining is good or bad. This issue is *how* we use our imagination. It is possible to use it in ways that lead us toward wholeness in Christ. For a recent treatment of this topic, see Veith, *Imagination Redeemed*.

4. A Pathway for Transforming of Our Feelings

As a way of distilling much of what I have said in this chapter, I want to lay out a pathway for the transformation of our feelings that involves five steps.[29]

First, we simply need to *recognize the reality of the feelings* that we have. In this step we seek to become aware of them, identify them, and name them.[30]

Second, we need to realize that *we are not these feelings* and *we are not our thoughts.* We stop identifying "us" as synonymous with "our feelings" and "our thoughts."

The neuroscientist Jon Kabat-Zinn, in an interview on "The Science of Mindfulness," addressed this issue directly. He describes what happens inside our bodies when our minds tell us stories about ourselves. Although he is specifically speaking of thoughts, it is clear that the feelings attached to those thoughts are also addressed:

> Well, if you're telling yourself a story about how horrible things are, even if the story is not quite true, your body is going to relate to it as if it is true, and it's going to pour stress hormones into the bloodstream—cortisol and the like—and your heart rate will go up and your muscles will contract and you will be in a fight or flight mode, or in a freeze mode if it's really terrifying—and all of this without really having there be a major threat. Just the thought in the mind is enough to generate that threat.[31]

Then he makes this observation that is quite freeing:

> Now if you're not sort of really intimate with thoughts as thoughts, then every thought that flits through your mind is potentially perceived as actually the truth. So, for instance the thought that "I'm not as good as she is" . . . or "people don't like me" or "I will never succeed" or "I'm over the hill now" or "It's all downhill from here" or "I'm too old" or "I'm too heavy" or whatever it is. [We have to realize that] all of these are just thoughts.
>   But [unfortunately] they are not related to as thoughts by most people. They are related to as the absolute truth. So one

29. Some of these thoughts are drawn from Willard, *Renovation,* 136–38.

30. There are a number of ways we can do this. Journaling is quite helpful to become aware of what is going on inside of us. Setting reminders at set intervals during the day can alert you to ask yourself, "what am I feeling right now?" Doing this over a three-four week time span will help turn this into a habit.

31. Kabat-Zinn, "Science of Mindfulness," 25:27:07 minutes.

of the ways in which you can actually deal with all the stress that we're facing, both the real events in our life and also the imagined ones that we create in the mind is to actually begin to differentiate between thoughts and other aspects of reality.[32]

What Jon Kabat-Zinn says here has tremendous implications for our spiritual well-being. *We are not what we think, and we are not what we feel.*

Think of your thoughts and feelings as clouds. Clouds pass over us all the time. Sometimes they move slowly, sometimes quickly. Some clouds are light and bright. Some are dark and depressing.

In the same way emotions and thoughts pass through us. But we are not those emotions or those thoughts. They will come, and they will go. We can become aware of them, and we can detach ourselves from them by naming them. Something powerful takes place when we label something.

If we become aware of our "self-speak" and disconnect who we are with what we are thinking, it will give us space to insert a new reality into our awareness. What Jesus and Paul suggest is for us to tell ourselves the truth about who we are in our relationship to God.[33]

The thoughts we have stored in our brains that tell us who we are based on negative experiences are not the real truth about us as followers of Jesus. Those thoughts present themselves to us as "the truth about who we are," evoking feelings of inadequacy, brokenness, and shame.

These things may be the *old truth* about us from our "BC" days— our days before Christ. However, the *new truth* about us is that because of Jesus, we have a new identity that brings with it new truths about ourselves. We need to increasingly live into this new reality by telling ourselves these new truths. This begins creating new recording tracks in our brains that can over time transplant the old recordings stored in our brains.

This will not be easy! The new recordings will compete for a place in our minds with the old recordings. But the more we use these new tracks, the more new feelings will begin to develop that are shaped by those truths. We will increasingly be shaped by the love, joy, and peace of knowing that we are beloved children of God.

32. Ibid.

33. The following are just a sampling of passages that I have found helpful for this: John 1:12; 15:15; Rom 6:12; 8:1, 15, 39. See also the helpful book by Backus and Chapian, *Telling Yourself the Truth.*

Third, if we discover emotions that are not in line with the teachings of Jesus, we need to agree with God to release those destructive feelings. This is where the battle begins. We name those emotions, and we tell God that we desire to give up these harmful emotions.

Fourth, we need to develop and practice positive habits of the mind and body. We need these to replace the negative habits of the mind and body that we have ingrained in our thinking and acting. You may need to map out a "personal plan" that specifically targets this in order to be intentional and concrete about it. (We'll talk about that later.)

Fifth, and finally: in order for you to follow through on it, it is vital for you to enlist a friend or group of friends to keep you accountable on a regular basis, even daily, if necessary.

This is the pathway to transform our feelings.

14

Our Bodies

"Take your everyday, ordinary life—your sleeping, eating, going-to-work, and walking-around life—and place it before God as an offering." (Rom 12:1 The Message)

IN THIS CHAPTER WE want to look at what the body is, how it relates to the previous dimensions, and how it can be transformed. Throughout the book thus far, we have discussed a good deal about how the body works, but now we will pull those bits together. We'll start with an overview of the body from the standpoint of neuroscience, and then we'll discuss the way the body relates to the other dimensions.

Overview

At a very basic level, our bodies are designed by God with capacities and processes to make sure it survives and thrives. *On the survival side,* when anything threatens us, warning signals are sent to alert us something is wrong. When we become conscious of it, we experience negative emotions, which we register as painful, driving us to deal with that pain by taking action. *On the thriving side,* when things are happening as they should, our body sends us—sometimes subtle, sometimes pleasurable—signals that all is well, and we should continue doing what we are doing.

This description indicates that all of the internal processes at work in us are compelling us to *use our body.* We are designed to *act,* to *do,* to *make,* to *perform* with our body.

Based on this overview, let's examine how the body interacts with the other dimensions in the cycle of human action.

The Body in the Cycle of Human Action

When we do anything—whatever that may be—that act begins with a *desire*, which originates in our *will*.[1]

Will [heart/spirit]

Our *will* is the starting point for all we do. However, our *will* has already been conditioned throughout the course of our lives to *will* in a certain direction and in certain ways based on how it has willed things in the past. In the process, our *will* has acquired a strong set of habits.

Will→ *Think*

When we desire something, our *will* triggers a process we generally call *thinking*. Thoughts don't just happen. They are willed into existence.[2]

Will→ Think → *Feel*

Further, what we *feel* flows out of the direction set by our willing and our thinking. These feelings, like our willing and thinking, have also been ingrained in us through the power of a lifetime of habitually feeling the same way about the same things.

Let's put all of these factors and build a flow diagram. Over the course of our lives, multiple influences have gone into shaping our will.

1. Dallas Willard touches on some of these ideas in *Renovation*, 142.

2. There are other images and thoughts that pop into our awareness without being willed, but that's another topic. I am talking here about the process of human intention.

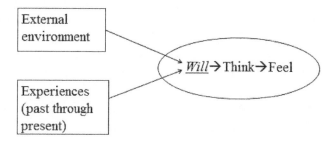

The present condition of our *will* has been shaped by everything we have experienced throughout our lifetime as well as by the environment we live in, even though we may not have been consciously aware of it: where we lived, our family, the social groups we were part of, etc.

Two dimensions of our being are particularly active here: our senses and our emotions—or, more accurately, emotional associations.

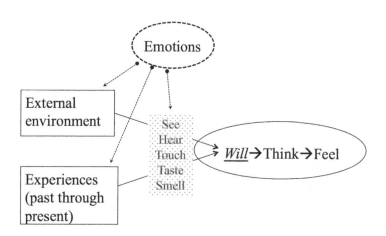

We experience everything in life through our *senses,* which get stored in our memory bank along with the emotions associated with those experiences. Recalling an event from the past leads us to re-experience those same emotions as well.

Our *will* acquires its present shape as a result of all of these factors. These factors are like a fully loaded truck barreling down the highway that can't stop or change the direction it is going in—they will drive our *will* to respond in the direction that all of these factors are compelling it to go in.

When the *will* experiences this pressure from these factors, it then turns and exerts pressure forward. It drives our present *thoughts* and *feelings* in a particular direction.

The process does not stop there. All of our willing, thinking, and feeling are designed to lead us to take *action* with our bodies.

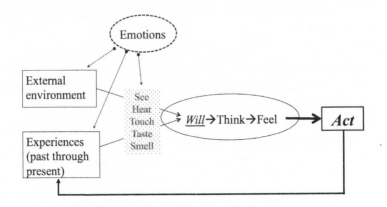

Like the momentum of that truck, all of these elements linked together exert pressure on us to *act* in certain, specific ways. It feels, at times, as if we can't stop ourselves from acting the way we do.

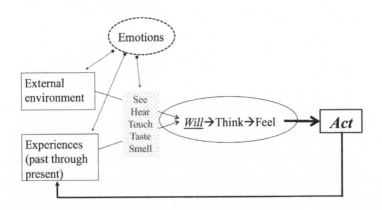

When the pressure of these forces moves us to act, this completes the entire cycle. This act, then, gets added to the stockpile of experiences that our will draws on to guide it in the future. The cycle continues and reinforce itself, shaping and strengthening who we are and what we are becoming.

This is the entire chain-link cycle of human action.

Character Is a Very Bodily Thing

It is out of this cycle of human action that our character is formed. Character is *that settled pattern of will, thought, feeling, and bodily actions that reflect what we have become as a result of how we have habitually lived our lives.*

Character anchors itself in our bodies. If you discover yourself *constantly* late for things, *constantly* angry in certain situations, *constantly* hurt, etc., it is because of the habituated responses you have *constantly* and *consistently* trained yourself in through the use of your body. For better or worse, this is now your character.

The beauty, however, is that our character is not set in stone. Change is always possible. We can be changed through the things that we do with our mind and body.

Leaning in the Wrong Direction

Unfortunately, we live in a world that in many ways is leaning away from God and is being manipulated and influenced by the rulers of this age (Eph 6:12). In addition, we often we find ourselves leaning away from God in our desires, thoughts, feelings, and actions.

Paul talks about our lean away from God in terms of "sin living in me" (Rom 8:17) and of "nothing good dwelling in my flesh" (Rom 7:18). By "flesh," he is not referring to the physical body, but the inclinations in our body that lead us away from God.

Is it possible to transform the inclinations of our bodies so that they naturally lean toward God? Let's explore that.

Learning to Lean in the Right Direction

How then can we transform our bodies so that they are naturally leaning in the right direction? The New Testament speaks directly to this topic in a number of passages. Notice particularly the way Paul speaks of how we can retrain our body to orient it toward God:

> Rom 12:1. Therefore, I urge you, brothers and sisters, in view of God's mercy, to *offer your bodies as a living sacrifice*, holy and pleasing to God—this is true worship.

Rom 6:11–13, 19. So you also must consider yourselves dead to sin and alive to God in Christ Jesus. Therefore, do not let sin exercise dominion in your mortal *bodies*, to make you obey their passions. No longer *present your members* to sin as *instruments of wickedness*, but *present yourselves* to God as those who have been brought from death to life, and present *your members* to God as *instruments of righteousness* . . . . For just as you once *presented your members* as *slaves to impurity* and to greater and greater iniquity, so now *present your members* as *slaves to righteousness* for sanctification. (NRS)

Col 3:5–12. *Put to death,* therefore, whatever belongs to your earthly nature: sexual immorality, impurity, lust, evil desires and greed, which is idolatry. . . . You used to *walk in these ways,* in the life you once lived. But now you must also *rid yourselves* of all such things as these: anger, rage, malice, slander, and filthy language from your lips. Do not lie to each other, since you have *taken off your old self* with its *practices* and have *put on the new self,* which is being renewed in knowledge in the image of its Creator. . . . Therefore . . . *clothe yourselves* with compassion, kindness, humility, gentleness and patience.

Note that Paul's language here focuses on the physical, referring to actions that we do with our *body* and its *members*. The image that both the Rom 6 and 12 passages evoke is of Old Testament sacrifices. With the coming of Christ, we no longer offer animals or grain. We offer our entire being to God by using our physical body in ways that are in line with loving God and loving others. The NLT expresses it this way: "use your whole body as an instrument to do what is right for the glory of God" (Rom 6:13).

We begin leaning our bodies in the right direction by replacing the old ways we used our bodies in the past with new ways that embody our devotion to God.

Take My Life and Let It Be

How we do this requires a unique response from each of us. It is not possible to give generic advice at this point. Each of us needs to reflect carefully on the concrete ways we presently use our body. I find it helpful to put the things we do with our body in two boxes: things that trip us up (our vices) and things that strengthen us toward God's way of living (virtues). Ask yourself two basic questions:

1. *(Dealing with my Vices)* What am I engaged in that is damaging me spiritually and hindering my relationship with God and others?

2. *(Strengthening my Virtues)* What can I be engaged in that strengthens me spiritually and develops my relationship with God and others?

Francis Ridley Havergal wrote a moving poem that later became a hymn entitled "Kept for the Master's Use," in which she describes her desire for each part of her life to be consecrated to God.[3]

> Take my life, and let it be
> Consecrated, Lord, to Thee.
> Take my moments and my days;
> Let them flow in ceaseless praise.
>
> Take my hands, and let them move
> At the impulse of Thy love.
> Take my feet, and let them be
> Swift and 'beautiful' for Thee.
>
> Take my voice, and let me sing
> Always, only, for my King.
> Take my lips and let them be
> Filled with messages from Thee.
>
> Take my silver and my gold;
> Not a mite would I withhold.
> Take my intellect, and use
> Every power as Thou shalt choose.
>
> Take my will and make it Thine;
> It shall be no longer mine.
> Take my heart; it is Thine own;
> It shall be Thy royal throne.

---

3. I was reminded of this hymn in Willard, *Renovation*, 172.

Take my love; my Lord, I pour
At Thy feet its treasure–store.
Take myself, and I will be
Ever, only, ALL for Thee.[4]

In the book she wrote about this poem, Frances Havergal takes each stanza of the poem and dedicates one chapter to exploring what it means to take each "member of our body" and present it to God in practical ways. (It's worth reading.[5]) I find it a helpful breakdown of categories so that we can examine our entire life. We can ask ourselves the two questions above:

1. What am I engaged in, in the area of _____ that is damaging me spiritually and hindering my relationship with God and others?

2. What are actions and activities that I can engage in in the area of _____ that can strengthen my relationship with God and others?

When you have identified the particular areas that need most work, you can develop a plan to diminish those vices and grow the virtues you most need. (In the final chapter we will talk in more detail about how that looks.)

Dealing with Your Vices: Agere Contra

An important strategy in dealing with what causes us most to stumble is replacing a vice with its opposite virtue. There is no set rule here. Instead, you will have to experiment to find what works best for you.

Notice what John Cassian (ca. 360–ca. 435 AD), one of the most well-known of the desert fathers, says about how to deal with our vices.

> For those who are anxious for the cure of their ailments [=vices] a saving remedy is sure not to be wanting, and therefore remedies should be sought by the same means that the signs of each fault are discovered .... When then anyone discovers ... that he is attacked by outbreaks of impatience or anger, *he should always practise himself in the opposite and contrary things*, and . . . accustom his mind to submit *with perfect humility* to everything

---

4. Havergal, *Kept for the Master's Use*, 6.

5. This book is also available on the Google Books website: https://books.google. com.

[and] . . . continually consider with all *sorrow of heart* with what *gentleness* he ought to meet them.[6]

Cassian makes the case that when we struggle (for example) with impatience or anger, we should especially develop humility, sorrow of heart, and gentleness—virtues that directly counter those vices.

This way of responding was also something St. Ignatius of Loyola advocated in his *Spiritual Exercises*. In one place he writes,

> Thus, if one's attachment leads him to seek and to hold [a religious position] . . . not for the honor and glory of God our Lord, nor for the spiritual welfare of souls, but for his own personal gain and temporal interests, *he should strive to rouse a desire for the contrary.* Let him be insistent in prayer and in his other spiritual exercises in begging God for the reverse, that is, that he neither seek such [a position], nor anything else, unless the Divine Majesty duly regulate his desires and change his former attachment. As a result, the reason he wants or retains anything will be solely the service, honor, and glory of the Divine Majesty.[7]

This practice advocated by Cassian and St. Ignatius often goes by the Latin phrase *agere contra*, which means to *act contrary* to the way you are inclined to act.

When we do this, it is important to avoid two dangers:

(1) This practice can be (and has been!) misunderstood to include inflicting physical pain on oneself—taking the cue from the Apostle Paul who "beat [his] body" (1 Cor 9:27, WEB).

(2) There is good reason to question whether "doing the opposite"— simply in the doing of it—is of any value in our personal and spiritual transformation.[8] Let me respond to both briefly.

Misunderstanding this practice: When Paul wrote "I beat my body," the context identifies specifically what he means: Paul is speaking of his desire to offer the gospel "free of charge" (v. 18) to the Corinthians, by not asking for their financial support, but instead, working with his own

6. Cassian, "The Conferences of John Cassian," 494–95.

7. Ignatius of Loyola, *Spiritual Exercises*, 9.

8. William Meissner comments about Ignatius's vigorous use of this concept: "One might be tempted to say that this was essentially masochism, in which the pilgrim's (i.e., Ignatius) sadistic and destructive impulses had been transformed into a punitive and guilt-inducing attack on himself." Meissner, *Ignatius of Loyola: The Psychology of a Saint*, 105.

hands. He explains to the Corinthians that the principle he operates under is to become all things to all people in hopes some might be saved (v. 22). It is in this context he uses the expression, "I beat my body," by which he means refraining from doing things that would harm the advancement of the gospel and living with self-discipline to ensure that would happen. It has nothing to do with inflicting physical pain on oneself.

Doing the opposite does not automatically change us. Physically doing the opposite will not automatically result in changing us. For example, a young boy who was misbehaving was directed by his mother to sit on a bench for a time-out. He refused. His mother threatened him with a worse punishment, so that he finally capitulated. As he was sitting down, he looked at his mother and said, "I may be sitting down on the outside, but I am standing up on the inside." You can do the right things for all the wrong reasons, and it will leave you unchanged.

Although practicing this concept of *agere contra* in the wrong way does not have the power to change us, there are ways of practicing it that can. Two things are critical.

First, our motivation needs to be healthy. Unfortunately, there is a lot of room for error at this point. Our desire for transformation may be driven by numerous false motivations:

- guilt—wanting to make good past wrong-doing;
- fear—being afraid of a God we believe is eager to punish us;
- shame—wanting to cover up or compensate for something that we don't like about ourselves (self-hatred, self-loathing);
- hypocrisy—wanting to look good on the outside;
- legalism—wanting to do the right thing, because we think this obligates God to accept us;
- pride—wanting to look better than others.

If we are driven by any of these (and similar) motivations, they will hinder our efforts to experience lasting change.

Second, our approach needs to be holistic and integrated, incorporating all the dimensions of our person. Just as all the dimensions of our being were involved in pursuing what was harmful, so we need to include all of the dimensions in pursuing what is good:

- **Will**: Our bodily transformation needs to be energized by a will that loves God and desires his ways above all else.

- **Thoughts**: Our bodily transformation needs to be supported by thoughts that are intentionally aimed at

  – filling our mind with thoughts/images/stories that speak of God's love for us and that evoke our love for him in return.

  – developing a deepening understanding of who God is, how he called us to live, and what his aims and intentions are for us, for humanity, and for this world.

- **Feelings**: When these thoughts are nurtured over time, they will begin to shift our feelings. Our feelings will gradually come into alignment with our new thoughts.

Some Examples of Change

This holistic way of countering our vices with its opposite virtue can transform us. Let me give some examples.

A Friend

Some time back, a pastor friend of mine was telling me about a terrible, horrible, no good, very bad day he had.[9] A number of things had gone wrong in the days leading up to this one. Then, on top of that, he was required to attend a meeting a few hours from his home. As he was driving in this rotten, no good, horrible mood, he noticed a car with a flat tire on the side of the road. He drove past it. As he passed it, he felt he should stop and help. He angrily ignored it, but the nudge came back. He ignored it some more, until finally, he couldn't ignore it, so he turned around. Now, he was even madder, because he had to turn around.

He stopped, helped the family, got back into his car, and continued his drive. But something had happened in the meantime. He could not believe the transformation that had come over him. He felt alive again, happy, and energized. His perspective, his passion, and his energy had returned.

9. The kind described in the children's book, *Alexander and the Terrible, Horrible, No Good, Very Bad Day* written by Judith Vorst.

Larry Crabb

In a dialogue with John Ortberg and Dallas Willard, Larry Crabb tells the story of how he also was in a bad mood one day.[10] He was supposed to lead a small group, but he simply did not want to go. What they had planned for that evening was for each person to share about what they appreciated in the others in the group. He sat down to write out his thoughts. As he focused on each individual and began to reflect on their positive qualities, he entered into his reflection and forgot about himself and his mood. At the end of his time of writing out his thoughts about each of these individuals, he couldn't wait to go to the group!

These are examples of how engaging our body has an effect on our emotions. But this is only short-term transformation. Does it work long-term? Yes. There are scores of illustrations of this from history and from my own personal life.

Saint Francis

In his autobiography, *The Testament*, St. Francis tells of how his physical revulsion of lepers was changed to what he calls "sweetness of body and soul."[11]

Three followers of St. Francis give more detail of how this happened:

> One day while Francis was praying fervently to God, he received an answer: "O Francis, if you want to know my will, you must hate and despise all that which hitherto your body has loved and desired to possess. Once you begin to do this, all that formerly seemed sweet and pleasant to you will become bitter and unbearable, and instead, the things that formerly made you shudder will bring you great sweetness and content." Francis was divinely comforted and greatly encouraged by these words.
>
> Then one day, as he was riding near Assisi, he met a leper. He had always felt an overpowering horror of these sufferers, but making a great effort, he conquered his aversion, dismounted, and, in giving the leper a coin, kissed his hand. The leper then gave him the kiss of peace, after which Francis remounted his horse and rode on his way.
>
> Some days later he took a large sum of money to the leper hospital, and gathering all the inmates together, he gave them

10. Willard, et al., "Fly on the Wall," 35.

11. Francis of Assisi, *The Writings of Saint Francis of Assisi*, 81.

alms, kissing each of their hands. Formerly he could neither touch or even look at lepers, but when he left them on that day, what had been so repugnant to him had really and truly been turned into something pleasant.

Indeed, his previous aversion to lepers had been so strong, that, besides being incapable of looking at them, he would not even approach the places where they lived. And if by chance he happened to pass anywhere near their dwellings or to see one of the lepers, even though he was moved to give them an alms through some intermediate person, he would nevertheless turn his face away and hold his nose. But, strengthened by God's grace, he was enabled to obey the command and to love what he had hated and to abhor what he had hitherto wrongfully loved.[12]

It was during the bodily act of St. Francis "making an effort" by dismounting, giving a leper a coin, and kissing his hand that something began to change in him. And it was his continual and repeated physical interactions with the lepers that his aversion was changed to sweetness.

Notice in this story how it was not simply the physical acts that St. Francis performed. This act was accompanied by a corresponding orientation of the will and thoughts that led him to choose to act. Then, as a result of this choice, the emotions followed the action.

Valia

For many years, my mother was the director of a Home for the Elderly in Connecticut, primarily populated with Slavic-speaking immigrants, many of whom had experienced the horrors of World War II. One lady, Valia, I recall vividly because she had a prosthetic hand, which as a kid, I had never seen before.

I don't recall Valia ever smiling. She kept to herself and silently walked from her apartment to the common meals and then back to her apartment. My mother explained to me that Valia had seen her entire family executed before her eyes. She had escaped, but had lost her hand in the process.

---

12. St. Francis, "Snapshots of a Saint," 18. This story of St. Francis was first recounted in the book, *Legend of the Three Companions*, which dates back to around 1246 AD, written by three of St. Francis's closest friends.

My mother saw that Valia was losing the will to live and was slipping into a depression. Without explaining what she was doing, my mother began to give Valia little tasks around the Home, for example, reading letters to others who could no longer read.

Over the next weeks and months, significant changes began to take place in Valia's appearance and energy level. She began smiling again.

"Carl"

"Carl" (not his real name) was a student in my spiritual formation class, who came from a broken home. His father had betrayed and then abandoned the family when Carl was in his late teens. The experience was still a deep wound for him.

One of the assignments I gave in my class was for the students to choose one area they wanted to grow in and develop a plan of specific things they could do to work on that. Carl decided for about three months to grow in inner peace in order to "move on with my life and leave behind the past traumas that were causing me to suffer daily."

There were three actions that he committed himself to do on a daily basis:

1. Pray for the people who have hurt me and for my own healing once a day for a minimum of 5 minutes.

2. In order to build my identity in Christ and break down my false belief systems, every morning I will look at myself in the mirror and speak out loud one lie I believe about myself and counteract it with the truth that Christ tells me.

3. In order to get professional support and tools to help me find my inner peace, I will go to counseling at least once a week.

At the end of the semester, I asked my students to respond to the question, "Did the steps, which you wrote and committed yourself to, help you grow in the way you had envisioned? Why or why not?" Here is how Carl responded:

> Yes they did. In the beginning of the process my daily action steps: telling a lie about myself and counteracting it with a truth, and praying at least five minutes, helped me tremendously. I started believing the truths about myself from God more and

more instead of the lies. I did not even have to look myself in the mirror by the end of the process because I was saying truths daily, multiple times in my head and when I talked to God. The praying at least five minutes daily helped me learn to pray more, especially for myself, something I never used to do.

Throughout the process though I struggled praying for those who hurt me, I was not sure how to pray for them, but now I have started praying a couple times a week for them. God is giving me the courage and the words when I do not have any.

Lastly though, I believe the counseling went above and beyond my expectations. . . . My main problem was not that I needed to forgive, which will be my next step, but first that I needed to detach myself from my father and others who keep hurting me. Counseling helped me see that and has been teaching me how to control my thoughts and feelings as well which has given me much more hope than I had before.

What can we learn from Carl and the other examples? Here are a few things that stand out to me:

1. Transformation is a process that takes time.

2. Transformation needs to involve the entire person, incorporating all of the dimensions in the process.

3. Transformation requires the "use" of the body. The body needs to be engaged in repeated practices over time that slowly begin reshaping the will, the thoughts, the feelings, and the body—as all of these together are dedicated to God and open to his Spirit working inside of us.

4. In the case of Carl, this process led to the formation of new ways of thinking and acting. The older habits of thinking and acting that kept Carl in a cycle of sadness and hopelessness were replaced by new habits of thinking and acting that led to increased joy in his relationship with God, himself, and others. He found his thinking transformed.

15

Our Relationships

"Loving God includes loving people. You've got to love both."
(1 John 4:21, The Message)

WE NOW TURN TO look at the one remaining dimension of our lives—the social dimension—and explore how this too can be transformed. Let's put our social relationships within the context of the other dimensions we have explored so far.

Our Social Relationships in the Context of the Other Dimensions

There are four essential elements of human nature we have discussed so far.

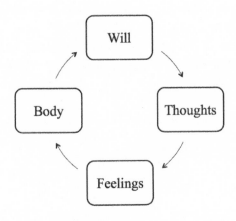

Our *will* is the choosing, decision-making center of our lives. Our first act of choosing begins with our *thoughts*. When we, over time, deliberately choose thoughts that are oriented toward God and his ways, this begins to slowly transform our *feelings*. When these dimensions are set in motion, they compel us to *act* in line with what we are feeling, thinking, and willing.

That is the journey of spiritual transformation that we have discussed so far, and it sets the stage for the next element: Our lives are fundamentally shaped by our relationships with others.

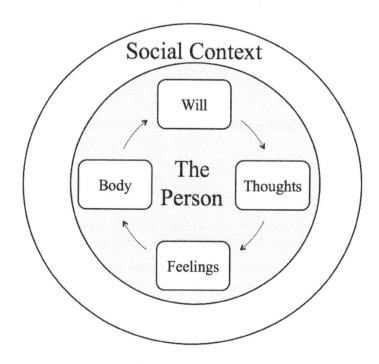

Since all we do as individuals is done in a social context, we need to explore how the relational dimension of our being fits into our spiritual formation.

We Are Wired to Imitate and Learn from Others

We noted in our look at neuroscience that we learn by imitating others. This forms the basis for the social dimension of our being. Since we are wired to imitate those with whom we are in relationship, we learn spiritual formation by observing those around us as they live their entire lives.

Much of this learning goes on under the radar of our conscious awareness. We see this clearly with children: a child observes the patterns of how her mother and father speak and interact and her brain interprets this to mean, "this is how I am to act and think and respond." This continues on into our teen years, often with a shift in focus: what else is "peer pressure" other than learning by imitation?

A scene in the movie 42, the story of Jackie Robinson, the first black player in professional baseball, illustrates this. The camera zooms in as Jackie Robinson takes his batting position. Then the camera pans out to a father and son in the bleachers. The father has hatred in his eyes and begins spewing racist rhetoric—as the son is watching. Then the son, with the same hate-filled look, repeats exactly what the father said.

The Bible and the Importance of Relationships

This characteristic of human nature to imitate others that is hard-wired within us confirms the wisdom of the Bible's many sayings about how important it is to choose your relationships carefully:

- "When you enter the land the LORD your God is giving you, do not learn to imitate the detestable ways of the nations there." (Deut 18:9)

- "Walk with the wise and become wise, for a companion of fools suffers harm." (Prov 13:20)

- "Do not make friends with the hot-tempered, do not associate with those who are easily angered, or you may learn their ways and get yourself ensnared." (Prov 22:24–25)

- "Do not be misled: bad company corrupts good character." (1 Cor 15:33)[1]

This truth is also reflected in many similar sayings throughout history:[2]

- "Every man is like the company he is wont to keep." (Euripides)

---

1. This is, by the way, actually a quotation from the Greek poet Menander, *Thais* 218.

2. *Collins Dictionary*, "Company."

- "A wise man may look ridiculous in the company of fools." (Thomas Fuller)
- "Tell me thy company, and I'll tell thee what thou art." (Miguel de Cervantes)
- "A man is known by the company he keeps."

The people we associate with fundamentally shape who we are and who we will become.

We Are Wired to Be in Relationship

Human beings are designed to be in relationships with others and cannot, in fact, survive without them. This is the central idea neuroscientist Matthew Lieberman wants to convey in his book, *Social: Why Our Brains Are Wired to Connect.* In fact, Dr. Lieberman claims that Abraham Maslow got it exactly wrong with his hierarchy of needs when he concluded that our *primary* needs are physiological (food, water, and sleep), and that our other needs—safety, social needs, esteem, self-actualization are "nice if you can get them."[3]

Yes, babies, when they arrive on the planet need food, water, and shelter to survive—but are utterly helpless to get it for themselves. They are absolutely dependent *on others* to provide for them. Lieberman explains it this way:

> What all . . . human babies really need from the moment of birth is a caregiver who is committed to making sure that the infant's biological needs are met. If this is true, then Maslow had it wrong. . . . Food, water, and shelter are *not* the most basic needs for an infant. Instead, being socially connected and cared for is paramount. . . . Love and belonging might seem like a convenience we can live without, but our biology is built to thirst for connection because it is linked to our most basic survival needs. . . . [O]ur need for connection is the bedrock upon which [all of our other needs] are built.[4]

Our need for relationship is embedded in our physiology to such an extent that we need to have physical touch to develop in a healthy way.

3. Lieberman, *Social*, 42.
4. Ibid., 43.

It is through physical touch that infants and adults experience relationships. A tender touch sends signals of nurture, care, and concern.

In a study conducted on newborns, who were then followed in their development over the first ten years of their life, Dr. Ruth Feldman, professor at Bar-Ilan University, and her colleagues documented the difference human touch makes on the development of children. She writes: "In this decade-long study, we show for the first time that providing maternal-newborn skin-to-skin contact to premature infants in the neonatal period improves children's functioning ten years later."[5] The study documented that children, who experience regular and high amounts of touch, when compared to children, who spent significant time in an incubator followed by low amounts of touch afterward,

> showed better cognitive skills and executive abilities in repeated testing from six months to ten years. At ten years of age, children who received maternal contact as infants showed more organized sleep, better neuroendocrine response to stress, more mature functioning of the autonomic nervous system, and better cognitive control.[6]

Children experience nurturing relationships through the physical touch of the mother. Although the extensive need for human touch recedes as we age, the need for nurturing relationships continues for the rest of our lives.[7] Why is it, after all, that social media apps and websites are exploding in the number of users—if not for this deep desire for connection with others?[8]

Research indicates that when we are in relationships that nourish and support us, we thrive as human beings. People live longer, are physically healthier, and experience more joy in life as a result of being in supportive relationships.[9]

We are Wired to Love

Another way of saying that we are wired to be in relationship is to say that we are wired *to love and be loved.* In an article entitled "The Neurobiology

5. Elsevier, "Loving Touch Critical for Premature Infants."

6. Ibid.

7. Lieberman, *Social*, 4.

8. On Facebook alone there are over one billion users!

9. Carnegie Mellon University, "How to Thrive through Close Relationships."

of Love," Dr. Semir Zeki explains that there are areas of the brain as well as patterns of brain activity that are designed to create deep bonds between individuals to ensure their well-being. These are particularly strong in infancy, but continue on throughout life.

Because this need for relational acceptance is so deeply embedded in us, when nurturing relationships are not present or when a significant relational break occurs (expressed either by rejection or physical and verbal abuse), our brain registers the emotional pain we experience in the same way it registers the pain of a physical injury. Matthew Lieberman explains that

> our brains [developed] to experience threats to our social connections in much the same way they experience physical pain. By activating the same neural circuitry that causes us to feel physical pain, our experience of social pain helps ensure the survival of our children by helping to keep them close to their parents. The neural link between social and physical pain also ensures that staying socially connected will be a lifelong need, like food and warmth. Given the fact that our brains treat social and physical pain similarly, should we as a society treat social pain differently than we do? . . . We intuitively believe social and physical pain are radically different kinds of experiences, yet the way our brains treat them suggests that they are more similar than we imagine.[10]

This explains why rejection by a spouse or close friend causes us intense emotional pain. Even the language we use to describe such experiences reflect this. "I was heart-broken." "That really hurt my feelings." "When she left me, I felt like I was punched in the gut." Conversely, when a relationship break has been repaired, or when someone shows us a gesture of kindness, we use similar expressions: "That was balm to my soul." "The relationship was healed."

Lieberman makes a perceptive comment about these expressions,

> Psychologists are discovering that language that sounds metaphorical is often less metaphorical than first supposed. When it comes to social pain, the language of physical pain is the metaphor [that is used] all around the world. This is true in Romance languages like Spanish and Italian, which share roots with English, as well as in Armenian, Mandarin, and Tibetan. It

10. Lieberman, *Social*, 4–5.

is unlikely that this metaphor would spring up again and again across the globe if there were no connection.[11]

It turns out that our metaphors for relational pain and pleasure mirror what is physically happening inside of us!

Acceptance: The Deepest Need of the Heart
Rejection: The Deepest Hurt of the Heart

Since God has wired us to need relationships for life, there are three tightly intertwined implications of this truth that we need to grasp, which relate to our spiritual formation as well as to our fundamental humanity:

1. *Relational acceptance is our deepest need.*

2. *When relational acceptance is present, it provides us with our deepest fulfillment*

3. *When relational acceptance is absent—or when we are rejected—it is the cause of our deepest pain.*

The effect of acceptance or rejection is especially deep and significant when it occurs at the beginning of life. Dallas Willard describes this eloquently:

> Most people know a great deal about being rejected, being left out, or just not received, not welcome, not acceptable. As the parent/child relationship is perhaps the most perfect illustration of a circle of sufficiency in human life, so it is also the place where the deepest and most lasting wounds can be given. If a child is totally received in its early years by its parents and siblings, it will very likely have a rootedness about it that enables it to withstand most forms of rejection that may come upon a human being in a lifetime. It will carry its solid relationship to and from its family members throughout life, being sustained by them even long after those loved ones are dead. It will receive a steady stream of rest and strength from them.
>
> By contrast, a small child not adequately received can actually die from it; or if it survives, it is very likely to be incapable of giving and receiving love in decent human relationships for the rest of its life. It will be perpetually "left out," if only in its

11. Ibid., 4.

imagination. And in this matter, imagination can have the force of reality.[12]

Receiving full acceptance as a child provides us with an inner stability that will most likely follow us throughout life. An article published in the *Journal of Social Cognitive & Affective Neuroscience* entitled "Time Spent with Friends in Adolescence Relates to Less Neural Sensitivity to Later Peer Rejection,"[13] documents that children who have strong relational bonds in their younger years have less pain when they experience rejection later on in life than children who had weaker relational bonds.

If someone did not receive that full acceptance in their early years, a sense of rejection may follow them for the rest of their lives. It may create a sense of instability and insecurity with *who they are as a person*, and as they subconsciously hunger for that missing full acceptance in their present relationships, they may become deeply disappointed at even the slightest hint of what they perceive as rejection, even when it was not intended.

Is there no hope, then, for someone who hasn't received full acceptance in their childhood? Let's explore the answer to this.

Good Will Hunting: A Parable for Overcoming Rejection

The film *Good Will Hunting* contains a powerful picture of the possibility of overcoming early childhood rejection. Matt Damon plays Will Hunting, a brilliant young man who didn't go to college and is working as a janitor at MIT. As a child, he had experienced severe emotional and physical abuse at the hands of his step-father. Now in his early twenties, Will runs into trouble with the law and is given the choice: either go to jail or get counseling. He opts for the counseling and begins meeting a psychotherapist by the name of Sean, played by Robin Williams.

In their sessions together, Will puts on a tough front—as if nothing affects him and as if he needs no one in his life. Sean tries to break through this front, without success.

After quite a number of sessions, we come to a scene that is the turning point of the film. The scene takes place in Sean's office. Sean is holding

---

12. Willard, *Renovation*, 180–81.

13. Masten et al., "Time Spent with Friends in Adolescence Relates to Less Neural Sensitivity to Later Peer Rejection."

Will's case file in which the audience can see photo-documentation of the physical abuse Will's step-father inflicted on him.

During the entire dialog in this scene, Sean looks deeply into Will's eyes, never taking his eyes off of him. With deep compassion Sean begins to speak:

> SEAN   I don't know a lot, Will. But let me tell you one thing. All this history . . . [pointing to a file folder documenting Will's past experience as a victim of abuse.]
>
> Look here, son.
>
> (Will, who had been looking away, looks at Sean.)
>
> SEAN   This is not your fault.
>
> WILL (nonchalant) Oh, I know.
>
> SEAN   It's not your fault.
>
> WILL (smiles) I know.
>
> SEAN   It's not your fault.
>
> WILL   I know.
>
> SEAN   It's not your fault.
>
> WILL (dead serious) I know.
>
> SEAN   It's not your fault.
>
> WILL   Don't [mess] with me.
>
> SEAN (comes around desk, sits in front of Will)
>
> It's not your fault.
>
> WILL (tears start) I know.
>
> SEAN   It's not . . .
>
> WILL (crying hard)
>
> I know, I know . . .
>
> [Sean takes Will in his arms and holds him like a child. Will sobs like a baby. After a moment, he wraps his arms around Sean and holds him, even tighter. We pull back from this image. Two lonely souls being father and son together.]

In a number of ways, this scene provides a powerful analogy for our relationship with God.

First, although the analogy is not perfect, since some of what happened in the past may have been our fault, nonetheless, what God says to us in the present, "The past is in the past. I don't hold anything against you. I accept you as you are with open arms."

Second, whatever has happened, no matter who was at fault, our "Father" speaks to us words of forgiveness and acceptance, which begin to heal the wounds of guilt and rejection.

Third, the transformation of our social dimension—and of the very core of our being—begins by grasping in the deepest part of our being that God is totally, utterly, and completely for us and that his love for us is limitless and unconditional. Transformation in our social dimension begins when we *experience* the love of God in this way. Knowing the love of God like we know a fact of geography will not transform us. Only the actual experiential knowledge of God's love will.

Fourth, notice that—and here we are stretching the analogy—God's forgiveness, love, and full acceptance of us is mediated through another human being. It is through the living example of a person that we can best grasp and enter into God's love. Here again, is the social dimension at work: we need others to put God's love on display for us.

Fifth, as we experience and live in the reality of God's love for us, we can extend that forgiveness, love, and full acceptance to others.

Sixth, and finally, what we see in the person of Sean (again, stretching the analogy) is someone whose love for Will remains unchanged regardless of what Will does. Whether Will rejects him or physically attacks him, Sean is (work with me here) so secure in himself that he is able to continue loving Will without resorting to fighting him, fleeing from him, or rejecting him.

Six Elements for Healing Relational Wounds

These six elements, I would suggest, form the basis for healing the wounds of relational rejection that we may have experienced:

1. Our Father accepts us as we are.
2. Our Father speaks words of forgiveness and acceptance over us that begin to heal the wounds of guilt and rejection.
3. Spiritual transformation begins when we grasp in the deepest part of our being that God is totally, utterly, and completely for us.
4. God's love is often mediated through another person who embodies God's love and acceptance of us.

5. The person who has experienced the love of God for themselves is then able to extend forgiveness, love, and full acceptance to others.

6. Someone who is secure in the love of God does not have to lash out in anger or withdraw in hurt, but is committed to being a blessing to others and relating to them with concrete expressions of goodness, grace, and mercy, no matter what they do.

I believe that these six elements make it possible for someone who experienced abuse and rejection as a child to move toward wholeness and relational healing with God, with ourselves, and with others.

Our Quest for Wholeness

In order for us to enter into experiencing these six elements that lead us to personal wholeness through our relationships with others and God, we need to engage in four primary tasks. These four tasks are the keys that will unlock our experience of these six elements.

Renewing our Picture of God

The first task is the most important of all, since everything else flows from it: we need to re-examine the picture of God that we have constructed throughout our lives and trade it in for a biblically healthier one.

Many people have absorbed destructive messages and images of who God is, which can cause severe trauma and doubt about the goodness and love of God. Let me recount three stories.

A close friend from college served as a missionary for a number of years in a desperately poor region of the world. He was committed, sincere, and passionate. Toward the end of his time on the mission field, he burnt out and went into a deep depression from which it took many years to recover. As he was visiting his elderly father, he opened his father's song book to sing with him and it opened to the song, "Nearer My God to Thee." These words, as he recounts, brought back in a flash "cob-webbed memories of my deeply religious youth when I was 'sold out to God' as we called it." His recounting of this experience is worth relating at length. He writes:

I spent hours in prayer and Bible reading, I listened to sermons and worship on the radio, on tape, and at church. I read Christian authors and talked with Christian friends.

[What I was trying to do was] reach an oasis, relief for my parched soul, but the God I sought was a mirage. The farther into the desert I pushed myself, year after year, the more lost I became, until I was crawling through the sand towards water that wasn't there, and I finally collapsed. Every step in the direction of a misconceived God is a step away from the true God.

I worshiped a God who was harsh and judgmental, and based on these assumptions, all my Bible reading and prayer and devotion simply drove me deeper into this skewed faith. I read verses about God's wrath and judgment that negated for me any verses about His gentleness and love. Sermons about God's kindness came across to me as soft and insubstantial, as merely a carrot to get me to work harder at being good so God would accept me. The more I sang "Holy, Holy, Holy" the more unworthy and rejected I felt—who could ever measure up to absolute perfection? I worked to strengthen my faith, but it was faith in God's power and omniscience and righteousness that were scrubbed of any scent of His patience and mercy and grace. That is, his power and omniscience and righteousness were frightening, not encouraging, the basis for his condemning me, not his rescuing me.

Love was there, but it was not foundational as these other attributes were. Fundamentally, God was pissed off at me and could only be mollified by the death of his son. Jesus kind of forced God into accepting me against his better judgment, bought God off so to speak. The harder I worked to be the person God wanted me to be, the more I realized how far short I fell. I heard Amy Grant's song "My Father's Eyes" and knew the look in those eyes: eternal disappointment.

This was not the kind of error that I could tweak my way out of. It was fundamental, all encompassing. It was not until my worldview, my belief system, crushed me beyond recovery that I was able to let go and discover the God in whom I now believe, a God of infinite grace. It has taken many years to unlearn, discard, loosen my fearful grip from my long held false securities and to cling stubbornly to my new faith, my new God, my new life and relationships . . . and even a new Bible and hymnbook. Nearer my God to Thee.[14]

---

14. Grace, "Happily Rejecting the God of My Youth."

A skewed picture of God can cause psychological scarring and intense emotional suffering! But, it can even cause physical damage. Dr. Timothy Jennings relates two encounters from his own life that reveal the devastating impact that having a distorted view of God can have on our physical, emotional, and spiritual well-being. He tells of a woman, who made an appointment at his medical practice because of infertility. When she came into his office, she was sobbing uncontrollably. After some time, between sobs, she was able to speak.

> "It's all my fault!" More tears.
> "What's your fault?"
> "I can't have children. Oh. God!"
> "Why do you say it's your fault?"
> More sobs, and with her face buried in her hands, she told me that when she was a teenager she had gotten pregnant and had an abortion. The abortion was routine . . . so I wondered why she couldn't have children.
> Then she said, "I can't have children because God is punishing me. My pastor told me that I murdered my child and as punishment God won't ever let me have children."[15]

Dr. Jennings then writes:

> As I sat listening to my patient cry, empathizing, I considered what her core problem was. Did her despair primarily stem from the fact that she had fertility problems, or from her belief about God and the perception of being punished? *Could her central psychological stress be arising not from her objective reproductive condition but rather a distorted view of God?* Does it make a difference to one's health to believe, as some had suggested, that God was punishing her for mistakes she had made? Would it be helpful, even healing, if she came to believe that, rather than punishing her, God was crying with her?[16]

Dr. Jennings also tells of an encounter with Sergeant Jones when Jennings was working as a division psychiatrist for the 3rd Infantry Division stationed in at Fort Steward, Georgia. In the 1991 invasion of Iraq, Sergeant Jones, an outspoken Christian, was placed in command of an Abrams battle tank, perhaps the most sophisticated and potent military ground vehicle at that time. With the invasion imminent, he anointed his

---

15. Jennings, *The God-Shaped Brain*, 19–20.
16. Ibid., 20. (My italics)

tank with oil, painted crosses on it, and prayed that God would protect him and his men.

After this, one thing after another seemed to go wrong. Just before the invasion was to commence, his commanding officer discovered his own radio was not functioning and so demanded that Sergeant Jones give him his radio, threatening arrest if Jones didn't give it to him. Then Jones discovered his night vision goggles did not work, leaving him essentially blind in battle. He requested that he be allowed to withdraw, but his commanding officers refused, even though Jones would have no idea what he would be shooting at.

Soon after the invasion began, they came under sustained, heavy enemy fire with such a ferocity that he and his crew felt that they would surely die. Although Jones ultimately survived, it was an extremely traumatic experience in which he felt completely abandoned by God.

Four years later, Sergeant Jones began to visit Dr. Jennings because of "nightmares, flashbacks, anxiety, sleep difficulty, relationship problems, tension, inability to concentrate, irritability, work problems, and depression."[17] After a number of sessions, Dr. Jennings thought he had some insight into the core issue. He told Sergeant Jones:

> You were a Christian. You made a public display of your Christianity. You put oil crosses all over your tank and dedicated yourself, your tank, and your men to God. You went into battle blind and deaf. And when your company came under attack, several other units were hit, but *not one bullet, shell, or piece of shrapnel damaged your tank.*

Dr. Jennings continued:

> After he had acknowledged each statement as true, I concluded, "Your Desert Storm experiences remind me of Daniel's experience in the lion's den."
>
> The man's eyes opened wide, his jaw dropped, and the realization was immediate. With his head in his hands, he sat sobbing for several minutes. When he left my office that day, he took with him a new outlook on life.[18]

The change in Sergeant Jones, Dr. Jennings recalls, was as dramatic as it was immediate. Sergeant Jones indicated a short while later that he didn't need to meet with Dr. Jennings anymore. Within months, his

17. Jennings, *Could It Be This Simple?*, 14.
18. Ibid., 15.

symptoms had virtually disappeared. He was honorably discharged, completed his college degree, became a high school teacher, served actively in leadership in his church and his relationship with his wife was strong and deep. Dr. Jennings asks:

> What had made the difference? Sergeant Jones had believed a lie. He had concluded that God had failed to answer his prayer, that the Lord had let him down. Now he realized the truth—that God had miraculously answered his prayer. It was the change in this belief that resulted in his recovery.[19]

In all these stories, the emotional, physical, and spiritual problems that these individuals had were directly connected to their picture of God and their beliefs about how God viewed them.

What Is a Healthy Picture of God?

This raises the all-important question, *what is a biblically healthy picture of God?* This is a challenging question since you can actually find texts in the Bible that might justify seeing God as a wrathful, vengeful, arbitrary God who is ready to pounce on anyone who does anything wrong.

Yet even in the Old Testament, God describes himself to Moses in terms that indicate his fundamental essence: "The LORD, the LORD, the compassionate and gracious God, slow to anger, abounding in love and faithfulness, maintaining love to thousands, and forgiving wickedness, rebellion and sin" (Exod 34:6–7). So significant is this description of God's character that it is cited ten times in the Old Testament.[20]

The New Testament makes clear that the point of departure for understanding who God is and how he views us is Jesus himself.[21] Hebrews and the Gospel of John show this truth most clearly. The writer of Hebrews describes Jesus as "the exact representation" of God's being (Heb 1:3). John writes that although no one has seen God directly, Jesus, "who is himself God and is in closest relationship with the father, has made

---

19. Ibid.

20. Ellison, *Exodus*, 180. Even though the passage in Exodus continues by describing God's responding to human sin with punishment, it is God's love and compassion that mark the essence of his character.

21. Roger Olson, a theology professor at Truett Seminary writes, "I know of no more important principle for Christian theology than that Jesus is the perfect if not complete revelation of God's character." Olson, "God and Children."

him known" (John 1:18). The Greek word behind "made him known" indicates a thorough explanation in order "to make fully and clearly known."[22]

Since Jesus is the best picture of the Father, any attempt to determine what God's character is like should begin with a close look at Jesus, and then from that vantage point we can reevaluate and reframe some of the troubling passages in the Bible. Greg Boyd explains it this way:

> The wholeness and vibrancy of our relationship with God depends on letting God define himself for us in Christ; we should not try to define God outside of or along side of Jesus Christ. Christ is our center, and everything in life must be viewed in relation to him. Our reading of Scripture must be carried out without looking even for a moment to the right or left of Jesus Christ. The Word incarnate is the fulfillment and complete expression of God's revelation in Scriptures . . . .
>
> Hence, we must never think of the revelation of God in Christ as merely *part* of God's total revelation. Rather, everything before Christ must be read in the light of Christ. All previous revelations are authoritative for the Christian insofar as they anticipate and point to God's definitive revelation in Christ.[23]

When we examine the life and teachings of Jesus as the absolute center point of our understanding of who God is and what he is like, we begin to see some core themes emerge that run through the entire New Testament:

- "God is love" (1 John 4:8, 16)

- "And I pray that you, being rooted and established in love, may have power . . . to grasp how wide and long and high and deep is the love of Christ, and to know this love that surpasses knowledge" (Eph 3:17–19).

- "Perfect love drives out fear." (1 John 4:18)

- "There is no longer any condemnation for those who are in Christ Jesus." (Rom 8:1, cf. 34)

- "Nothing can separate us from his love." (Rom 8:39)

- "While we were sinners, Christ died for us." (Rom 5:8)

22. Louw and Nida, *Greek-English Lexicon of the New Testament based on Semantic Domains*, 339.

23. Boyd, *Is God to Blame?* 28–29, 30.

God *is* love—infinite love from the infinite Father for his finite children. Everything about God flows out of this loving essence of who he is.

Jesus told a story to help us understand God's love. We know this story as the parable of "The Prodigal Son." In a shocking display of disrespect and rejection toward his father, a rebellious son asks for his inheritance, and the father consents. (In the culture of Jesus' day, this would be tantamount to wishing the father dead.) With a wad of cash in his pocket, the son heads into the world to fulfill his every wish for pleasure. At the end of his escapades, with empty pockets, an empty stomach, and an empty heart, the son decides to return to his father, in hopes of being taken in as a servant.

The father, however, love-sick for his son, has been watching every day, hoping he might return. When the son appears on the horizon, the father runs toward him, casting aside all concern about the shame, humiliation, and reproachful looks he would get from the townsfolk. The son can't even get his apology out before the father envelops him in a loving embrace.

This story communicates Jesus' understanding of the character of God as one who loves lavishly and welcomes us back again and again and again when we stumble, reject him, or turn our backs on him. Any time that we "come to our senses" and turn toward him, he runs toward us with open arms.

Recognizing that this is the true picture of what God is really like can cause healing to begin in us. Dr. Jennings relates the findings of Andrew Newberg's research on the brains of Buddhist and Christian monks during their contemplative meditation practices. Although both groups experienced significant growth, Dr. Jennings recounts that

> the greatest improvements occurred when participants meditated specifically on a God of love. Such meditation was associated with growth in the prefrontal cortex (the part of the brain . . . where we reason, make judgments and experience Godlike love) and subsequent increased capacity for empathy, sympathy, compassion and altruism. But here's the most astonishing part. Not only does other-centered love increase when we worship a God of love, but sharp thinking and memory improve as well. In other words, worshiping a God of love actually stimulates the brain to heal and grow.
>
> However, when we worship a god other than one of love— a being who is punitive, authoritarian, critical or distant—fear circuits are activated and, if not calmed, will result in chronic

inflammation and damage to both brain and body. As we bow before authoritarian gods, our characters are slowly changed to be less like Jesus. Truly, by beholding we are changed, not only in character, but our neural circuitry as well (2 Cor 3:18).[24]

In teaching a course on spiritual formation for over a decade, I have come to recognize that a person's inner image of God is the single biggest factor impacting their physical, emotional, relational, and spiritual well-being. If our picture of God is not in alignment with the image that Jesus presented of his Father in heaven—the picture embodied in the Parable of the Prodigal Son—then it will negatively impact our lives. The further our image diverges away from the image of God portrayed in Jesus, the more severe damage it will do in our lives.

If you want to pursue this topic of reshaping your understanding and picture of God, here are some resources that I have found helpful.

Greg Boyd, *Is God to Blame: Beyond Pat Answers to the Problem of Human Suffering* (Downers Grove, IL: IVP, 2003).

Timothy Jennings, *The God-Shaped Brain: How Changing Your View of God Transforms Your Life* (Downers Grove, IL: IVP, 2013).

Henri Nouwen, *The Return of the Prodigal Son: A Story of Homecoming* (New York: Image, 1993).

Renewing Our Image of Ourselves

In our quest for wholeness, it is also critical that we reexamine the picture we have of ourselves.

The image we have of God is closely connected with our self-image. The story of the Prodigal Son illustrates this. Upon his return home, the son, who had previously felt like a failure who could only be, at best, a servant, begins to form new ideas about his own identity, value, and significance through the relationship with his lavishly loving father. All he needs to do is receive the identity of immense value that his father offers him.

A simple way to capture this is to watch a mother cradling her newborn with all the tenderness and love she has. From an economic

24. Jennings, *The God-Shaped Brain*, 27.

standpoint, the little kid is not worth much. In addition, he sucks up his parents' time, make a mess, and is often an inconvenience and interruption. Yet, when you watch a mother looking at her newborn, you see love being poured into that child. The child, filled with the mother's love, responds with smiles and coos—reflecting love back to her.

The Bible portrays God as having this type of love for us. King David uses this same metaphor to describe his relationship to God: "I hold myself in quiet and silence, like a little child in its mother's arms, like a little child, so I keep myself" (Ps 131:2, NJB).

When we experience being fully embraced by God just as we are—with all our shortcomings, faults, and failures—we experience deep satisfaction within, which makes it possible for us to flourish.

Developing a Posture of Blessing Others

A ripple effect of love occurs at this point: knowing that God accepts us as we are, we can accept ourselves as we are. And because we accept ourselves as we are, we can extend that acceptance to others. This enables us to interact with others in a way that blesses them—no matter who they are or what they do.

In Jesus' Sermon on the Mount, he teaches that we are to love even our enemies and then gives the reason why: "But I tell you, love your enemies and pray for those who persecute you, that you may be children of your Father in heaven. He causes his sun to rise on the evil and the good, and sends rain on the righteous and the unrighteous" (Matt 5:44–45).

Jesus' rationale for loving our enemies is that this is what God himself does: he does good indiscriminately to "good" people and to "bad" people, because it is in the very nature of God to "bless" others. In the same way, our posture when we encounter anyone who comes across our path should be a posture of blessing.

The two typical responses when we encounter people we don't like or don't get along with are normally "fight" or "flight". We either go into attack mode or we avoid them. Jesus, however, doesn't advocate either of those options. He calls us neither to attack nor to withdraw, but to choose a third way: *to bless*.

Blessing our "enemies" has little to do with how we feel about those who are against us. Blessing someone is a decision to do good to them, to wish them well, and to speak well of them.

Now, obviously, God calls us to wisdom and discernment. Serial killers and abusive people should not be allowed to continue harming us or others. Consequently, blessing others does not mean that you can't call the police on an abusive person and have a restraining order put out on them. The best thing for them in this moment would be to stop from causing even more harm.

But you can still bless them and do good to them, and even speak caring words of compassion to them. We can learn to view people like Jesus did when hanging from the cross. He looked down at the people who had put him there and said: "Father, forgive them. They don't know what they are doing."

An acquaintance of mine, let's call her Jane, illustrated how we can bless others who are causing us grief. Jane was co-leading a couple's group in a church I once attended. Another woman in the group was negative and critical toward her and others, causing tensions in the group. But Jane was a godly woman, who wanted to follow the way of Jesus.

This cantankerous person was running a service project and needed help with the set-up and tear-down process. Jane volunteered to help, and over the course of the month, as they worked together, Jane's acts of kindness and blessing transformed their relationship—and began transforming the other person.

Unfortunately, not every attempt to follow Jesus' teaching about blessing our enemies results in a happy ending. You can seek to bless another person, and find that they still continue to be abusive and hateful.

What do you do in cases like that? This happened to some close friends of ours. A person with a troubled past entered our friends' lives. The wounds from this person's past led him to inflict wounds on the people around him. Numerous conversations over the years and even joint counseling did not improve the situation.[25]

Eventually, our friends came to a point where they felt that it was best to separate themselves from this person, since continuing the relationship enabled this person's abusive behavior. However, our friends disciplined themselves not to get caught up in constantly thinking about the unkind things this man had done to them. With God's help, they sought to truly wish this person well in their hearts. They prayed for

25. In observing this couple, we have learned that reconciliation is not always possible and that it doesn't always take two to have a disagreement. Sometimes the problem really does reside within one person.

God's blessings on him, and they committed themselves to not speak ill of him to others.

When we intentionally choose a response of blessing others, it enables us to become free of hatred and fear. We may find that this choice actually transforms our animosity into empathy and genuine concern for the other.

Developing Relationships That Sustain Us

The third task that will unlock our experience of the six elements we mentioned earlier is becoming rooted in nurturing Christian community. Spiritual wholeness begins and spiritual transformation takes place by developing a network of intentional relationships that shape us spiritually in positive ways.

Being with other followers of Jesus in various contexts of work, play, and worship begins to reinforce the values and priorities of Jesus in us. Through such relationships we absorb, by imitation, how to live a life of discipleship. Corporate worship and small group Bible studies immerse us in the story of God and his world, and our lives become shaped by the shared practices of communion, baptism, and worship liturgies that we participate in—whether they are of a more formal nature or a more open nature.[26] Through the accountability relationships that living in community can provide, we receive correction and guidance and encouragement for our lives.

In short, we need to incorporate intentional relationships with other followers of Jesus in order to "hold unswervingly to the hope we profess . . . consider how we may spur one another on toward love and good deeds, not giving up meeting together, as some are in the habit of doing, but encouraging one another—and all the more as you see the Day approaching" (Heb 9:23–25). This passage, perhaps more than any other in Scripture, captures the reason why we need Christian community and underscores that spiritual transformation is essentially social in nature.

---

26. The works of James K. A. Smith speak compellingly of this: *Desiring the Kingdom; Imagining the Kingdom.*

Conclusion to the Transformation of the
Dimensions of the Person

We are at the end of our journey of surveying the spiritual transformation of all of the dimensions of the human person: spirit (heart/will), mind (thoughts and feelings), body, and human relationships.

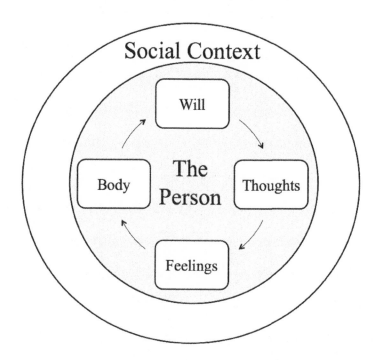

Together, these dimensions comprise the entire person. While we have, up to now, looked at these dimensions somewhat in isolation from each other, in the final two chapters, we'll bring all of the threads together and talk about pathways to change that incorporate all of these dimensions into a coordinated, holistic plan.

PART 4

Developing our own Spiritual Formation Plan

Transforming Every Dimension of Our Being

IN THIS FINAL PART, I will lay out a process you can use to develop your own plan for spiritual development. Developing such a plan requires the development of a new set of habits that will help move you in the direction you want to go. In the next chapter, we will look at what the science of habit formation has to teach us. In the final chapter, we will integrate what we learn about habit formation into a process for spiritual transformation that you can use.

16

Spiritual Formation Is Habit-Forming

Understanding the Science of Habit Formation

HOW CAN WE TRULY change things in our lives? I doubt that many of us are aiming at mere temporary or superficial change. We want lasting and pervasive change that begins in the core of our beings and flows through all of our dimensions.

In pursing that kind of change, it is important to remember that God made each human being as an integrated whole. There is no division between the "spiritual" and the "physical" dimensions of who we are, because everything that is sacred partakes of the physical and everything physical affects the sacred.

We see this reflected in the sacrament of communion. In the physical acts of eating bread and drinking wine, spiritual things take place within us. So also, when we read Scripture in a community Bible study group and discuss what it means for our lives, that reading and discussing are physical acts. The acts of eating bread, drinking wine, and reading Scripture are (or can be) both physical and deeply spiritual ones at the same time—acts that have the power to change us.

Since our spiritual dimension is bound up with our physical dimension, we need to think about developing consistent ways of desiring, thinking, feeling, and living that shape us in positive ways spiritually. Whenever we speak of acquiring "consistent ways" of doing anything, we are talking the language of habit formation.

Life Is Habit-Forming

The *American Psychologist* published an important article reviewing scholarly literature on the nature of habits entitled, "The Unbearable Automaticity of Being." The authors claim that only an average of 5 percent of what we do on any given day of our lives is a result of intentional and conscious choice. *A puny 5 percent!* They conclude that "most of daily life is driven by automatic, nonconscious mental processes."[1]

That means (even I can do the math on this!) the left-over 95 percent of what we do—spiritually or otherwise—is done by the habits we have developed. We live most of our life on autopilot.

Whether or not this is a disheartening thought all depends on the habits we have formed. If we have developed damaging or unproductive habits, this fact is discouraging—and frightening! But it will be great news to us if we have developed life-enriching habits.

It is a basic design feature of the human body to form habits. Life would, in fact, be impossible without this feature. Imagine if we had to consciously think about every action we needed to perform. We would get nothing done and would remain in a state of perpetual mental exhaustion. Looking at it this way makes it clear that it is a good thing that much of our life runs on autopilot.

But hurray for the 5 percent of our lives not driven by our subconscious habits—because it is this 5 percent that has the power to influence, shape, and redirect the 95 percent! This 5 percent is the key to unlocking and transforming the 95 percent! Our present habits don't have to have the final word on who we will become. Change is possible, if we consciously mobilize the 5 percent to help us develop better habits in the 95 percent of our lives.

Imagine having 95 percent of our lives automatically doing what Jesus calls us to do, instead of having 95 percent of our lives driving us toward destructive things.

The philosopher A. N. Whitehead made this comment about a healthy civilization: "It is a profoundly erroneous truism . . . that we should cultivate the habit of thinking of what we are doing. The precise opposite is the case. Civilization advances by extending the number of operations *which we can perform without thinking about them.*"[2] A. N.

---

1. Chartrand, "The Unbearable Automaticity of Being," 464.
2. Quoted in ibid.

Whitehead argues that societies flourish because they naturally and automatically do the things that encourage, sustain, and advance goodness.

In the same way, as followers of Jesus, we want Christ's goodness and way of life to flow out of us naturally and automatically so that we are doing what he wants us to do because it has gotten into our bones. That means, for example, it is possible to develop a habit so that you naturally and reflexively respond to abuse and mistreatment like Jesus did on the cross and say, "Father forgive them"—without gritting your teeth and muttering curses under your breath.

The Science of Habit Formation

How do we form new ways of thinking and living? How do we overcome negative habits—especially when our "old self" doesn't really want to? It is easy to neglect the importance of integrating the social dimension into the process of developing new habits. An excellent book that addresses this is *Change Anything: The New Science of Personal Success*. Although the title reads like a self-help book, the book is actually based on broad social science research with over 5,000 individuals. The five authors, all researchers, carefully studied the dynamics of acquiring new habits and shedding old ones, and they identified "six sources of influence" that lead to changed habits.[3] It is worth summarizing them and then integrating these into our plan for spiritual change.

Source 1: Personal Motivation

The journey of developing new habits begins with learning to "love what you hate." This step focuses on developing the powers of our imagination to envisage a new future that is more compelling than accepting the status quo. (Recall what we said earlier that we think in images.) We have the ability to imagine who we want to become in our relationship with God. This vision, when kept before our inner eyes, can begin to draw us toward it.

I confess. I am a chocaholic! When I see semi-sweet chocolate from Europe in the grocery store, I'm drawn to it like a magnet. That's how images work: they draw you toward them. The more beautiful and tantalizing they are, the more they compel you to follow them.

3. Patterson, *Change Anything*, 14.

You have the God-given capacity to imagine "the transformed you" in your life with God. The more beautiful and compelling picture you draw, and the longer you sustain that picture in your awareness, the more the desire will grow in you to pursue what you are envisioning.

It's easy to get stuck, if you seek to use the negative side of this principle. Instead of proactively painting a picture of the desired positive habit, some folks think fixating on what they want to avoid will produce change. However, the more you focus your time and attention on what you don't want to do, the stronger your desire becomes to have what you are trying to avoid! It is much more effective to create an image of the positive that compels you to follow it.

Here are two tools to help you do this:

1. *Visualize it.* Either find a person you want to emulate and visit with them, or literally close your eyes and imagine what you would like to be in Jesus. Imagine this in living color, in 3-D, with Dolby surround sound. The authors write, "The more vividly you imagine the visit, the more powerfully it can influence you."[4]

2. *Write it out.* After you have visualized it, then write out what you visualized using the most vivid and compelling language you can so that it inspires and energizes you. Spend time working on it until it helps you "catch fire." Then put it in a prominent place where you can regularly see it in order to "stoke the fire."

Source 2: Personal Ability

The second source for creating a new habit is to develop new skills. Though at this point many people tend to focus on working up their will-power, this is a dead-end strategy bound to fail. *Trying* harder won't work, but *training* will.[5] *Trying* will not transform us. It will only discourage and frustrate us. *Training*, however, leads to transformation.

Training means deliberately practicing a new set of behaviors (skills) that will slowly take us in the direction we want to go. As in piano playing, or tennis, so in spiritual formation—practice makes perfect.

---

4. Ibid., 64.
5. Ortberg, *The Life You've Always Wanted*, 45–62.

It is especially important to "practice for crucial moments," when we are weak and prone to fail. Three things help us practice for these crucial moments, that I will then clarify through an illustration.[6]

1. Break the skills into small pieces, practicing each skill in short intervals.
2. Get immediate feedback from a friend and evaluate your progress.
3. Prepare in advance for potential setbacks that you might encounter.

Practicing in advance for crucial moments needs to go hand-in-hand with retraining our will. The authors write:

> What far too few people know is that *will is a skill*, not a character trait. Willpower can be learned and strengthened like anything else, and (no surprise here) it is best learned through deliberate practice.[7]

The authors relate the story of how a woman named Martha, who re-trained her will by practicing for crucial moments. Martha was overweight and wanted to avoid processed sugars and empty calories. She knew one of the places she blew it was in the coffee shop, where she regularly orders a double chocolate mocha—"with lots of syrup and whipped cream, please." She knows avoiding the coffee shop would be difficult to maintain in the long term, especially since she meets many of her close friends there regularly.

How could she go into the coffee shop and order an espresso without cream or sugar? She had to develop a plan.

First, she analyzed when she was most vulnerable, who was with her, and what normally took place.

Second, she talked in advance to the people she normally went to the coffee shop with and told them what she was trying to do so that they could support her in her plan.

Third, Martha deliberately placed herself in the tempting situation in order to experience wanting the double chocolate mocha without giving in to it.

Fourth, Then Martha deliberately practiced the "distraction" tactic. The authors describe this tactic:

6. Patterson, *Change Anything*, 74.
7. Ibid., 76.

Instead of riveting her view on the caloric concoctions and dreaming of how they might taste (her usual tactic), Martha averts her eyes. Next, she steps back and reads a poster on the wall. Then she starts a conversation with a friend. As Martha continues to wait, she pulls out her cell phone and checks her e-mail. She also shifts her emotions by slowly reciting her Personal Motivation Statement in her mind and thinking about each word.[8]

There is solid research that indicates the distraction tactic works as a way to avoid temptation. There is another line of evidence relating to our cravings which the authors bring in at this point: researchers have documented that our cravings and desires, even strong ones, "usually subside over fifteen to twenty minutes."[9] Knowing these two things can help us succeed in the battle with our temptations.

Fifth, after a few successes doing this for a while, Martha practiced this again, but in some of the more difficult situations that she had identified. Knowing how challenging that would be, she deliberately had a coach nearby. The goal was to challenge herself with "reasonably tempting situations and to develop the skill to survive them."[10]

This is, admittedly, a touchy and potentially dangerous area. Research into substance abuse indicates this often does not work, particularly because of nature of the substances themselves. Martha needed to know her limits—what she could and couldn't handle—and develop her strategy accordingly.

What the authors of *Change Anything* identify as the key to success is "deliberate practice in risky situations [by determining in advance] to have a coach nearby. As you're building [willpower] by learning how to delay and distract yourself, involve a trusted friend who is empowered to pull you out of a situation if the temptation turns out to be too much."[11]

It is often at these two points that the spiritual formation process fails: (1) We haven't developed new skills or put those skills into practice in a thought-through way, and (2) we haven't integrated friends or coaches into the process.

8. Ibid.
9. Ibid., 78.
10. Ibid., 79.
11. Ibid.

Sources 3 and 4: Turn Accomplices into Friends

These next two sources build on our need to be in relationships with others. The authors understand *accomplices* as people who are "partners in crime"—people who, when you are around them, often lead you into temptation. They may not have bad intentions, but generally when you're with them, you end up blowing it.

The goal is to enlist your accomplices to help you in your desire to change, so that they become your "friends" who support and encourage you in your desire to change.

In the process of turning accomplices to friends, you will have to define a "new normal" for yourself. It will require a change of behavior on your part—and, at times, on their part as well. You may need to hold a "transformation conversation" where you lay out your plan for them and ask for their assistance.

Along with friends and accomplices-turned-friends, your desire to form new habits and break old ones can get a turbo boost if you intentionally find new friends who have the same vision and desire that you do.

Source 5: Develop New Incentives

Another source of developing new habits successfully is the practice of setting small, incremental goals combined with frequent small, tangible rewards for yourself along the way to celebrate the successes of your effort.

Alcoholics Anonymous use a chip award system for their weekly meetings. The chips have different colors indicating whether a person has been sober for one month, three months, six months, etc. Those who reached a goal of sobriety are invited to come forward and get a chip. As they do, everyone claps, cheers, and hugs them—celebrating this accomplishment with them.

Source 6: Control Your Environment

The final source of developing new, positive habits is taking into consideration the physical environment we live in. Where we live, play, and work plays a crucial role in the success or failure of our venture to change.

Embedded in our environment are cues that trigger us to engage in certain behaviors.

If you are struggling with your weight, but spend large amounts of time in restaurants, chances are good that your weight will not go down. Also, many people have gone through successful detox treatments at a clinic, only to return home and relapse. Why? The cues in the environment call out to them to do what they always have done in those particular locations with particular people. Unless they change their environment, relapse is almost pre-programmed.

How can we control our surroundings in ways that assist us in developing new habits and avoiding old, destructive ones? The authors identified four ways:

1. *Build fences*: Develop rules for yourself of what you do, when you do it, and where you do it. Talk them through with a trusted friend or coach. This can't be the only source for change, but in concert with the other five sources, it can be a powerful aid.

2. *Manage distance*: Keep things close to you that help you do the right thing, and keep things far away from you that cause you to fall. Ice cream in your home fridge is going to be harder to avoid eating than ice cream at the grocery store.

3. *Change cues*: Put up visual cues in places you are likely to look at regularly that will remind you of what you are working on and motivate you: your bedside stand, kitchen, bathroom, desk, or pop-up reminders on your phone and computer.[12]

4. *Engage your autopilot*: Develop new routines and "standing commitments" that naturally and gently lead you down a path that encourages and supports your desire for change. The authors claim that "the more you structure good choices as the default in your life, the easier change becomes."[13]

---

12. Cues are not limited to what we see. Charles Duhigg explains that "cues can be almost anything, from a visual trigger such as a candy bar or a television commercial to a certain place, a time of day, an emotion, a sequence of thoughts, or the company of particular people" (Duhigg, *The Power of Habit*, 25). We can develop cues that work for us.

13. Patterson, *Change Anything*, 129.

Summary

These six critical sources, which the authors of *Change Anything* have identified in their social science research for forming new habits apply to change in any realm of human life, including the spiritual.

These sources of forming new habits dovetail with what we have learned from neuroscience about how we function as human beings. They also fit with what we discovered in our chapter on the biblical foundations for the process of spiritual formation. We can use insights both from the field of neuroscience and from the social sciences to assist us in our journey toward being transformed into the image of Christ.

17

Putting It All Together:
Laying Out a Process for Spiritual Growth

Developing Your Own Plan for Spiritual Growth

IN THIS CHAPTER I will incorporate the insights I have been highlighting and lay out a process that you can use to develop your own plan for spiritual growth. Before I dive into that, I need to address two topics that will help you start well and avoid some pitfalls that could derail you. Then, I'll close the chapter with the story of how "Rick" developed his plan and put it into practice.

Starting Well

In working with individuals as they develop their own personal plan for spiritual formation,[1] I have noticed two things that hamper people at the outset.

Tendencies That Could Derail Us at the Start

First, some people see so many areas of deficiency in their lives that it immobilizes them, leaving them discouraged and hopeless. They give up before they even start, thinking, "It's just no use! I'll never change!"

---

1. The language of having a "Personal Plan for Spiritual Growth" comes from Randy Frazee's *The Christian Life Profile Assessment Tool Workbook*. This work has also been influential in the process of spiritual formation that we lay out below. He has published two further books that expand and complement the workbook: Frazee, *Think, Act, Be like Jesus*; Frazee, *Believe*.

Others have the opposite tendency: they are so excited and eager for change that they dive in head-first, trying to tackle everything at once. The result is that they become exhausted and overwhelmed by trying to work on so many things simultaneously. Gradually, they too get discouraged because they see no progress.

Two crucial, yet quite simple principles help us avoid both of these tendencies.[2]

- Be precise about what you want to change.
- Focus on tackling only one thing at a time.

There have been multiple studies that point to the impossibility of multi-tasking and the danger of attempting to accomplish too many goals at once.[3] Although we are tempted to think, *"I can do more than just that one little thing!"*, personal experience and research indicates you will progress faster if you focus on making one small change at a time. When you have mastered one area so that it becomes more of a "settled condition" of your life, you can move on to the next area.

The beauty of beginning with only one thing in the realm of the spiritual life is that it will have a ripple effect on the other things that you want to see transformed in your life. Each small victory will encourage and strengthen you as you pursue transformation in the other dimensions you have your eye on.

Where Do We Begin? Identifying Your Starting Point

The second thing that hampers people when they become serious about their spiritual growth is that they often struggle with the question, "where do I start in my desire to become like Christ?" The goal of becoming like Christ sounds simple at first, but when you begin to think more deeply about what that actually means, there are so many facets to consider that this can also overwhelm you. Let me lay out three ways to select a starting point, in hopes that maybe one of them will resonate with you. These are not mutually exclusive, so your decision about where to start might even incorporate all three suggestions.

2. Although these two principles are not identified as such in the book, *Change Anything*, they are implicit throughout and create the framework of the entire process of change:

3. See the many research studies that the Brain, Cognition, and Action Laboratory have conducted on this at http://www.umich.edu/~bcalab/projects.html.

One simple, direct way of determining where to start is to pray over a period of time (perhaps a few days or a week) asking God, "what do you want me to work on?" As you open your heart for an answer, seek to be sensitive to impressions and thoughts that come to you.

A second way goes hand-in-hand with the first. Reflect back on your life over the past several months. Are there impressions you have had about the way you are living, your character, your thoughts, etc.? Do certain impressions crop up repeatedly in your mind accompanied by the thought, "You should work on this *sometime*"?

That is how God has often worked in my life. In a particular season of my life, I begin to become aware of a pattern of failure in one specific area, and that still small voice of God's Spirit whispers to me, "this is something you need to work on." I have never heard an audible voice telling me this, but rather it is simply a growing impression within me as I seek to be open to the Spirit within me.

A third suggestion for a starting point comes from Randy Frazee's *Christian Life Profile Assessment Tool Workbook,* in which he suggests that becoming like Christ means having the same beliefs, practices, and virtues Jesus had. He suggests a "top ten" in each category.[4]

Beliefs	Practices	Virtues
Trinity	Worship	Love
Salvation by grace	Prayer	Joy
Authority of the Bible	Bible study	Peace
Personal God	Single-mindedness	Patience
Identity in Christ	Biblical community	Kindness/goodness
Church	Spiritual gifts	Faithfulness
Humanity	Giving away my time	Gentleness
Compassion	Giving away my money	Self-Control
Eternity	Giving away my faith	Hope
Stewardship	Giving away my life	Humility

Randy Frazee suggests that you identify your weakest item on this list and then create a plan to improve in just that one area. He advocates enlisting a few people to help you discern what your weakest point is,

4. Although we could quibble with some of these and could certainly extend this list, they are a good place to start.

using a tool that he calls a "one another assessment." For this assessment, you choose people who know you well and whose opinion you trust and respect to rate you from 0 to 5 on 40 statements which are designed to reveal how strong or weak you are in the virtues of Christlikeness that are listed in the chart above. Then you combine what they've said about you with your own self-assessment to come up with one area out of the 30 to start working on.

As you decide what area to focus on, it is important to be walking closely with Jesus, inviting him to direct where you should start.

The virtues are a good place to start, since Jesus and other New Testament authors indicate that the virtue of love is to be the primary hallmark of all followers of Jesus, and—as we saw in Gal 5—all the other virtues are facets of love and flow out of love.[5]

Process of Spiritual Formation: Developing Your Personal Plan for Spiritual Growth

The process of spiritual formation that takes into consideration the findings of neuroscience and social science research needs the following elements to be successful:

1. Have the right personal motivation for change.[6]

2. Evaluate yourself: where do I presently stand in my spiritual development?

3. Get feedback from others: how do those closest to me view where I presently stand in my spiritual development?

4. Select one target area to work on.

5. Design a personal plan for spiritual growth that identifies new practices you can engage in that have the potential to lead to spiritual change. As you design your list of these new practices, it is important to integrate the following.

   a. This set of practices needs to engage your entire being: heart, thoughts, emotions, body, and personal relationships.

---

5. This comes out in many passages in the New Testament. Some of the key ones are John 13:34–35; 15:12; Rom 13:8; 1 Cor 13:13; Heb 10:24; Jas 2:8; 1 Pet 4:8.

6. For this, see the discussion in chapter 14, in the section, "Dealing with Your Vices: *Agere Contra*."

b. Remember that you need to engage in these practices regularly and repeatedly over a period of time in order to reshape all of your dimensions in a way that establishes a "new normal" for how you live your life.

6. Include in the preparation and the implementation of this plan a support system of frequent and regular connections with key friends, allies, and coaches, who know of your desires. Invite them to keep you accountable in the process.

7. Reassess your environment:

a. Analyze your surroundings, looking for triggers that lead you into engaging in harmful behavior patterns as well as those that lead you into engaging in beneficial behavior patterns. Your environment includes the physical spaces you live in: your bedroom, your home, your work environment, and places you go in your free time. Analyzing your environment is not only about location, but about particular situations and times when you tend to engage in harmful or beneficial behavior patterns.

b. Intentionally restructure your environment to support triggers for beneficial behavior patterns encouraging your spiritual growth, and minimize or eliminate triggers that lead you back into harmful behavior patterns.[7]

What follows below is a pathway that integrates all these factors into a comprehensive process you can use to take concrete steps toward your own spiritual development. Having said that, each person is unique. As you read and reflect on the steps below, you may need to adapt it to fit your own context and personality. Feel free to adjust the process—but remember that all of these elements are vital for lasting change to take place.

7. This is an element that is often not on our radar screen for our spiritual development. Spiritual transformation often requires the intentional transformation of our environment. We may have developed sinful or destructive patterns—negative activities—that are connected with particular locations and times, both in our home as well as outside of it. Changing geography, changing room or room arrangement, in places you are prone to falling, may help strengthen you not to fall. This is, in fact, the problem with those with addictions going into a rehab center. They can become "sober" in the center, but as soon as they are in their old environment, all the "cues" that trigger their desire for that addiction are still there, leading them to succumb to the power of the addiction.

Step 1 Evaluate Where You Stand in Your
Own Spiritual Development

I would like to suggest three helpful tools determine where you stand spiritually. The first one is the "Self-Assessment" in Randy Frazee's *The Christian Life Profile Assessment Tool Workbook*. This assessment has 120 questions keyed to the thirty "core competencies" we mentioned earlier, which are self-scored to show your areas of strength and the areas of weakness.

The second tool is a set of self-assessments developed by Dr. Michael Zigarelli, Professor of Leadership and Strategy at Messiah College.[8] These assessments (he calls them surveys) have been developed with careful academic rigor and have been used by almost 20,000 individuals. Depending on what you want to work on in your life, you can choose one of three self-assessments:

- The Christian Character Index (thirty-five questions)

- The Obstacles to Growth Survey (forty questions)

- The Love for God Scale (thirty-four questions)

These evaluations by Dr. Zigarelli can be filled out on-line and are immediately scored, showing your areas of strength and weakness.

The third tool is the "Spiritual Growth Planner" Adele Calhoun has developed in Appendix 1 of her book, *Spiritual Disciplines Handbook*, in which she helps a person identify the area they have the strongest desire to grow in from the following categories:[9]

- Worship the Trinity

- Open yourself to God

- Relinquish the false self and idols of your heart

- Share your life

- Hear God's Word

- Incarnate the love of Christ

- Pray your life

Any of these three assessments can be integrated into the steps below.

8. These assessments, which Dr. Zigarelli calls "surveys" are kindly available free of charge at http://www.assess-yourself.org/surveys/.

9. Calhoun, *Spiritual Disciplines Handbook*, 256–63.

Step 2 Get Feedback from Others

Since we are often blind to our own strengths and weaknesses, we need others to encourage us by pointing out areas we are doing well in and lovingly helping us see areas that need to be nurtured.

A guest visited our home recently and asked about the paintings hanging on the wall and other items we had on our cabinets. I realized that I had not "seen" those things for quite some time, even though I walked past them every day. It took a guest to help me notice them again. Without the insights of others, we may remain blind to areas we need to grow in.

All three tools mentioned in Step 1 can be used for this as well. The *Christian Life Profile* calls these "One Another Assessments," and suggests giving them to three people who know you well, and who would give you feedback specifically on the way they see you living out the ten virtues.

Although the assessments developed by Dr. Zigarelli and Adele Calhoun don't specifically have the equivalent of a "One Another" assessment, you could ask a few individuals close to you to respond to the same assessment you are taking about yourself.

This step often makes people a bit uncomfortable. Our culture tells us we should "mind our own business." Yet Scripture moves in a counter-cultural direction by encouraging us to invite others to speak into our lives. We see this, for example, in the follow Scriptures:

- "Wounds from a sincere friend are better than many kisses from an enemy." (Prov. 27:6 NLT)

- "Let a righteous man strike me—that is a kindness; let him rebuke me—that is oil on my head. My head will not refuse it." (Ps 141:5 TNIV)

- "In the end, people appreciate honest criticism far more than flattery." (Prov 28:23 NLT)

- "Those who flatter their neighbors are spreading nets for their feet." (Prov 29:5 TNIV)

We need the honest feedback of those who know us so that we can live life well. How can we go about getting such feedback? Here is a suggestion of how to invite someone to give you feedback in a way that doesn't threaten you or cause the relationship to become awkward. You could say something along these lines:

I am working on personal project right now. I feel the need to be more intentional in my spiritual growth, and I am trying to discern my strengths and also discover the areas I need to grow in. Can I have your help? Could you fill out a survey/assessment for me that is aimed at helping me figure out where I stand spiritually—both where I am strong and where I need to grow?

In addition, many have found this especially beneficial to do this as a joint project in a small group. If everyone is eager to dig deep and grow, if the relationships are deep, and if the trust levels are strong, then the process of doing this together can be very powerful. (When these factors are not present, however, people may resist doing this.)

Step 3 Debrief with the Person Giving You Feedback

After your friends have finished their feedback, it is helpful to have a conversation with them about it. Two primary questions are important to talk through:

- In what areas do you see strengths in my life?
- What areas do you think I could use some work on?

Although we might feel hesitant to have this conversation, in all my years teaching spiritual formation, my students consistently tell me that these conversations were rich and rewarding. They felt affirmed and valued, and the conversation often led to a deepening of the relationship as well as an offer to pray for them and stand by them throughout the process.

Step 4 Reflect on Your Strengths and Areas You Need to Grow In

After you have gotten the feedback from your own assessment as well as the assessments from your friends, the next step is to reflect on what you have discovered about yourself from comparing your assessment with those of your friends and the conversation you had with them.

There are two purposes of this step: to affirm you by identifying areas you are strong in, and to identify one area you sense God wants you to improve in.

I have found the questions in the *Christian Life Profile* to be helpful and have modified them and built on them.[10]

10. Frazee, *The Christian Life Profile Assessment Tool Workbook*, 48–49.

Affirm where you are strong

1. List the two or three top areas of strength that you identified in your assessment of yourself. What strikes you about these strengths? Jot your thoughts down.

2. List the two or three top areas of strength that your assessors identified in their assessment of you below and summarize what they communicated to you about them. What strikes you about these strengths? Jot your thoughts down.

3. What strikes you when you compare the strengths that your assessors identified with the ones you identified? Any overlap? Differences? Reflect on what you learn from this.

Reflect on the areas you need to grow in

4. List the two lowest areas that you identified in your assessment of yourself. What strikes you about them? Jot your thoughts down.

5. List the two lowest areas that your assessors identified in their assessment of you, and summarize what they communicated to you about them. What strikes you about these growth areas? Jot your thoughts down.

6. What strikes you when you compare the growth areas that your assessors identified with the ones you identified? Is there any overlap? Are there differences? Reflect on what you learn from this.

Identify the one area you desire to grow in

7. After a time of reflection and prayer, identify the one area you wish to grow in and indicate why you have chosen this area.

Envision how you see yourself changing

8. Describe how you envision yourself, with God's Spirit empowering you, to be thinking, acting, and responding to others at the end of this process. How do you want your entire person to be re-shaped when you conclude this time? In a visually rich and descriptive way, using all of your senses, describe this "new you in Jesus" that you desire to become as a result of this process.

This last step is critical to the success of this process. In our discussion of neuroscience, we talked about how we are transformed by what we see. The more we see ourselves in the transformed state that we are trusting God to work in us through his Spirit, the more this image can orient us and motivate us as we go along. The neuroscientist Kristen Hansen explains why:

> Our imagination is one of the most powerful tools to achieve our goals. Recent research has tested the power of imagination and found that the same regions in our brain light up whether we imagine it or actually do it. New neural pathways are developed in our brain just by imagining and these contribute significantly to achieving our goal—whether the activity involves shooting baskets, flexing muscles or learning music.
>
> The process of neuroplasticity . . . is generated not only by doing, but also by imagining. The key to neuroplasticity is attention. If we pay regular attention to our goals, our brains can change in as little as a few weeks, enough to be seen on a brain scan.[11]

Step 5 Develop Your Plan for Spiritual Growth

All of these steps up to now are designed to prepare you to develop your own plan for spiritual growth.

Once you have identified the one area you wish to grow in, the next—and critical—step is to identify specific activities or practices you think will help you grow in this one area. A helpful resource, with marvelous descriptions of spiritual practices you may wish to consider, is Richard Foster's classic book, *Celebration of Discipline*, which identifies thirteen spiritual practices Christians have used throughout the centuries. Another excellent resource for many additional spiritual practices is Adele Ahlberg Calhoun's *Spiritual Disciplines Handbook*. In addition, in the Appendix, I have listed some spiritual practices that my students have developed, which they found to be particularly helpful.

As we learned from neuroscience and social science research, it is important to select activities you can integrate into the routine of daily life over a longer period of time. For my busy students, I suggest a minimum of three activities—or action steps—that they can engage in on a daily or weekly basis. Depending on your lifestyle, you may want to choose more

11. Hansen, "The Neuroscience of Goal Setting."

than three. The more activities you can integrate into your daily life that target your spiritual growth area, the more effective the process will be.

In addition, you may choose other activities that are "one offs"— things you do only once, like reading an article or a book on a topic, but most of your action steps should be things that last long enough or take place repeatedly enough to begin to reshape you.

Based on research about goal setting, it is important that your goals be concrete and tangible, not just vague wishes. The following statements are unhelpful as action steps:

> "I will be less abrasive in my speech and conduct, especially to those I am comfortable with."
> "I want to become more patient with my roommate."

Why aren't they helpful? Because you can't know if or when you have accomplished it—or when you have even practiced it!

In contrast, goals that are concrete and tangible have five characteristics:

> S—Specific (an observable behavior)
> M—Measurable (how many? how long?)
> A—Attainable (with the resources available, such as time, money, etc.)
> R—Relevant (to the aims and intentions you wish to achieve)
> T—Trackable (by a specific dates)[12]

A good action step—or goal statement—lets you know clearly if and when you have accomplished it. Here are some examples of SMART action steps:

- "In order to work on developing compassion, I will volunteer at St. Joseph's hospice center on a weekly basis (minimum two hours per visit) for three months."

- "In order to stretch myself in giving, I will donate $10 per month to a missionary organization for the next year."

By formulating goals this way, you know exactly *what* you are working on, *how* you will accomplish them, and you will know *when* you have accomplished them.

Here is a sample format for writing goals that incorporates all the aspects of what a SMART goal should include.

12. Pyle and Seals, *Experiencing Ministry Supervision*, 60.

"In order to work on _____, I will (engage in) _____. I will do this ____ times per _____ (day/week). I will begin this on _____ and continue this until _____."

You may wish to use this as a guide to make sure all the components of a well-formulated goal are included. Even though it's not absolutely necessary to use this format, my students have found it useful because it helps them be precise about what exactly they will be doing. However, if you find this too restrictive, develop something that works for you.

In choosing action steps, it is important to take the following into consideration:

- Select goals that fit who you are, your personality, and your daily rhythm. If you are, for example, a night owl, it would not be wise to make a goal of getting up at 4:30 in the morning to pray.

- Select a limited number of goals and do not be overly ambitious. If you set too many goals and you do not keep them, you will feel disappointed and guilty.

- You may discover, over time, that some of your goals are artificial, not productive, too ambitious, too vague, etc. Feel free to modify them accordingly so that they truly are a help to you. These action steps should be a pathway to transformation. If you sense they are not serving that purpose, evaluate them and consider how you could modify them to make them more effective.

Another aspect of planning good action steps for the purposes of spiritual growth is to select practices that are *proactive* and not *reactive*.

A *proactive* action step
- is independent of a situation;
- is something you do in advance of a situation that you struggle with;
- prepares you for a situation that you will most likely encounter.

A *reactive* action step
- is dependent on a certain situation to occur;
- requires you to constantly watch for that situation to occur, and then react to it in the way that you intended—by which time it is often too late!

An example of a *reactive* action step is, "when my child/spouse/colleague irritates me, I will pray for them." An example of turning this into a *proactive* action step is, "Since I know my child/spouse/colleague irritates me at times, I will spend five minutes each morning journaling my prayers about this person and writing out what I appreciate about them."

Step 6 Identify an Accountability Partner and Other "Allies"

Selecting an accountability partner (or partners) at the beginning of the process and then meeting at least weekly with them throughout the process is critical for the success of this process. In feedback from my students, this was often the most important factor determining the success or failure of their personal plan for spiritual growth.

In my spiritual formation classes, I ask my students to meet with an accountability partner for a minimum of fifteen minutes each week where the accountability partner

- reviews the action steps the person has identified;
- asks how they are doing with the goals they have set for themselves;
- discusses with the other person whether the action steps are realistic and effective, and if not, assists them in revising them;
- encourages and prays for the person.

In addition to having an accountability partner, my students are part of a small group that meets weekly, where the group members are all intentional about each other's spiritual growth. An accountability partner and a small group make a powerful combination that aids in the transformation process.

Step 7 Scanning and Adapting the Environment

The final step is to reevaluate the environment and see if changes should be made. If someone, for example, is struggling with pornography, then thinking through ways to change the environment (moving the computer into an open space instead of the bedroom, installing a filter, switching to a cell phone that has no internet access, etc.) would be vital. It is wise to enlist the accountability partner in thinking this through practically.

"Rick" and His Plan for Spiritual Formation

In the final section of this chapter, I would like to show you how this process works by using an example of someone who went through this process. We will call him "Rick."[13]

In Rick's plan for spiritual growth, the strengths he identified were prayer, Bible Study, and faithfulness. The two individuals he selected to provide him with feedback identified his strength as being hopeful. Rick was a bit surprised. He wrote,

> It surprised me that this was a strength of mine. I didn't think it would be. I am glad that others see this in me, because it is something I endeavor to have. I think that is cool that everyone was in agreement on this.

Rick was quite encouraged to get this feedback from others, and it showed him that God was at work in his life.

When Rick looked at the areas where his own lowest scores were, he identified compassion, peace, and self-control. He commented, "These have been extreme struggles I have gone through and I know very well I need to work on." When he examined the relationship between these lowest areas he made this observation:

> I think self-control and compassion are closely related. Without self-control you can't have compassion. This problem also ties into peace. Without one you can't have the other. It seems a lot of spiritual things work like this: when you have an issue in one area, it seeps into the rest of your being.

Interestingly and significantly, both of his assessors also identified peace and self-control as areas that most needed to be developed in Rick's life. In reflecting on the conversation Rick had with them, he wrote:

> It is crazy how they are the exact same as the ones on my personal assessment. These were people who know me best, and I know these are areas I definitely need to improve on. I am grateful for this opportunity to strengthen my weaknesses in order for my relationship with Christ to be closer!

The meeting with these close friends and their feedback to him on this helped Rick to see clearly that these were some things that God

---

13. This example is partially composite. The identities have been masked and some of the details have been changed for the purpose of anonymity.

might want him to work on. And so, when Rick identified the one thing he wanted to work on, he wrote:

> Peace is the area I would like to spend time on improving. It has been a weakness of mine for a while. I sense God wants me to rest in his peace, and a big part of that is getting free from my fears.

When Rick envisioned how he wanted to be changed at the end of the semester, he expressed it this way:

> At the end of this three-month process, I want to be completely reliant on God for everything. I don't want to look to friends or material things. I want to keep my eyes and heart focused on my Savior. I want to be totally and completely free from my fears that are gripping me. God told me two weeks ago that this is something that he wants for me. I will not be able to go further in my spiritual journey with these holds on me. I want to be a person who walks with confidence in Jesus and not be controlled by anything of this world. That is what true peace looks like to me.

When it came time to write out the action steps that would help Rick work on developing peace in his life, here are the four action steps he selected:

1. I will spend thirty minutes a week in quiet, just listening. This will help me achieve the goal of peace, since I have a fear of being alone. I think practicing solitude on a regular basis will take me a long way on my goal of living without fear or anxiety.

2. I will read one chapter of my Bible every night before I go to sleep. This will help me to overcome any fear the enemy throws in my face. I want to know Jesus as my *Prince of Peace*.

3. I will keep a weekly journal of what God has been telling me that week. Keeping a journal will allow me to see what God has done, and will allow me to prepare for and overcome other situations I encounter. My journaling will focus primarily on obtaining peace and becoming free from my fears. If these fears creep up again, my journal will make it possible to look back and be reminded of what God did for me in the past.

4. I will listen to sermon podcasts three times a week of a pastor I
   highly respect. My goal is to remind myself of who I am in Christ
   and to keep the devil from tearing me down and telling me I am
   worthless.

Over the weeks and months, I could see that Rick was making a
concerted effort to work on these areas. His reports to me of his meetings with his accountability partner documented the slow, incremental
changes. In one of his earliest reports, Rick wrote,

> I read my Bible before I went to bed and I practiced thirty min-
> utes of solitude. This week I was a lot more diligent in doing it
> than the previous week. I allowed for more intimate time with
> my Savior in order to focus on Him. The steps that I developed
> and committed myself to are helping me to stay on track and
> focus on having time with Jesus.

A few weeks later, as Rick reflected on the spiritual practices he had
planned, he felt he needed to change them a bit. He explained:

> I tried to incorporate forgiveness into my week. I intentionally
> began to take steps to forgive those who have hurt me in the
> past. In addition, I also increased my time in the Word. I am re-
> alizing now how important it is to hide God's word in my heart
> in order to deepen my identity in Him.

Throughout the process, Rick began seeing the power of immersing
himself in Scripture as well as the value of increasing the time spent in
this practice.

Then, in the next week, a break-through came for Rick as he was
practicing the spiritual discipline of solitude. Rick confessed,

> Honestly this spiritual discipline was the hardest thing I have
> ever had to do. I have an extreme fear of being alone. It wasn't
> until two weeks ago that God started working on my heart about
> conquering this fear.

Rick went on to explain this fear of being alone began as a child and
was often so intense, he could not be separated from his mother. As Rick
grew older, the fear intensified. He could only handle a twenty-minute
time-frame of being alone before he would start to feel panicky. When
it came to practicing the spiritual discipline of solitude, Rick wrote the
following:

For the first time in my life, I spent a thirty-minute period by myself away from all people and noise. It was a terrifying experience for me. I thought to myself "never again!" When it came time for me to practice this discipline again, I was extremely hesitant. Then something unexpected happened: I became ill and was "forced" to be in solitude—whether I wanted to be or not. It was in this time that I felt the presence of the Lord in my apartment in a powerful way. I laid in silence because I no longer could sleep and I sat and listened. I didn't shake or tremble. I just lay still in the presence of my King. For the first time, I felt liberated.

A little later Rick elaborated in more detail about what had transpired.

In this time, God impressed on my heart this verse that I had been memorizing, "my freedom from fears and agitating passions and moral conflicts be multiplied to you in [the full, personal, precise, and correct] knowledge of God and of Jesus our Lord" (2 Pet 1:2 AMP).

Through this verse, God seemed to be speaking directly to me. He told me that he wanted me to be completely free of my fears. As a result, I took this exercise in solitude as an act of obedience.

It was not an easy task. After about twenty minutes I began to shake, and as I attempted to focus on praying I was completely overwhelmed and feeling all alone. After about an hour I was shaking and crying. As much as I wanted to give up, I persevered through because I knew I needed to work on this.

I began praying, even though I was still shaking and choking back sobs. I prayed that God would make himself real to me and heal the past hurts that caused this. As I began talking to my Father, I felt a peace come over me. When I began focusing on him, my fear lessened. This went on for the rest of the time, just sharing time with my Father. Afterwards, I felt a sense of accomplishment and peace.

Although my fear is not completely conquered, I have come a long way from where I was at the beginning of this process. Moments like these build my confidence. I am excited for the time when this fear is completely gone from me. I don't want to be restricted from things of God because of my overwhelming fear of being alone. I know that a process of healing is taking place. Even though at times it is excruciating, I am happy because I know the end result will be worth it.

This experience signaled a turning point in Rick's experience with God and with his sense of peace. This "victory" encouraged him from this point on, and he became increasingly energized in his journey toward transformation. Yes, there was ebb-and-flow, but in general, he was experiencing clear progress. There were also other factors going on in his life that contributed significantly to his spiritual growth.

When Rick reviewed his progress at the end of the time-frame he had set for himself, this is what he had to say:

> As I followed through on my action steps, after the third week I started to notice a change in me. How clever of God to help me by putting me in heightened situations which required me to trust him.
>
> Practicing my action steps went well most of the time because I invested in them. It was challenging to do this, however. Because of the scars in my life from my past, I had built up a strong desire to protect myself, my heart, and ultimately my whole being. Past painful experiences and relationships taught me to harden my exterior. Despite this, I believe through this process God opened my heart. That was an incredible insight and realization in my practice.
>
> Because I am a goal-oriented person, it would at times frustrate me when I did not see immediate results. I noticed, however, as the weeks went on, I have been growing stronger in the area of being by myself. I don't find the feeling of panic coming on so quickly. This may seem like very small progress, but to me it's a giant leap.

This was the experience of Rick over the course of about two and a half months of intentional focus on one area he wanted to grow in. It was exciting to see the transformation happening week by week in his life.

I hope that this gives you an idea of what can happen when we target one area of growth at a time, and then concentrate on developing practices that help us grow in that one area. Growth in one area of our lives can then have a ripple-effect into other areas of our lives.

A Closing Word

WE HAVE COME TO the end of our journey, but in many ways, the journey has only just begun. Let's review our journey. It began (Part 1) by wrestling with what spiritual formation is and what it is not. At the outset, we defined Christian spiritual formation as *the redemptive process of intentionally forming our interior and exterior life so that so that we increasingly take on (acquire, develop) the character of the inner being of Christ himself.*

We then sought to place spiritual formation on the backdrop of the story of God and his world. Keying in on God's original intentions for humanity, we saw that spiritual formation is about restoring human beings to what God had intended for them all along—that human beings, as in one large family, would reflect God's character and values, and share in his life. This was something that was only made possible through Jesus, the true image bearer of God and the one who gave us eternal life and empowers us through his Spirit. We then turned to look at what the Bible had to say about the *goal, dynamics,* and *process* of spiritual formation.

Part 2 looked at what modern brain research is discovering about how the brain and body function—with a particular emphasis on those topics relevant to spiritual formation. This look provoked some questions, one of which was this: as brain research discovers more and more about the mechanisms of change, what role does the Holy Spirit have? We argued that the Spirit is still the primary agent at work both in creation itself and also in the restoration of creation. He is working "in the background" of all of reality to conform and restore every last inch of it to what it was meant to be. The Spirit is at work in the wider world, but he is also at work within us—doing all he can both through natural processes as well as supernatural processes to empower us to become conformed to the image of Christ.

In Part 3 we looked at each dimension of the human person (heart, thoughts, emotions and feelings, body, and relationships) and discussed what they were and how change takes place in each of them. As we did this, we brought in insights from brain research along the way.

Part 4 is where we took all the things we had looked at and asked: how can we use this information to develop pathways for spiritual growth? We first drew on modern research regarding how habits develop, arguing that much of the process of spiritual formation is about developing habits that aim our lives in the direction becoming more like Christ. We then rounded out the book by suggesting a process we can use to tailor-make a pathway for our own spiritual development, and by providing the example of how "Rick" did this.

☩

At the beginning of the book, I noted the words of Dallas Willard: "Everyone receives spiritual formation, just as everyone gets an education. The only question is whether it is a good one or a bad one."[1] My hope, in the book that you have just read, is that you not only understand what spiritual formation is all about, but that you now also have the tools you need to help you make significant strides on your journey toward spiritual growth.

---

1. Willard, "Spiritual Formation in Christ," 254.

Appendix

Sample Action Steps

For the Personal Spiritual Growth Plan

BELOW ARE SOME ACTION steps individuals have developed to help them work on their target area for spiritual growth.

Growing in the area of "putting God first"

- In order to work on my relationship with God, I will read God's Word and pray about the Scripture. I will do this five times per week for a minimum of fifteen minutes.

- In order to work on being a part of the community of believers, I will engage in fellowship, through a fellowship group or talking to a close Christian friend. I will do this once a week for a minimum of thirty minutes.

- In order to work on my thought life, I will pray and journal about my thoughts. I will do these things twice a week for a minimum of fifteen minutes.

Growing in the area of "joy"

- Once a day, look back and focus on an event and ask, "Where was God in that?" Journal it each day. Write, but no legalism. End with prayer.

- Purposefully find 7 verses that relate to "Joy" and "Trust with the Lord," and memorize one verse a week. Put them in a prominent place where I will see them daily. Repeat the verse before bed and when I rise in the morning.

- I will make a list at the end of every day of every positive thing that the Lord did for me that day. I will reflect on these in prayer and thank God for giving me all that he has (15 minutes of prayer). It's hard to focus on the bad if you're constantly reflecting on the good.

- Every day for the rest of the semester, I will get to work 15 minutes early and pray in my car before I go into work. I will ask God to help me stay in a state of joy during my shift.

- I will print off 2 verses that have to do with joy, and I will memorize them. I will recite them to myself every morning before I start my day.

Growing in the area of "my identity in Christ"

- In order to find my identity in Christ, I will spend at least 20 minutes per week in solitude in which I reflect on who Christ is and who He has made me to be.

- In order to stop comparing myself to others, I will write down one thing that I like about myself each morning and pray for 15 minutes that God would help me to remember this throughout the day.

- In order to find my identity in Christ, I will look up one new Scripture each week that focuses on our identity and then spend 10 minutes each day meditating on it for the rest of the week.

Growing in the area of "peace"

- In order to work on forgiving those who hurt me, I will call both of them once a week, and talk to them for a minimum of five minutes (If they do not respond, I will text them a nice message).

- In order to forgive the things of my past and be free of its bondage and pain, I will pray for the people who have hurt me and for my own healing once a day for a minimum of 5 minutes.

- Throughout the next few months I will work through the 12 Steps of the forgiveness process for as many people who have hurt me as I can.

Growing in the area of "prayer"

- Wake up at 7 am on Monday, Wednesday, and Friday and at 8:30 on Tuesday and Thursday in order to seek God's face in devotion and prayer for 20 minutes.

- Revel in God's creation as I walk to each class, choosing three specific things in nature each day to thank God for in the form of prayer, such as a birds' chirp or the simple yet wonderful shape of the clouds.

- Conclude each night with more prayer, this time for 10 minutes, lifting up very specific things that have come up throughout the day. I will put a sign that says "PRAY" on the ceiling above my bed.

- In order to get better at the Christian discipline of prayer, I will look up one verse on prayer each Sunday as my prayer verse for the week and pray through it daily.

Growing in the area of "reading my Bible"

- So that reading my Bible will become a real habit, I will daily read one chapter from the Bible and reflect on it for at least 10 minutes.

- In order to better understand what I have been reading, twice a week (on the weekends) I will look up and read an article that corresponds to what I am reading.

- I will pray about what I have read and the things I have gained from it after each time, so that I will be relying on the Holy Spirit to produce fruit from what I have read.

- I will choose 3 highlighted verses at the end of each week to memorize, and I will write them out at the beginning and the end of each day of the following week. This is so that I won't just read and forget. If I memorize it, it can affect me long-term and I can continue growing from what I've read later in life.

Bibliography

À Kempis, Thomas. *The Imitation of Christ*. Translated by Ronald Arbuthnott Knox and Michael Oakley. San Francisco: Ignatius, 2005.

Alfeyev, Metropolit Hilarion. "Deification in Christ." Online: http://hilarion.ru/en/2010/02/25/1081.

Anderson, Neil T. *The Bondage Breaker*. 2nd ed. Eugene, OR: Harvest House, 2000.

——. *The Steps to Freedom in Christ*. 3rd ed. Ventura, CA: Gospel Light, 2004.

——. *Victory Over the Darkness: With Study Guide*. London: Monarch, 2002.

Arichea, Daniel C., and Howard Hatton. *Handbook on the Letter from Jude and the Second Letter from Peter, UBS Handbook Series*. New York: United Bible Societies, 1993.

"Babies 'Cry in Mother's Tongue.'" *BBC News*. November 6, 2009. Online: http://news.bbc.co.uk/2/hi/health/8346058.stm.

Backus, William D., and Marie Chapian. *Telling Yourself the Truth*. Minneapolis: Bethany Fellowship, 2000.

Bartholomew, Craig G., and Michael W. Goheen. *The Drama of Scripture: Finding our Place in the Biblical Story*. 2nd ed. Grand Rapids: Baker Academic, 2014.

Bauckham, Richard. *Jude, 2 Peter*. Word Biblical Commentary. Waco, TX: Word, 1983.

Bauer, Walter, et al., eds. *Greek-English Lexicon of the New Testament and Other Early Christian Literature*. 3rd ed. Chicago: University of Chicago Press, 2000.

Beilby, James K., and Paul R. Eddy, eds. *Divine Foreknowledge: Four Views*. Downers Grove, IL: IVP, 2001.

——. *Understanding Spiritual Warfare: Four Views*. Grand Rapids: Baker Academic, 2012.

Borg, Marcus J., and N. T. Wright. *The Meaning of Jesus: Two Visions*. San Francisco: HarperSanFrancisco, 1999.

Boyd, Gregory A. *Is God to Blame? Moving Beyond Pat Answers to the Problem of Evil*. Downers Grove, IL: IVP, 2003.

Burridge, Richard A. *Imitating Jesus: An Inclusive Approach to New Testament Ethics*. Grand Rapids: Eerdmans, 2007.

——. *What are the Gospels? A Comparison with Graeco-Roman Biography*. 2nd ed, The Biblical Resource Series. Grand Rapids: Eerdmans, 2004.

Calhoun, Adele Ahlberg. *Spiritual Disciplines Handbook: Practices That Transform Us*. Downers Grove, IL: IVP, 2005.

Carnegie Mellon University. "How to Thrive Through Close Relationships." *Medical News Today*, September 9, 2014. Online: http://www.medicalnewstoday.com/releases/282158.php.

Carson, Donald A. *The Gagging of God*. Grand Rapids: Zondervan, 1996.

Cassian, John. "The Conferences of John Cassian." In *Sulpitius Severus. Vincent of Lerins. John Cassian.* New York: Christian Literature Company, 1894.

Chartrand, Tanya L. "The Unbearable Automaticity of Being." *American Psychologist* 54: 462–79. Online: http://www.yale.edu/acmelab/articles/bargh_chartrand_1999. pdf.

Collins Dictionary. Online: http://www.collinsdictionary.com/dictionary/english/ company.

Cox, D. Michael, and Brad J. Kallenberg. "Character." In *Dictionary of Scripture and Ethics,* edited by Joel B. Green, 127–30. Grand Rapids: Baker Academic, 2011.

Cron, Lisa. *Wired for Story: The Writer's Guide to Using Brain Science to Hook Readers from the Very First Sentence.* New York: Ten Speed, 2012.

Cyril of Alexandria. *Commentary on John.* Library of the Fathers 48. London: Rivington. Online: Online: http://www.tertullian.org/fathers/cyril_on_john_12_book12. htm.

Damasio, Antonio, and Gil B. Carvalho. "The Nature of Feelings: Evolutionary and Neurobiological Origins." *Nature Reviews Neuroscience* 14 (2013) 143–52. doi: 10.1038/nrn3403.

Damasio, Antonio R. *The Feeling of What Happens: Body and Emotion in the Making of Consciousness.* New York: Harcourt Brace, 1999.

———. *Self Comes to Mind: Constructing the Conscious Brain.* New York: Pantheon, 2010.

Damon, Matt, and Ben Affleck. "Good Will Hunting (Script)." Online: http://www. thescriptsource.net/Scripts/Good%20Will%20Hunting.pdf.

Davids, Peter H. *The Letters of 2 Peter and Jude.* The Pillar New Testament Commentary. Grand Rapids: Eerdmans, 2006.

Davies, W. D., and Dale Allison. *A Critical and Exegetical Commentary on the Gospel according to Saint Matthew.* The International Critical Commentary on the Holy Scriptures of the Old and New Testaments 3. New York: T. & T. Clark, 2004.

Doidge, Norman. *The Brain that Changes Itself: Stories of Personal Triumph from the Frontiers of Brain Science.* New York: Penguin, 2007.

———. "Dr. Norman Doidge on Neuroplasticity." *Big Ideas,* April 29, 2012. Online: http://tvo.org/video/176666/dr-norman-doidge-neuroplasticity.

Dowd, Damien, and Jocelyn Proulx. "Neurology and Trauma: Impact and Treatment Implications (Research Summary)." Online: http://umanitoba.ca/centres/resolve/ media/Neurology_and_Trauma_Research_Summary.pdf.

Duhigg, Charles. *The Power of Habit: Why We Do What We Do in Life and Business.* New York: Random House, 2012.

Dunn, James D. G. *The Epistle to the Galatians.* Black's New Testament Commentaries. London: Continuum, 1993.

———. *The Epistles to the Colossians and to Philemon : A Commentary on the Greek Text.* The New International Greek Testament Commentary. Grand Rapids: Eerdmans, 1996.

Duvall, J. Scott. *Experiencing God's Story of Life and Hope: A Workbook for Spiritual Formation.* Grand Rapids: Kregel, 2008.

Edsall, Sidney, et al. "Childhood Trauma." In *Clinical Child Psychiatry,* edited by William M. Klykylo and Jerald Kay, 275–94. England: John Wiley & Sons, 2005.

Ellison, H. L. *Exodus, Daily Study Bible—Old Testament.* Philadelphia: Westminster, 1982.

Elsevier. "Loving Touch Critical for Premature Infants." ScienceDaily. January 6 2014. Online: http://www.sciencedaily.com/releases/2014/01/140106094437.htm.

Fee, Gordon D. *God's Empowering Presence: The Holy Spirit in the Letters of Paul.* Peabody, MA: Hendrickson, 1994.

Feinberg, John S., et al. *Predestination & Free Will: Four Views of Divine Sovereignty & Human Freedom.* Downers Grove, IL: IVP, 1986.

Fishbane, Mona. "Wired to Connect: Neuroscience, Relationships, and Therapy." *Family Process* 46 (2007) 395–412. doi: 10.1111/j.154300.2007.00219.x.

Foster, Richard J. *Life with God: Reading the Bible for Spiritual Transformation.* New York: HarperOne, 2008.

Frazee, Randy. *Believe: Living the Story of the Bible to Become like Jesus.* Grand Rapids: Zondervan, 2015.

———. *The Christian Life Profile Assessment Tool Workbook.* Updated Ed. Grand Rapids: Zondervan, 2015.

———. *Think, Act, Be Like Jesus: Becoming a New Person in Christ.* Grand Rapids: Zondervan, 2015.

Friberg, Timothy, et al. *Analytical Lexicon to the Greek New Testament.* Baker's Greek New Testament Library. Grand Rapids: Baker, 2000.

Grace, Janathan. "Happily Rejecting the God of My Youth." August 9, 2014. Online: http://janathangrace.org/2014/08/09/happily-rejecting-the-god-of-my-youth/.

Green, Joel B. *Body, Soul, and Human Life: The Nature of Humanity in the Bible.* Studies in Theological Interpretation. Milton Keynes, UK: Paternoster, 2008.

Guigo II. *The Ladder of Monks: A Letter on the Contemplative Life and Twelve Meditations.* Translated by Edmund Colledge and James Walsh. Garden City, NY: Image, 1978.

Habermas, Ronald T. *The Complete Disciple: A Model for Cultivating God's Image in Us.* Colorado Springs, CO: NexGen, 2003.

Hackmann, Ann, and Tanja Michael. "Intrusive Re-experiencing in Post-Traumatic Stress Disorder: Phenomenology, Theory, and Therapy." *Memory* 12 (2004) 403–15. doi: 10.1080/09658210444000025.

Hansen, Kristen. "The Neuroscience of Goal Setting." Online: http://www.evancarmichael.com/Leadership/6238/Neuroscience-of-Goal-Setting.html.

Hanson, Rick. *Hardwiring Happiness: The New Brain Science of Contentment, Calm, and Confidence.* New York: Random House, 2013.

———. 2014. "Taking In the Good." *Greater Good*, November 1, 2009. Online: http://greatergood.berkeley.edu/article/item/taking_in_the_good.

Havergal, Frances Ridley. *Kept for the Master's Use.* New York: Dutton, 1882.

Henderson, Tom. "Babies Pick Up Mothers' Accents in the Womb." *Parentdish.com,* November 6, 2009. Online: http://www.parentdish.com/2009/11/06/babies-pick-up-mothers-accents-in-the-womb/.

Iacoboni, Marco. "Neurobiology of Imitation." *Current Opinion in Neurobiology* 19 (2009) 403–15. doi: 10.1016/j.conb.2009.09.008.

Interlandi, Jeneen. "Mysteries Of Memory: New Research Explores how the Brain Records and then Recalls Events." *Newsweek* 152 (2008) 64.

Jeeves, Malcolm A. *Minds, Brains, Souls, and Gods: A Conversation on Faith, Psychology, and Neuroscience.* Downers Grove, IL: IVP Academic, 2013.

Jennings, Timothy R. *Could It Be This Simple? A Biblical Model for Healing the Mind.* 2nd ed. Chattanooga, TN: Lennox, 2012.

————. *The God-Shaped Brain: How Changing Your View of God Transforms Your Life.* Downers Grove, IL: IVP, 2013.

Jewett, Robert. *Paul's Anthropological Terms: A Study of Their Use in Conflict Settings.* Arbeiten zur Geschichte des antiken Judentums und des Urchristentums. Leiden: Brill, 1971.

Johnston, Robert K. *God's Wider Presence: Reconsidering General Revelation.* Grand Rapids: Baker, 2014.

Jowers, Dennis W., ed. *Four Views on Divine Providence.* Counterpoints: Bible & Theology. Grand Rapids: Zondervan, 2011.

Kabat-Zinn, Jon. *Full Catastrophe Living: Using the Wisdom of Your Body and Mind to Face Stress, Pain, and Illness.* Rev. ed. New York: Bantam, 2013.

————. "[Unedited Cuts from 'Opening to Our Lives and a Science of Mindfulness'] Jon Kabat-Zinn with Krista Tippett." *OnBeing.org*, December 27, 2012. Online: http://www.onbeing.org/program/opening-our-lives/138/extraaudio.

Kahneman, Daniel. *Thinking, Fast and Slow.* New York: Farrar Straus and Giroux, 2011.

Kolk, Bessel A. van der. "The Neurobiology of Childhood Trauma and Abuse." *Child & Adolescent Psychiatric Clinic North America.* 12 (2003) 293–317.

Barrett, Matthew, and Ardel B. Caneday, eds. *Four Views on the Historical Adam.* Counterpoints: Bible and Theology. Grand Rapids: Zondervan, 2013.

Lane, William. "Hebrews." In *Dictionary of the Later New Testament and Its Developments*, 443–58. Downers Grove, IL: IVP Academic, 1997.

Legrenzi, Paolo, and C. A. Umiltà. *Neuromania: On the Limits of Brain Science.* New York: Oxford University Press, 2011.

Lewis, C. S. *The Great Divorce.* New York: Macmillan, 1946.

Lieberman, Matthew D. *Social: Why Our Brains Are Wired to Connect.* New York: Crown, 2013.

Llewelyn, S. R. "Ammonius to Appolonios (P.Oxy. XLII 3057) The Earliest Christian Letter on Papyrus?" In *New Documents Illustrating Early Christianity*, edited by Llewelyn, S. R. 169–76. Grand Rapids: Eerdmans, 1997.

Louw, Johannes P., and Eugene Nida. *Greek-English Lexicon of the New Testament Based on Semantic Domains.* New York: United Bible Societies, 1988.

Mampe, Birgit, et al. "Newborns' Cry Melody Is Shaped by Their Native Language." *Current Biology* 19 (2009) 1994–97. doi: 10.1016/j.cub.2009.09.064.

Mangis, Michael W. *Signature Sins: Taming our Wayward Hearts.* Downers Grove, IL: IVP, 2008.

Masten, Carrie L., et al. "Time Spent with Friends in Adolescence Relates to Less Neural Sensitivity to Later Peer Rejection." *Social Cognitive & Affective Neuroscience* 7 (2012) 106–14. doi: 10.1093/scan/nsq098.

McDonald, H. D. *The Christian View of Man, Foundations for Faith.* Westchester, IL: Crossway, 1981.

McElroy, Molly. 2013. "A First Step in Learning by Imitation: Baby Brains Respond to Another's Actions." *UW Today*, October 30, 2013. Online: http://www.washington.edu/news/2013/10/30/a-first-step-in-learning-by-imitation-baby-brains-respond-to-anothers-actions/.

McGarry, Joseph. "Formed by the Spirit: A TAT of Spiritual Formation in Christ." Paper presented at the annual meeting of the Evangelical Theological Society. San Diego, CA, November 20, 2014.

McGowan, Kathleen. "The Neuroscience of the Seven Deadly Sins: Brain Researchers are Finding the Sources of our Nastiest Temptations." *Discover Magazine*, October

5, 2009. Online: http://discovermagazine.com/2009/sep/05-i-didnt-sin-it-was-my-brain.

McKnight, Scot. *Embracing Grace: A Gospel for All of Us*. Brewster MA: Paraclete, 2005.

———. *The Jesus Creed: Loving God, Loving Others*. Brewster, MA: Paraclete, 2004.

Means, Patrick A. *Men's Secret Wars*. Grand Rapids: Baker, 2006.

Meissner, W. W. *Ignatius of Loyola: The Psychology of a Saint*. New Haven: Yale University Press, 1992.

Middleton, J. Richard. *The Liberating Image: The Imago Dei in Genesis 1*. Grand Rapids: Brazos, 2005.

Morris, Leon. *The Gospel according to Matthew*. The Pillar New Testament Commentary. Grand Rapids: Eerdmans, 1992.

Murphy Paul, Annie. "What We Learn Before We're Born [Transcript]." *TED.com*, November 2011. Online: http://www.ted.com/talks/annie_murphy_paul_what_we_learn_before_we_re_born/transcript?language=en#t-233530.

Newberg, Andrew B., and Mark Robert Waldman. *How God Changes Your Brain: Breakthrough Findings from a Leading Neuroscientist*. New York: Ballantine, 2009.

Olson, Roger E. "God and Children: Would Jesus (God) Command Their Slaughter?" *Roger E. Olson: My Evangelical Arminian Theological Musings Blog*, August 2, 2014. Online: http://www.patheos.com/blogs/rogereolson/2014/08/god-and-children-would-jesus-god-command-their-slaughter/.

Ortberg, John. *The Life You've Always Wanted*. Grand Rapids: Zondervan, 1997.

Osborn, Ronald E. *Death Before the Fall: Biblical Literalism and the Problem of Animal Suffering*. Downers Grove, IL: IVP Academic, 2014.

Palmer, Parker J. *Let Your Life Speak: Listening for the Voice of Vocation*. San Francisco: Jossey-Bass, 2000.

Patterson, Kerry. *Change Anything: The New Science of Personal Success*. New York: Business Plus, 2011.

Peterson, Eugene. *Eat this Book: A Conversation in the Art of Spiritual Reading*. Grand Rapids: Eerdmans, 2006.

Pilcher, Helen. "The New Witch Doctors: How Belief Can Kill." *New Scientist*, May 12, 2009, 30–33.

Plantinga, Cornelius. *Not the Way It's Supposed To Be: A Breviary of Sin*. Grand Rapids: Eerdmans, 1995.

Pyle, William T., and Mary Alice Seals. *Experiencing Ministry Supervision: a Field-Based Approach*. Nashville: Broadman & Holman, 1995.

Randall, Michael. "The Physiology of Stress: Cortisol and the Hypothalamic-Pituitary-Adrenal Axis." *Dartmouth Undergraduate Journal of Science*, 14 (2010). Online: http://dujs.dartmouth.edu/fall-2010/the-physiology-of-stress-cortisol-and-the-hypothalamic-pituitary-adrenal-axis#.VVsoTflViko.

Richards, John. *But Deliver Us from Evil: An Introduction to the Demonic Dimension in Pastoral Care*. New York: Seabury, 1974.

RJS. "Fairness Tastes Like Ice Cream." *Jesus Creed Blog*, July 3, 2014. Online: http://www.patheos.com/blogs/jesuscreed/2014/07/03/fairness-tastes-like-ice-cream-rjs/.

Robinson, David L. "Brain Function, Mental Experience and Personality." *The Netherlands Journal of Psychology* 64 (2009) 152–67. Online: http://www.visio-moralis.co.uk/mind_and_brain/publications/pdf_files/NJPemotionsPaper.pdf.

Saint Francis. *The Writings of Saint Francis of Assisi*. Translated by Paschal Robinson. Philadelphia: Dolphin, 1906.

Saint Ignatius of Loyola. *The Spiritual Exercises of St. Ignatius: Based on Studies in the Language of the Autograph.* Vintage Spiritual Classics. New York: Vintage, 2000.

Schwartz, Jeffrey, and Sharon Begley. *The Mind and the Brain: Neuroplasticity and the Power of Mental Force.* New York: HarperCollins, 2002.

Seliger, Janna. "The Spiritual Atheist—Finding Spirituality without Worship." *iBuzzle Blog*, n.d. Online: http://www.buzzle.com/articles/the-spiritual-atheist-finding-spirituality-without-worship.html.

Shreeve, James. "Beyond the Brain." *National Geographic* 207.3 (2005) 1–12. Online: http://science.nationalgeographic.com/science/health-and-human-body/human-body/mind-brain/.

Smith, James K. A. *Desiring the Kingdom: Worship, Worldview, and Cultural Formation.* Cultural Liturgies, Vol. 1. Grand Rapids: Baker Academic, 2009.

———. *Imagining the Kingdom: How Worship Works.* Cultural Liturgies, Vol. 2. Grand Rapids: Baker Academic, 2013.

Smith, Martin L. *The Word is Very Near You: A Guide to Praying with Scripture.* Cambridge, MA: Cowley, 1989.

St. Francis. "Snapshots of a Saint: Stories that Reveal Francis's Intense, Complex Personality." *Christian History* 42 (1994) 18–21. Online: http://www.christianitytoday.com/ch/1994/issue42/4219.html?start=2.

Sternberg, Esther M. *Healing Spaces: The Science of Place and Well-being.* Cambridge, MA: Belknap, 2009.

Stone, Lawson. "The Soul: Possession, Part, or Person? The Genesis of Human Nature in Genesis 2:7." In *What about the Soul? Neuroscience and Christian Anthropology*, edited by Joel B. Green, 47–62. Nashville: Abingdon, 2004.

Szalavitz, Maia. "Explaining Why Meditators May Live Longer." *Time*, Dec. 23, 2010. Online: http://healthland.time.com/2010/12/23/could-meditation-extend-life-intriguing-possibility-raised-by-new-study/.

Tallis, Raymond. *Aping Mankind: Neuromania, Darwinitis and the Misrepresentation of Humanity.* Durham, UK: Acumen, 2011.

Thiselton, Anthony C. *The Living Paul: An Introduction to the Apostle's Life and Thought.* Downers Grove, IL: IVP Academic, 2009.

Toews, John E. *The Story of Original Sin.* Eugene, OR: Pickwick, 2013.

Vang, Preben, and Terry Carter. *Telling God's Story: The Biblical Narrative from Beginning to End.* Nashville: Broadman & Holman, 2013.

Vanhoozer, Kevin J. *The Drama of Doctrine: A Canonical-Linguistic Approach to Christian Theology.* Louisville: Westminster John Knox, 2005.

Veith, Gene Edward. *Imagination Redeemed: Glorifying God With a Neglected Part of Your Mind.* Wheaton, IL: Crossway, 2015.

Waltke, Bruce K. "*Nefesh.*" In *Theological Wordbook of the Old Testament*, edited by R. Laird Harris, et al., 2:587–91. Chicago: Moody, 1980.

Walton, John H. *Ancient Near Eastern Thought and the Old Testament: Introducing the Conceptual World of the Hebrew Bible.* Grand Rapids: Baker Academic, 2006.

———. "Creation in Genesis 1:1—2:3 and the Ancient Near East: Order out of Disorder after *Chaoskampf.*" *Calvin Theological Journal* 43 (2008) 48–63.

———. *Genesis 1 as Ancient Cosmology.* Winona Lake, IN: Eisenbrauns, 2011.

———. *The Lost World of Genesis One: Ancient Cosmology and the Origins Debate.* Downers Grove, IL: IVP Academic, 2009.

Wells, Rebecca. "Dahlins." *Ya-Ya Blog*, n.d., 2004. Online: https://web.archive.org/web/20040607131849/Online: http://www.ya-ya.com/update.htm.

———. "Dear Sweetnesses." *Ya-Ya Blog*, June 3, 2004. Online: https://web.archive.org/web/20040607131849/Online: http://www.ya-ya.com/update.htm.

Wells, Samuel. *Improvisation: The Drama of Christian Ethics*. Grand Rapids: Brazos, 2004.

Wenham, Gordon J. *Exploring the Old Testament: A Guide to the Pentateuch*. Vol. 1. Downers Grove, IL: IVP, 2003.

Willard, Dallas. *The Great Omission: Reclaiming Jesus's Essential Teachings on Discipleship*. San Francisco: HarperSanFrancisco, 2006.

———. *Renovation of the Heart: Putting on the Character of Christ*. Colorado Springs: NavPress, 2002.

———. "Spiritual Formation in Christ: A Perspective on What It Is and How It Might Be Done." *Journal of Psychology & Theology* 28 (2000) 254–58.

Willard, Dallas, et al. "Fly on the Wall: A Conversation about Authentic Transformation among Dallas Willard, Larry Crabb, and John Ortberg." *Conversations* 1 (2003) 28–39. Online: http://dallaswillardcenter.com/wp-content/uploads/2014/04/aflyonthewall.pdf.

Witherington, Ben. *Letters and Homilies for Hellenized Christians: A Socio-Rhetorical Commentary on 1–2 Peter*. Vol. 2. Downers Grove, IL: IVP Academic, 2007.

Wright, N. T. *Jesus and the Victory of God, Christian Origins and the Question of God*. London: SPCK, 1996.

———. *The New Testament and the People of God, Christian Origins and the Question of God*. London: SPCK, 1992.

———. *Paul for Everyone: Romans Part One (Chapters)*. London: SPCK, 2004.

———. "Romans and the Theology of Paul." In *Pauline Theology, Vol. 3 Romans*, edited by David M. Hay and E. Elizabeth Johnson, 30–67. Minneapolis: Fortress, 1995. Online: http://ntwrightpage.com/Wright_Romans_Theology_Paul.pdf.

Name/Subject Index

Scripture Index

OLD TESTAMENT

Made in the USA
Coppell, TX
25 September 2021